CHAOS DAEMONS

It is an age where the darkest dreams of Humanity are surpassed daily by the stark horrors of their reality. The galaxy overflows with nightmares made flesh. Yet even in these dread times there are powers of such inimitable malevolence that the mere knowledge of their existence must be suppressed, lest it shatter the resolve of all Mankind. But innocence is not the same as safety. Through the tattered veil of the real, from amidst the roiling madness and infinite corruption of the warp, the daemons of Chaos spill forth to claim the souls of the ignorant and the dreadfully enlightened alike, and to plunge all of reality into final and everlasting damnation.

CONTENTS

PRODUCED BY THE WARHAMMER STUDIO

With thanks to the Mournival and the Infinity Circuit for their additional playtesting services.

Games Workshop Ltd, Willow Rd, Lenton, Nottingham, NG7 2WS

WARHAMMER.COM

INTRODUCTION

You have opened the book. Already, you have read too much. You have no choice now but to press on, to learn of the roiling otherspace of the warp, of its malevolent denizens and of the Dark Gods of Chaos that compete to rule over its infinite and insane depths. If you are fortunate, you may bind these daemons to your will and lead them to conquest… for a time, at least.

The daemons of Chaos burst from the pandemonium of warp space to despoil and corrupt all that mortals hold dear. Unbound by even the most fundamental laws of realspace, these malevolent terrors unleash infernal powers upon their victims. Worlds writhe and transmute into unclean hellscapes at their touch. Storms of conjured sorcery mutate mortal foes into deformed abominations, or unmake their flesh and burn away their souls. Even the bravest of warriors may die from sheer terror at the sight of daemonic entities bearing down upon them, and most who do not will surely lose their minds.

To command these unholy hosts on the tabletop is less a case of marshalling a conventional army as it is channelling the cruelty and ambition of the Dark Gods of Chaos made manifest. Khorne, the Blood God, wrathful and warlike; Tzeentch,

the Changer of the Ways and Architect of Fate; Nurgle, the Plague God, ruin of all; Slaanesh, the Dark Prince, master of excess and obsession. These four and other, lesser demigods besides send forth diabolic legions whose freakish aspects and arcane war engines echo the entities that give them form. Some daemon armies comprise only the empyric soldiery of a single Dark God. Others may see the hosts of two rival deities compete in a harvest of mortal souls, or might even hurl the daemons of all the Chaos Gods together into a mingled tumult of madness and horror. As ever with the chaotic energies of the warp, the only constant is utter inconstancy.

For the tabletop strategist, the anarchic composition of daemon forces is only the beginning. Here is an army whose troops can flicker into being all across the battlefield, drawing ever closer to

their victims as the veil of reality thins. The unfettered fury of the warp wreathes the daemon hosts as they surge to battle, conjuring unnatural storms to lash the enemy army and transmogrifying the very battlefield beneath their feet.

Equally, for those wishing to build and paint a truly unique force, daemons have much to offer. Their aesthetic ranges wildly from the baroque to the techno-organic, from savage to the elegantly sinuous or the putrid and foul. Though the hosts of the Dark Gods tend towards those colours that best evoke their masters' essential natures, in truth there are no hard-and-fast rules to such beings of unfettered Chaos. Your army is yours to build as you see fit, and to paint in whatever hues you so desire. After all, so many daemonic bargains begin with the illusion of boundless power and freedom. Read on to seal the pact…

It begins with the slightest flaw, be it the subtle
whisper stoking ambition, the frenzied fury of
battle, the despair of inescapable entropy or the
desire for change. All it takes is a single chink
in the armour of reality – a vulnerable mind,
a tainted soul – to unleash all the legions of
the warp.

To fight these supernatural terrors is to do battle
with one's own darkest nature. Daemons wrought
from despair, obsession, fury and cunning stalk
through manifesting storms of misery and infernos
of lust. Malevolent entities shudder in and out of
reality, shrugging off hails of gunfire as though the
shots had never been loosed. Heartbeat by frantic
heartbeat, they close in from all sides.

Those who stand and fight face a nightmarish
battle against creatures that cannot truly be slain,
and that delight in tormenting their victims and
breaking their minds. Those who flee fare no better.
There is no escaping such tireless malevolence.
Even death is no release, for to die at the talons of
the daemons of Chaos is to feel one's soul torn free
and plunged into eternal torment.

The Nature of the Daemon

Far have I seen and far have I wandered, beyond the tattered veil of this thing we call reality, into the wondrous realm that in our limited Human fashion we call the warp. To have ascribed such a banal moniker to this infinite sea of souls – this endless dimension of boundless energy – is as damning an indictment of my species as ever I have known.

It is said that it is a mirror of reality, which reflects and reshapes all of the emotions, the desires, the needs and wants of all living beings that have ever been or will ever be. If that is so then this is a mirror of the divine, which furnishes apotheosis upon all that it captures in its depths. So powerful are the roiling currents of warp space, which the learned call also the empyrean or the immaterium, that they can even tear through the veil and spill into reality as raging warp storms. One day, by the blessings of the Dark Gods, they may consume all of realspace in such a manner.

To look upon the daemon legions of the Dark Gods is to see glorious damnation made manifest. The hosts of Khorne march beneath brazen icons and howl their bloodlust as they brandish smouldering blades aloft. The legions of Tzeentch coruscate with kaleidoscopic flame, capering and gibbering even as they endlessly mutate. Nurgle's clades lumber to war amidst roaring storms of plague flies, some slouching slump-shouldered and grim, others ebullient in their festering and malevolent mirth. Those of Slaanesh, meanwhile, advance with deceptive grace, wreathed in perfumed clouds and glittering illusions that drive mortals wild with want even as they repel and dismay.

Myriad beings dwell within the warp, predatory sentiences wrought from empyric energy that perceive the souls of living beings as shimmering lights and are drawn ravenously toward them. Our clumsy Human scripture names these things daemons; it warns of the threat they pose to body and soul.

Yet no prayer book dares make mention of the warp's greatest denizens, the Dark Gods of Chaos. Praise be to these divine powers, amongst whose infernal pantheon the greatest are Khorne the Blood God, Nurgle the Plague Lord, Tzeentch the Changer of the Ways, and Slaanesh the Dark Prince of Excess. Since the dawn of existence have these gods sought primacy, both over the sterile tracts of realspace and also in the Great Game that they have waged always against one another. Across the ever-changing battlefields of the warp impossible wars play out as the Dark Gods' daemon legions march against one another over landscapes most Humans would perceive as nightmarish.

Ever do the four great siblings scheme against one another, the power of each rising and falling in relation to their divine rivals, yet never one rising to true rulership over the others. So it has always been and must always be, and as ever more of the warp spills into our own unworthy realspace so the Great Game may be played out in our realm also.

It is true that each dark sibling has legion mortal followers scattered across the Imperium and beyond. Yet we are as nothing, mewling worms compared to the daemons that comprise the legions of the Gods. Each daemon is drawn from the essence of its patron god, a spark extracted from a veritable constellation and imbued with sentience and purpose of its own. All daemons, it is said, seek to further their patron god's agenda for ultimately they are extensions of its being and can be claimed back as easily as they were fashioned should they fail their master.

Yet even the lowliest daemon is cunning and powerful in its own right, a supernatural entity that hungers for mortal souls and seeks always to corrupt and to destroy. Some may whisper blandishments and honeyed lies into mortal dreams to get their way, others rage and tear like wild beasts, each according to their essential natures, but ultimately all daemons seek to gain access to realspace and – in so doing – to sow the seeds of its absorption into the warp.

Whether they emerge in intermingled hordes from some shuddering rent in the veil of reality, or march forth in legion strength under the banners of their almighty masters, the daemons of Chaos claim more of our own undeserving reality with every passing day. Glory to the Dark Gods for surely, soon, in this age of infernal miracles, there shall come a day when they reign triumphant at last…

Hereabove find laid down but an extract from the dreamseeings and visionwalkings of Maelos the Seer, the Eighth Eye, in which the truths are spoken that must not be put to words.

TO PIERCE THE VEIL

Composed as they are of the stuff of the warp, daemons cannot enter – nor even exist in – realspace at will. The tangibility of mortal reality, and the temporal and physical laws that govern it, are anathema to their chaotic nature. Yet there are many ways for malevolent entities to break through the veil that separates the warp from realspace, or for unwary pawns to invite them in.

Mass daemonic incursions are apocalyptic events most often triggered by warp storm activity spilling into realspace, or else by a rift opening between reality and the warp. In either case, it is the flood of empyric energy pouring from the beyond that sustains the daemon legions. They use it to manifest and sustain physical forms so that they can interact with the stuff of reality, and to power their infernal sorceries and vile weapons of war. As a rule, once the warp storm activity peters out or the rift is sealed – often by the desperate sacrifices of those with the knowledge to do so – the incursion ends as the daemons fade, wither, and are banished back to the warp.

However, there are other paths by which daemons may enter realspace. Rather than descending on a world en masse,

entities may slip through the veil by themselves to achieve subtler ends. Even a single daemon is a jagged splinter lodged in the skin of realspace. Over time its corruption spreads until the weakened weave of the veil tears and another grand incursion begins.

One common route by which a daemon may gain access to realspace is by possessing a mortal being. Unfortunately for the galaxy at large, there are many ways this can occur. Those with psychic abilities – either fully realised or nascent and as yet unguessed – are particularly vulnerable to possession. Their souls form shimmering beacons in the warp that draw daemonic entities to them like sharks scenting blood. Each time a psyker accesses their powers they open a conduit between their mind and the immaterium. It takes but an instant of incaution or bad

luck for a daemon to force itself through that doorway and take possession of its victim, body and soul.

Psykers are not alone in facing the danger of possession. Daemons whisper into mortals' dreams. They play upon ambition, hatred and desire. They trouble the tortured thoughts of the insane and the desperate, offering respite in return for living flesh. They haunt cursed places and wait for sentient prey to read the incantation, unlock the door, spill blood upon the altar, or whatever other ritual precondition permits them to pounce. Strangest of all, there are those mortals who willingly offer themselves up as hosts for daemonic possession. They make such bargains in the belief the grateful daemon will grant them supernatural might. Yet those who allow themselves to be possessed learn too late that this is not a

relationship of symbiosis, but instead the worst sort of malign parasitism.

Once a Daemon has seized a mortal shell they assume absolute control. The victim's physical form becomes the daemon's to mould at will. The host's personality is typically thrust into some small, dark corner of their own mind, imprisoned and forced to watch as the daemon pursues whatever diabolical agenda it desires. Some possessor daemons are subtle things who pick their victims with care then exploit their position and influence to advance cunning schemes in realspace. A priest, a politician, a military commander, or perhaps the Tech-Priest who alone holds the activation runes for a city's plasma generatora; all such individuals can be immensely useful puppets. Other daemons are savage and bestial, swiftly mutating their host's tortured flesh into nightmare shapes more pleasing to their grotesque sensibilities before embarking upon murderous rampages. In either instance, the possessor daemon can cause immense damage before it is banished back to the warp, usually through the destruction of its mortal host. Some of the worst and most inexplicable atrocities in galactic history have been perpetrated by daemons who had claimed the bodies of mortal beings.

DARK CONJURATIONS

Daemons may also be summoned through complex and dangerous rituals or sorcery. Many are the forbidden tomes and grimoires that speculate upon the nature of such rites, about what it is that sustains daemons summoned in this way and why the utterance of words and the giving of offerings can bring them forth. D'kael the Loathed suggested in his *Apocrypha* that it was the sheer belief of those working the ritual, coupled with the evocation of a daemon's true name, that drew the entities from the warp into realspace. Tamarys the Thrice-accursed wrote in *The Chronicles of Damnation* that even the least daemon is a sort of demigod, capable of taking the tiniest fragment of reality and crafting itself a physical avatar. The *Maleficum Abjurum*, much prized by the inner circles of the Imperial Ecclesiarchy, preaches that malign entities manifest only thanks to

the inherent corruption and impiety of the heretic. There are those organisations and eldritch beings in the galaxy who possess greater understanding of the nature of daemonic summoning, but knowledge is power in an age of ignorance, and is not shared lightly. For most who summon daemons – or must battle those that others have summoned – it is enough to know that the creatures manifest from the raw stuff of the warp, and possess all the inherent supernatural strengths and weaknesses that entails.

Daemons summoned by cabals of cultists or sorcerers may further be constrained to do the bidding of the ones who summoned them, though it is a tremendously difficult and uncertain process. There are those amongst the Dark Mechanicum and the Heretic Astartes who have even mastered the ability to channel the essence of a summoned daemon into a war engine or ward-engraved artefact. Binding a daemon into such a physical object effectively imprisons it within that one fixed fragment of reality. It further forces the daemon to imbue its prison with power, be it the infernal furnace that drives a baroque Daemon Engine to war or the coruscating arcs of corrupt energy

that render daemonic blades, hammers, guns and grimoires so deadly.

Daemons do not take well to enforced captivity. To them, mortals are ephemeral playthings to be used, tortured and discarded on a whim. To instead be conjured and compelled by such fleeting and limited beings is the gravest insult. From the moment they are summoned, a trammelled daemon will bend all its considerable powers to the act of escape. Some rage and fight, burning out warding runes, ripping free of hexagrammatic chains and smashing their prisons asunder before falling upon their hapless would-be jailers. Others are more subtle, seeking to corrupt those who wield the blade in which they are trapped, or who read from the pages of the tome to which they have been bound. Promises of power, plaintive appeals for mercy, dire threats of retribution – a daemon will employ whatever ruse is most in its nature to escape its imprisonment. In many cases it will go further, finding ways to manipulate mortal playthings even from within its prison and eventually fooling them into not only granting its freedom, but also exacting revenge upon its summoners or triggering a full-blown daemonic incursion.

Daemons summoned to the battlefield by devoted worshippers or the diabolists of the Heretic Astartes bear less rancour towards their summoners. They have had the door thrown wide to admit them, and are rarely under any geas to serve the ones who conjured them. Daemons unleashed in this way may form the vanguard for a much greater incursion. Unless confronted by those with the lore and power to properly combat the infernal hosts, these daemonic cohorts will soon work their foul magicks upon reality and force the fault line wider so that more of their ilk can pour through. More than one populous hive world or precious forge complex has been swallowed by the warp after downtrodden cultists summoned daemons into its depths. Meanwhile, a handful of entities summoned in extremis to act as allies in battle have, on a tragic number of occasions, succeeded in plunging both their summoners and their foes into the abyss.

Inquisitor Thrax cleared his throat and dictated the last section of his report.

'The mutants have been eradicated throughout the Chapter. The tainted command personnel have been slain. The Chapter Master chose to take his own life rather than face his deserved fate. The creatures he summoned have been banished, or have returned to the warp. Significant cerebral reconditioning continues amongst those Adeptus Astartes deemed salvageable and penitent duties will be assigned in due course.'

'For now the most important consideration is that the unfortunate lapses of the last months have been cleansed. This heresy is ended and the warp entities banished back to the immaterium. Full casualty reports are attached. I can now confidently claim that the reformed Grey Slayers Chapter of the Adeptus Astartes will prove more loyal in future, as they did in the past.'

'Praise to the God-Emperor and the Holy Ordos!'

'Thrax, Inquisitor Ordinary, This day of etcetera etcetera. Make a good copy and then return so that I may seal the dispatch.'

'Yes, Lord Inquisitor.'

Thrax sat down at the former Chapter Master's desk. He had a mind to keep it for his own. The workmanship had a certain naive charm. The inlay work was particularly fine for a backward world, such intricate patterns, such a pleasing arrangement of woods and techplastics. One could almost believe that it all meant something. His finger idly traced across the surface, following the line of a swirl and loop…

In the warp something stirred. Its true name had almost been used. Soon it would be spoken, and the way opened. The summoning was happening. It could feel the drawing together of power and intent…

Thrax was thinking hard, and now his finger barely moved. The Chapter Master had been weak, a fool. But the power he had tapped! Properly used, in the service of the Emperor, could it not make him the best, the greatest, of all the Inquisitors? His finger moved across the desktop again, following the inlay…

Soon… Soon…

Thrax reached the end of the techplastic line. He half-turned towards something in the corner of his eye. And then he knew…

NOW!

There was a knock on the door. The scribe had returned. 'Inquisitor Thrax, I have the copy of your report, Lord.' His voice filled with doubt. 'Inquisitor… Thrax? My Lord?'

In a rush of mandibles and heaving flesh, Inquisitor Thrax feasted.

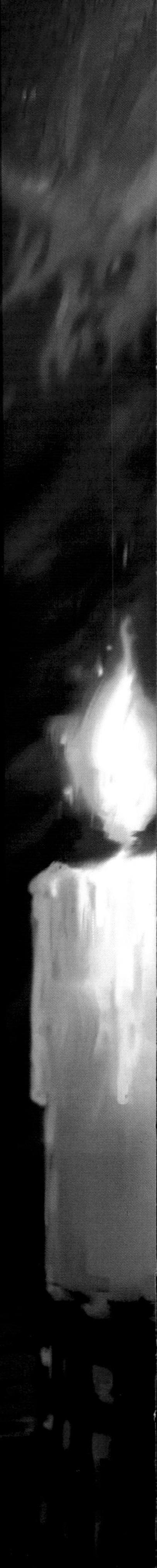

THE WAR UNENDING

Those Humans who know something of Chaos speak of the Long War, the conflict that has raged between loyalists and Chaos-worshipping traitors since the dark days of the Horus Heresy. Yet those of still greater insight understand there is a more fundamental battle being fought, a war for spiritual sanctity and Humanity's survival in which even the most elite warriors and draconian measures are barely sufficient to hold damnation at bay.

Locked away in rune-sealed and secret vaults lie records that tell of the Imperium's darkest hour, when Warmaster Horus fell to the temptations of the Dark Gods. His corruption began a civil war that brought Humanity to its knees, unleashed traitor hordes and daemon legions upon countless worlds, and saw the Ruinous Powers come as close to victory over realspace as they have in aeons. This apocalyptic conflict also saw the Emperor consigned to the life-preserving technologies of the Golden Throne. This, more than anything else, impressed upon the surviving Imperial leadership that the threat of Chaos demanded nought but the most drastic measures to combat.

Both the Inquisitorial Ordo Malleus and the Grey Knights Chapter knew their genesis in that dark time. Since their inception, these organisations have fought the insidious influence of daemons and striven to stave off the spiritual collapse of the Imperium. Yet theirs is a war whose cost long ago spiralled too high to tally, and in which there is scant hope of final victory.

The Ordo Malleus is amongst the greatest of the Holy Ordos of the Inquisition, that shadowy body that fights hidden wars against the greatest threats to Mankind. Its Inquisitors – who often go by the title of daemon hunter – wield absolute authority to requisition armies, go where they please, access forbidden lore and employ any weapon they believe will bring them victory over their foes. The Grey Knights, meanwhile, are an entire Chapter of Space Marines trained and equipped to battle daemons. Silver-clad psychic templars all, they are entrusted with arcane lore and incredible weaponry that allows them to take the fight to the diabolic and the infernal.

Both organisations appear mighty when their assets and abilities are considered in isolation. Indeed, with the resources, intelligence, and near-absolute authority they wield, the Ordo Malleus and Grey Knights are amongst Mankind's most potent agents in the war against the dark denizens of the immaterium.

Yet when set against the eternal malevolence and infinite power of the daemon legions, it soon becomes clear how finite a shield even these mighty forces are.

Every day, across the vast span of the Emperor's realm, amidst the uncountable masses of Humanity, daemonic forces are at work. Whispers and promises from beyond the veil thread themselves through the pliant minds of the vulnerable, the jaded and the despairing. Human populations and rogue psykers turn against the Imperium at the urging of supernatural corrupters. Full-blown daemonic incursions erupt upon worlds that appeared loyal right up until the day of their own personal apocalypse. Warp storms rage. Infernal legions spill from their depths to slaughter their way across the stars.

In the face of such an omnipresent threat, the Ordo Malleus and Grey Knights must strive to counter those dangers they deem greatest. They cannot possibly be everywhere at once. This is doubly true amidst the shadows of the Imperium Nihilus, where entire systems were as good as lost the moment they were severed from the guiding light of the Emperor's Astronomican.

Yet even such triage measures are not enough. Those who battle the daemonic menace must also propagate ignorance to serve as their greatest ally and weapon both. Even the slightest inkling of the true threat posed by the warp is considered too perilous for Imperial citizens or soldiers to possess. Knowledge leads to questions, then to doubt and fear. Soon enough, it is claimed, panic and rebellion would follow, throwing wide the very gates that hold back the infernal tide.

Rather than risk such wholesale corruption, many Inquisitors would rather exterminate entire planetary populations and liquidate regiment after regiment of Astra Militarum soldiery after the slightest contact with daemonic forces. Even Space Marines are not beyond such purges. However, they are so precious to the embattled Imperium that – where possible – intensive psycho-reindoctrination is used to scour knowledge of daemons from their minds and reconsecrate their souls. So it is that much of Humanity believe the heretical worshippers of the Dark Gods to be deluded lunatics, and any manifestations of their patently false beliefs to be chance mutation, or the work of xenos or witches.

While the murder of trillions of citizens is surely a sign of desperation, such methods have helped the Inquisition to keep Humanity blinkered against the true daemonic threat for countless millennia. Yet even here the corrupting influence of Chaos can be seen. Though ignorance may serve as a shield, it also leaves the vast majority of Mankind singularly unprepared to recognise or defend themselves against daemonic influence. Secrecy and inexplicable acts of genocide further serve to sow mistrust and acrimony amongst the disparate Imperial organisations, not to mention seeing countless souls condemned to death where they might otherwise have lived. And now, as the Great Rift splits the heavens and the ghastly truth becomes ever harder to conceal, so ever more frantic and bloody measures are required to maintain the Imperium's greatest lie.

It is already too late for me. But if you follow these instructions, if you ward yourself against the thing that dwells within these malevolent pages, you may yet survive. Heed my warnings. Follow the steps. Protect yourself and your comrades, and above all, for the love of the God Emperor, DO NOT LET IT ESCAPE!

KHORNE

Khorne is known across the galaxy as the Blood God, the Lord of Battles and the Great Butcher, amongst countless other titles. He is the patron of warriors – whether they worship him consciously or not – and the wellspring of all conflict, hatred and bloodshed. The daemons of Khorne are embodiments of his murderous rage and raw martial might.

Territorial aggression, uncontrolled anger and the urge to violence are amongst the most basic and common drivers of most mortal species. As they develop, civilisations may claim to have left such barbarity behind. Yet even the most advanced star-spanning empires make war upon their foes. Perhaps their peoples and their holdings require defending against less enlightened invaders. Maybe they desire new territories into which they can expand. Champions fight for their lords, their honour or their faith. Warriors do battle to defend their homes and families, or to cast down those they believe their enemies. Drunkards brawl in void-dock taverns. Assassins strike from the shadows. Feted generals direct mighty armies in countless campaigns of conquest. No matter the cause, no matter the scale, the result is the same. Every violent act and expression of rage or hate flows into the warp. There, it empowers the entity that mortals know as Khorne, the Blood God.

Myriad civilisations throughout the galaxy and across the span of millennia have offered worship to Khorne. He is a patron of warriors, a deity easily perceived to be a source of strength and catalyst to conquest. Moreover, all too many peoples throughout the long and tragic history of the galaxy have been quick to anger and ready to hate. Entire alien empires have risen and fallen in service to the Blood God, inevitably ending amidst calamitous violence and vast loss of life.

Some, like the Abdori Harrow-clans or the arachnoid Svekka, were barbarous and feral species, drawn to the brute strength and ferocious aspect of Khorne. Others, such as the sombre Palatorinate of Enkh, began as noble and highly advanced beings who were drawn into Khorne's worship during their quest for martial excellence.

Countless Human cultures, too, have offered praise to Khorne. Indeed, many still do, either in secret within the bowels of Imperial society or else openly upon renegade worlds long sundered from the guidance of the Ecclesiarchy. On Korlin II he is known as Khargg the Red Hound. To the Blood-sects of the Reaving Stars he is Ohrne, the Endless Howl. The skinner-gangs of the Cthartek underhives know him simply as the Bladesman, honouring him by flensing the skulls of their rivals and piling them in pyramids. Meanwhile, the self-proclaimed Prophets of Fury know him as the Skullstar, whose furious glare guides their slaughter-fleets to each new battleground.

Khorne is depicted in many different aspects across the span of the galaxy. He is rendered in gory cave paintings, in mosaics of brass and bone, or on the billowing banners of those renegade Space Marines who worship him – the dreaded World Eaters chief amongst them. Yet there are aspects to Khorne's portrayal that appear repeatedly, even amongst cultures separated by immense gulfs of space and time. Many envision him as a towering warrior with the head of a snarling hound. He is said to wear a mighty suit of brass and blackened iron, and to bellow his demands for bloodshed while seated on a brass throne atop a colossal mountain of skulls. Those who worship Khorne believe that every worthy head they take is added to that pile, and that – when their time comes – their own skull will be added. Furthermore, every sect or civilisation ever to depict Khorne shows him with a dread weapon at his side. Most often this is a vast, two-handed battle blade. Others may envision an axe, a halberd or whatever strange local melee weapon seems most in keeping to them. Whatever the case, Khorne's blade is always said to be a huge and terrible thing, war itself wrought in bloodied iron that can cut reality itself asunder with a single swing. It has been called Woebringer, Warmaker and the End of All Things.

THE MARK OF KHORNE
Khorne's rune is seen on countless battlefields, gladiatorial arenas and bloody murder scenes the galaxy over. It most closely resembles a stylised skull, though there are those who claim that it also echoes the immense, brazen gates of Khorne's great fortress. Often this design is borne into battle by those who worship the Blood God, or by the daemons fashioned from his fury and might. It may be wrought from hellforged brass or blackened and blood-spattered iron, and festooned with the dangling skulls of mighty foes slain by the champions of Khorne. It may be blazoned across tattered banners of flayed skin, daubed onto tank hulls with molten metal or boiling blood, or even scarified or branded into the flesh of Khorne's servants. Regardless of how it is rendered, the mark of Khorne sends a clear message to all of the slaughter to come. In the heat of battle, with carnage all around, such icons have been known to radiate palpable bloodlust and to stoke the fury of those who fight in their shadow.

On some aspects of his nature, all worshippers agree. Khorne disdains trickery, and hates sorcery and psykers worst of all. Khorne's true altar is the battlefield, and his sacrament is an endless tide of flowing blood. Most importantly, Khorne bestows his greatest favour upon those who butcher without restraint, and even turn their blades upon their allies in battle. Such slaughterers, it is said, show their understanding of Khorne's most fundamental tenet; he cares not from whence the blood flows, only that it does.

DAEMONS OF KHORNE

There can be no mistaking Khorne's daemons as they surge from the warp to do battle. Furious manifestations of living brass, corded muscle and bloodied bone, they embody all the Blood God's boundless rage and his unending need for battle.

Brazen horns howl to herald these daemons' onset. Their clamour fills the skies, loud as crashing thunder and echoing from all directions. Feral war cries rip through vox networks and burst from comm-beads, so sudden and deafeningly loud that they burn out entire channels and rupture eardrums.

The ground shudders and cracks, chasms yawning wide to vomit boiling blood and clattering masses of skulls. Ragged rents split the fabric of reality, infernal firelight swelling from within. Carmine mist billows, blood-warm and heavy with a coppery stink, alive with prowling, half-seen shapes with eyes like burning coals. Warriors feel sudden fury grip them. Their discipline and training crumble before the inexplicable urge to turn their weapons upon comrades they have known and valued for years. The sky darkens with whirling ash, or else catches light as flames race through the boiling clouds.

Then come the daemons, falling upon their victims like an avalanche. Bloodletters lope into battle hissing their hatred, hacking away with their forge-hot hellblades, which they wield with terrifying savagery and skill. Every blow lops another head from enemy shoulders. As the blood of their victims forms lakes upon the battlefield, still more Bloodletters claw their way up from beneath its surface to charge into battle.

Bloodcrushers smash everything in their path with single-minded ferocity, the brass-skinned Juggernauts shrugging off firepower that would reduce battle tanks to scrap. Skull Cannons clatter into position, the wail of damned souls filling the air as macabre ammunition is stuffed into the weapons' crunching jaws. The air shudders as the cannons fire, raining screaming skulls down upon the foe to detonate in brimstone blasts.

Yet even as warriors are butchered, even as shocking violence reduces everything to bloodied meat, still a special kind of terror is reserved for the Bloodthirsters. These are the ultimate champions of Khorne, the generals and war leaders of his infernal legions. Towering giants clad in baroque armour and borne aloft upon vast, leathery wings, they are the damnation of Humanity made manifest. Where their gaze falls even the bravest of enemies quail in mindless terror, and wherever the Bloodthirsters strike with their massive, brazen weapons, even the mightiest armour is torn apart.

WAR ZONE:
TARTORA

'Eight, the sacred number be, of Skull Lord 'pon his brazen throne. Eight the bloody rivers and eight the legions cruel. Eightfold the damned upon the endless fields of battle, and eight-times-eight eight times again the legions loosed from iron gates. Ever eight, though none knows why, nor asks upon that road of skulls…'

- Extract from the writings of Maelos the Seer

For eight hundred years, the fortress world of Tartora stood watch over the Carmynus Sub-sector. So heavily fortified was Tartora, so massively garrisoned and replete with orbital lasers and deep-void missile silos, that its castellans had long claimed it was unconquerable. Yet when the Orks of Waaagh! Gozmod invaded, Tartora's very might proved its undoing.

When the Ork invasion fleet approached Tartora, the garrison troops were already filled with fury. The greenskins came fresh from overrunning the hive worlds of Styxen and Hador, and the dishevelled refugees from those planets had brought tales of massacre and cruelty to the defenders of Tartora. Unable to take the fight to the xenos, the frustrated soldiery had been forced to wait for the Orks to come to them. Stoked by the sermons of Tartora's preachers, the garrison's hate for their enemies blazed like a bonfire in the warp.

Then came the greenskin onslaught, and the bloodletting began in earnest. Dozens of ramshackle ships were blasted apart before they reached Tartora's atmosphere. Their wreckage blazed through the planet's skies, streaking them with fire. Waaagh! Gozmod was a vast horde, however, and despite the megatonnes of ordnance being hurled into space by the Tartoran guns, hundreds of invasion craft crowded in upon the world. Massive dropships thundered down to crash-land all across the surface. Some collided with crackling shield domes and were dashed to ruin before making planetfall. Many more slammed down amidst Tartora's endless networks of trenches, bunker complexes, ferrocrete fortresses and gun emplacements.

The shock waves of the greenskin craft hitting home were enough to kill those defenders stationed too near, and to trigger earthquakes that shattered bulwarks and toppled curtain walls. Then came the Orks, pouring from the blazing wreckage of their craft in an endless tide. Shaken but unbowed, the soldiery of the Tartoran defence regiments rallied swiftly and brought their full fury to bear upon the invaders.

What followed was week upon week of constantly escalating butchery that saw hundreds of miles of trenches clogged with alien and human corpses alike. Days-long artillery bombardments pulverised greenskin warbands trapped in ferrocrete canyons until all that remained was cratered ruination overflowing with blood and blackened meat. Ork war engines smashed open Imperial fortifications, allowing howling greenskins to pour through the breach and hack apart thousands of cornered Imperial Guardsmen at a time.

As the bestial bellow of the Blood God rang through Tartora's skies, every priest preaching words of hate found their vox-horns and hailers turning to molten brass that flowed out to encase them. Cocooned in searing-hot metal, the priests were transformed into tormented gargoyles, compelled to howl the wrathful praises of Khorne the Blood God through brazen speakers, and to endure ceaseless agonies from then until the end of time.

Day after day the furious preachers bellowed exhortations to hatred through Tartora's laud hailer network, their pious sermons mingling with the crash of artillery, the cacophony of war cries and the screams of the wounded and dying. Finally, on the eighth hour of the eighty-eighth day of unending slaughter, the dreadful clangour of war melded into a single monstrous howl, which echoed around Tartora loud enough to shatter every window, crack the walls of every bunker and send rapidly widening fault lines racing across the planet's surface. Sulphurous fumes and infernal forge-light spilled up from those yawning rents. Then came a seemingly endless tide of the daemons of Khorne, surging up from the hellish netherworld below. They had been drawn from the warp to Tartora by the hatred and bloodshed that had engulfed it so completely, and now they would reap a monstrous tally for their wrathful god.

As blazing brass skulls the size of dropships trailed flames across the heavens, the Bloodthirster Agoth'Kar led its daemon legions into battle beneath a driving carmine downpour. Ork invaders and Human defenders alike fought and died beneath the blades of the brazen host, or else fled in mindless terror only to be transmuted into statues of brass and bone as punishment for their cowardice.

Manufactorums and Mekboy workshops alike burst into unholy flame, their mechanisms mutating into vast brazen forge-engines. From within these emerged Daemon Engines of Khorne that fell upon Human and Ork with equal fervour.

Millions of miles of trenches criss-crossed Tartora. Suffused now with infernal energies, many transformed into vast maws of gnashing brass teeth. Others flooded with boiling gore or molten metal. Wave upon wave of warrior daemons erupted from these unholy portals.

Long had the mighty Bastion Adamant stood against the tides of Orks surrounding it. At the coming of Khorne's daemons the fortress split and warped, its defenders vomited forth and forced to meet infernal and alien foes alike at close-quarters for the Blood God's pleasure.

Vast reservoirs of purified aqua turned blood-red and brackish at the coming of the daemons. Those who, in desperation, drank from them were possessed by a berserk and murderous rage that saw them turn upon their allies with blades, nails and teeth.

TZEENTCH

An ever-shifting multiplicity of concepts are considered to fall within the purview of Tzeentch, as is only appropriate for this strange Chaos God. Sorcery; fate; mutation; trickery; prophecy; infinite knowledge; boundless change – Tzeentch is said to preside over all of these things and more.

There are many reasons that mortals fall to the whispered temptations of Tzeentch. Within dank underhive slums, bond-sworn to sweltering manufactorums, or mutated since birth and forced to hide amongst a society that reviles them, Humans are robbed of power over their own lives. They long for something, anything, to change. Gradually that longing becomes a desire for the power to force that change to manifest. Perhaps these desires are altruistic, the wish to feed one's starving family, or the honest need to change the hand fate has dealt. Other motivations are more selfish and spiteful: a bullying overseer with all the power, who needs to be taught a lesson; a desire to gain the insights needed in order to ensure some criminal enterprise succeeds. All such fervent wishes for change provide opportunities that Tzeentch's daemons exploit. In the most psychically empowered of minds, these wants may be enough to open the way for entities to flow from the warp. In others, they are sufficient to see lost individuals hear and obey the voices that whisper through their dreams, or to steer them into dangerous cults that soon see souls pledged to the Changer of the Ways.

Nor is it only the downtrodden who wish for change. Even the greatest men and women can discover there are limits to their ability to understand, or to alter the galaxy to their liking. Nobles and planetary governors yearn for the ability to out-politick and out-scheme their rivals, or to improve the lot of those they serve. Learned scholars and powerful sorcerers wish always for more knowledge, greater understanding, the unlocking of forbidden lore; no matter how good or evil their intentions might be, this thirst for insight leads them into the clutches of Tzeentch. Generals and priests, Inquisitors and prophets alike, all have sought proscribed lore and thus been ensnared by the Architect of Fate.

No matter why people turn to the worship of Tzeentch, or how intentionally they do so, every mortal race empowers him. All those who plot, who trick their rivals or ambush their enemies, all who prize knowledge and understanding over brute force, who inscribe or study arcane lore – all are worshipping. Tzeentch has countless faithful scattered across the galaxy. Some form cults and covens sequestered within forbidden libraries or lurking in fanes in the wilds. Others are cunning manipulators hidden in plain sight amidst high society, or even renegade warbands of the Heretic Astartes, most notably the cults of the Thousand Sons and their Daemon Primarch Magnus the Red.

It is easy to see why so many give their allegiance to the Architect of Fate. His daemons whisper secrets into the minds of his faithful, insights they could not possibly glean by other means, and forbidden lore that renders them powerful. His champions' mortal forms undergo incredible changes that are hailed as boons and proof of Tzeentch's favour: coiling and crushing tentacles; the ability to breathe gouts of warpflame; glassy scales harder than bonded ceramite; diaphanous wings; the power to hypnotise with but a glance; labyrinthine and inhuman mental architecture. All these and infinite other blessings may manifest within the bodies of those who offer their souls to the Changer of the Ways. Then there are the sorcerous powers bestowed upon so many of Tzeentch's worshippers. These allow them to hurl blasts of mutating fire, to scry the maddening strands of the future, or to transmogrify the very fabric of realspace.

Such boons are not freely given. It is said of Tzeentch that he is the Great Conspirator, the master of enigmatic and ineffable plans of such complexity and galaxy-spanning scope that none but he himself can comprehend them. Every one of his mortal servants, no matter how powerful they might think themselves, is but another puppet. Each is but the

THE MARK OF TZEENTCH

Tzeentch's rune takes the form of a stylized staring eye set within a barbed and serpentine curve. While its shape remains constant, its nature is ever-changing. In one place the Mark of Tzeentch may be formed from dancing warpflame or coiling tendrils of mutant flesh. In another, it might manifest as a delicate crystalline sculpture swimming with unnameable colours, a flowing sigil of quicksilver studded with heliotrope crystals, or as an inconstant manifestation whose entire aspect and composition alters with every passing moment. It is borne as a hidden tattoo upon the flesh of Tzeentch's worshippers. It is brandished as a flickering mass of raw sorcery by daemonic entities, hoisted high upon standards of shimmering silver to unleash the power of rampant change upon foes in battle. In arcane cryptonumeracy, the sacred number of Tzeentch is nine. Thus his rune is sometimes branded ninefold times, or enchanted to be visible through nine overlapping dimensions. Sometimes it is even witnessed upon nine consecutive nights in the chaotic nightmares of those who are soon to be the victims of unwilling possession, taken by Tzeentchian daemons that stalk them through the warp.

tiniest of cogs within an impossibly complex machine intended to bring about eventual victory for the Architect of Fate. Snared in this eternal web, mortal worshippers are in truth trapped worse than ever they were before they sold their souls. More often than not their fate is simply as the conjurers or screaming conduits by which Tzeentch's daemonic hosts pour into realspace.

THE MANY FACES OF CHANGE

There have been as many differing depictions of Tzeentch rendered by mortals as there are stars in the heavens. Some envision an enlightened being of illuminating flame, a constellation of all-seeing eyes, or an impossibly intricate puppeteer tugging at the strings of fate. Often he is envisioned as a towering figure whose sunken visage is embedded low in his chest, and whose skin crawls with myriad faces that leer, mock, lie and contradict. Great horns are depicted curling from Tzeentch's head, crackling with arcane fire, while about him wheel endless expanses of sorcerous energy and overlapping, fractured realities. He is said to be able to observe the fates and machinations of any mortal being from any moment in time amidst these whirling images, and to hear the thoughts, hopes, plots and schemes of every living thing within his mind.

There are those who believe that Tzeentch's realm within the warp manifests as a vast crystal labyrinth through which his daemonic legions prowl. Supposedly replete with bizarre libraries, weird mirror-realms and fractal mazes of infernal madness, this convoluted infinity is said to dance with the fires of change and to grow and branch ever further as Tzeentch's power swells. Within the Ordo Malleus archives there are indeed numerous references to extrusions from just such a labyrinth. It is recorded tearing through the skin of realspace during especially apocalyptic incursions by the daemons of Tzeentch. Dark rumour and recorded visions insist that somewhere in the labyrinth's uttermost depths lies the Impossible Fortress, wherein Tzeentch lurks and plots within his Hidden Library. Whatever the truth, entire worlds and vast regions of space have been swallowed into the ever-changing and beautiful mass of the crystal labyrinth, or left impossibly altered after its tunnels retreat back to the warp. Meanwhile, legions upon legions of daemons have been seen to spill from within its shimmering depths.

Those daemons of Tzeentch are every bit as bizarre and mind-bending as their patron deity. The greatest of their number are the Lords of Change, which manifest as avian horrors with cruel talons, kaleidoscopic wings, flowing robes and eyes like windows into the abyss. They are embodiments of Tzeentch's boundless cunning, devious manipulators and conjurers of illusion whose touch brings mutation. Their sorcerous powers eclipse those of the mightiest mortals. The Lords of Change serve as the generals of Tzeentch's daemonic legions and the arch-magisters of his infernal covens. Many also work his will upon realspace by possessing mighty individuals and secretly abusing their power, or by posing as demigods to be worshipped by – and to utterly corrupt – primitive peoples.

The closest thing to foot soldiers in the Tzeentchian hosts are the Horrors. These weird humanoid daemons possess rubbery and malleable bodies with leering faces set into their chests, lurid pink flesh, and gangling arms that end in wicked talons or gross fungoid digits. They spill toward the enemy in a shimmering tide, tumbling and writhing over and about one another as they cackle, wail and gibber cacophonously. As manifest motes of Tzeentch's power, each Horror possesses formidable sorcerous abilities and can hurl mutating warpfire to twist and burn their victims. Moreover, should a Pink Horror be slain they are not banished, but instead split into two smaller Blue Horrors that gurgle and jabber with foul-tempered spite even as they continue to assail their victims. Lesser again are the Brimstone Horrors, swarming imps of living warpflame that cluster about their foes and engulf them in crawling fire.

As warriors struggle to hold back this surging tide of sorcery and madness, even stranger entities engulf them from all sides. Blade-winged Screamers flow through the air, slashing and sinuous. Flamers of Tzeentch bound into battle, spraying tongues of mutating warpflame from myriad yawning maws. With every moment the daemons' victims are twisted and ruined in body and mind, until nothing remains but pleading eyes and screaming maws dotted amidst heaving masses of unclean mutant flesh.

WAR ZONE:
GARMESH

The ancient hive world of Garmesh was once the beating heart of the Mathenda Sub-sector. Shifting trade routes, depleted resources and a string of incompetent planetary governors drawn from the noble Clan Habeyl saw the world decline until its populace languished in poverty, while their indolent rulers hid in their spire fortresses and ignored their people's plight.

It was amidst a climate of resentment towards Governor Habeyl VII that nine individuals formed a cabal in the underhive. Each had experienced the awakening of psychic abilities after the coming of the Great Rift, and had been drawn together by visions in their dreams. Believing the God-Emperor had appointed them champions, they pooled their powers as the dream voice bade them, and beseeched their master's aid. To their shock, a winged being of blazing light manifested in their midst. This entity offered them its blessings, magnifying their psychic abilities ninefold. It told them they had the power to change their world beyond recognition, and that – if they employed their newfound powers to the full – all would know their blessings. Blinded by faith and hope, the nine psykers named themselves the Heralds of Change, and set about mounting a sorcerous insurrection.

The Heralds' magnified powers allowed them to read thoughts and enslave the wills of their unwitting foes. They could glimpse the future, conjure changes in the fabric of reality and unleash upon their oppressors the curse of mutation for which so many underhivers had long been hunted and culled. At first their growing coalition of hive gangs and zealous militia fought against the enforcers who sought to stamp them out. Later, as the faith of the Heralds of Change took hold throughout the hives of Garmesh, many amongst the authorities and the manufacturers' guilds, and even some of the planet's Ecclesiarchal preachers, joined the cult.

By the time Habeyl VII could be made to grasp the scale of the disaster unfolding on his world, the fires of rebellion had become an inferno. Gripped by fear, the planetary governor ordered astropathic distress calls sent. He and his fellow nobles locked themselves away in their spire fortresses. They demanded that their household guards hold back the onslaught until help could arrive. Well-armed, and dug in behind massive fortifications, it appeared as though the nobles' guards would do just that.

Faced with failure and the deaths of their followers when they were so close to victory, the desperate Heralds of Change combined their powers once more. It was all as the Lord of Change Tz'Keth'K'Zar had foreseen when he had first appeared to his unwitting pawns and bestowed his gifts upon them. Conjuring the name of their God-Emperor, the Heralds of Change beseeched aid once again from their benefactor. Tz'Keth'K'Zar was only too pleased to answer.

As one, the nine Heralds were consumed by raging pillars of warpfire. The flames raced between their blazing bodies before erupting into a nine-sided warp gate. Out from that inferno spilled the daemon legions of Tzeentch. They brought anarchy and madness with them. The skies of Garmesh filled with kaleidoscopic clouds that whirled faster and faster about the world until those who looked upon them were driven insane. The worst afflicted fell, not down but upwards into the yawning skies with despairing screams, to be swallowed by the maelstrom.

The architecture of the hives sprouted weird extrusions and rearranged itself metaphysically so that soon no one could know where any doorway, crawlspace or processional might lead. Gravity; time; relative position and causality – all melted away like ice before a flame as the power of Tzeentch waxed across the world. Rebels and governor's guards alike found themselves lost in impossible mazes, trapped on stairways that never ended, or attempting to fight while standing vertiginously upon sheer walls or arched ceilings. Wherever the hosts of Tzeentch advanced, rampant change spread before them. Solid stone became feathered flesh. Doorways became fanged maws, or crystal mirrors into which damned souls tumbled for eternity. Fortifications transmuted into brittle glass, while those behind them were driven mad or mutated beyond recognition by the daemons' powers.

By the ninth hour after the incursion began, all hope was lost…

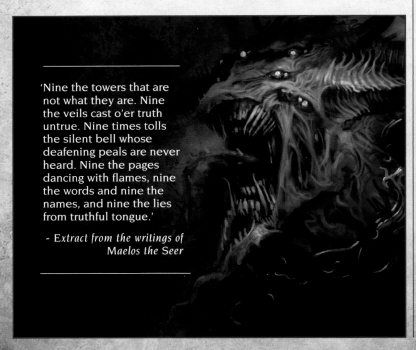

'Nine the towers that are not what they are. Nine the veils cast o'er truth untrue. Nine times tolls the silent bell whose deafening peals are never heard. Nine the pages dancing with flames, nine the words and nine the names, and nine the lies from truthful tongue.'

– Extract from the writings of Maelos the Seer

When the forward vid-feed flickered to life, Shipmistress Endara frowned at the image it displayed. She had expected to see a world wreathed in polluted haze, only the spires of Garmesh's hive cities jutting above the murk like craft sailing a tainted sea. Instead, the bridge of the Hopeful Saint was painted with the riot of colours thrown off by the planet's flickering weather systems.

'As though it were aflame,' breathed her second, Mister Thrend. Endara shot him a look, not liking the glassy quality of his gaze or the way the strange lights reflected in his pupils. She cleared her throat pointedly.

'Vox, have you established a link with Governor Habeyl's High Sanctum?'

The pause before her voxman answered only deepened Endara's unease. Her crew were Navis Imperialis veterans with several decorations to their name. They had manned their frigate through sterner tests than rescuing some unctuous planetary governor from the wrath of his mistreated subjects. They didn't hesitate. They didn't stare in bewilderment.

'Vox,' she barked again. The man turned to look up at her command dais, his expression dismayed.

'I... Yes ma'am, but... I can make no sense of what I'm hearing.'

'Route it to my earbead,' she said.

An instant later, Endara wished she hadn't. The cacophony that erupted through the vox was appalling. If it had simply been a wall of noise, that would have been bad enough. Yet amidst the confusion of babbling and screaming were threaded distinct pleas for help, brittle splinters of mirth, mathematical formulae chanted with a desperate intensity.

'Governor?' she tried, knowing her hail was futile, a single note drowned in a madman's symphony. 'Governor Habeyl, lord, can you hear me? This is- '

The din vanished, replaced by a sibilant singsong voice. It took Endara a moment to recognise the words to the lullaby her nursemaid used to sing to her when she was an infant and the nightmares came. A song that, so far as she knew, the nursemaid had invented herself and never repeated to another living soul.

Endara tore the bead from her ear with a shaking hand. Before she could draw breath to issue orders, or decide what in Throne's name those orders might be, the image on the vid-screen shuddered and expanded until its kaleidoscopic hues drowned the bridge.

'God-Emperor, what is happening?' croaked Mister Thrend, reeling back from the insane blare of light. That was when Endara saw the distorted figures emerging from within the blinding haze, saw the first eruptions of fire streak from their hands to engulf her bridge crew. Shipmistress Endara fumbled for her laspistol, but even as she did so the tide of light poured through her eyes to flood her mind, and her torments began in earnest.

NURGLE

Nurgle is the Plague God. He is most often depicted as a hulking and leprous abomination, a mountain of disease-bloated flesh whose pustulant innards spill through his splitting hide amidst a miasma of rot and droning plague flies. Nurgle, they say, hunches over his noxious cauldron and delights in brewing nightmarish contagions to unleash upon the peoples of realspace.

At first glance it might seem that few mortal beings would choose to worship Nurgle, and that those who do must surely be mad. The ragged preachers of Nurgle's feculent faith cannot promise martial might on a par with that embodied by Khorne. They do not offer the boundless cunning and sorcerous potency of Tzeentch, nor even the hedonistic pleasures or obsessive fulfilments of Slaanesh. Nurgle's remit is plague. His boons are in themselves supernatural maladies, daemonic parasites and disfiguring mutations. Who but a nihilistic lunatic would willingly offer worship to the author of such woes?

Yet disease, decay, entropy and the despair they bring are fundamental facts for populations and armies across the galaxy. On world after world, crops fail, food spoils and sickness and starvation follow. Overcrowded field hospitals are hotbeds for swift-spreading infections and feeding grounds for rapacious parasites. Languishing in foetid slums, pinned down and wounded amidst the contaminating filth of no man's land, ravaged by noxious bioweapons and alien phages, souls beyond number confront the inescapable fact of their own mortality. Some cling to faith and hope until the last. Most pass beyond the

limits of their endurance and cry out in their delirium for salvation no matter its source. Whether they suffer until the end or their will gives way, they all empower the Plague God.

It is said by the worshippers of Nurgle that – for all the cruelties he heaps upon realspace – he is at heart a fond-hearted and grandfatherly deity. There are few whose supplication he would refuse, nor deny his rancid gifts. Thus, the worshippers of Nurgle become willing hosts for all his most grotesque contagions precisely in order to survive their touch. They take into themselves that which would otherwise be their destroyer, becoming one with it, and glorying in the unholy vitality and resilience such a gruesome bargain grants. Each mortal who makes this pact becomes another vector for Nurgle's supernatural contagions, and another catalyst to furthering the Grandsire's power.

In truth, succumbing to the worship of Nurgle is indeed a kind of madness. His mortal worshippers exult in all the repugnant signs of disease and mutation that should instinctively repel them. They willingly spread his plagues far and wide, even to comrades

in arms or loyal friends they would previously have sought to protect. They do this in the certainty they are sharing Nurgle's priceless gifts, echoing their deity's boundless generosity. The most fervent of Nurgle's mortal worshippers recognise that even amidst the misery of disease and the ruination of decay, new life is born. Squirming parasites and filth-grubbing nematodes; grotesque, spore-spewing fungi; clouds of flies vast and dense as thunderheads; mutant viral strains and ravenous bacteria – all such progeny of rot proliferate where Nurgle's touch is felt.

THE GARDEN OF NURGLE

Nurgle's realm within the warp is described in mouldering, maggot-riddled grimoires and Ordo Malleus dataslates alike. Many are the luckless mystics and gibbering heretic witches who claim to have looked upon that noxious netherworld in their visions. Most call it the Garden of Nurgle, at the heart of which squats the vast canker of his manse. In truth, it is likely that neither Human words nor Human imaginations can come close to accurately portraying the raw malignancy of the empyric reaches in which Nurgle's powers coalesce.

THE MARK OF NURGLE
The Mark of Nurgle is known also as the tri-lobe, for it comprises three bloated spheres arranged in a distorted triangle. As often as not, the mark manifests in the form of plague symptoms. Three fatted boils; three pustules straining fit to burst; three reddened weals or crater-pocks in flesh; three coiled maggots, bulbous flies' eyes or leech-like maws; all these and myriad other horrors appear upon the hides of Nurgle's servants or bubble up from the armour plates of war engines dedicated to his glory. At other times the tri-lobe is wrought in verdigrised bronze or rusting steel, blessed with libations of bile and pus before being raised high above the reeking ranks of armies, mortal or daemonic. This awful mark may appear spontaneously upon the flesh of livestock, in the alchemical swirls of chem-factories or in the visions of luckless astropaths – a curse mark that promises plague and pestilence to follow. Even to look upon Nurgle's mark can cause mortal beings to suffer spontaneous outbreaks of disease; in battle such decaying icons borne by Nurgle's daemonic foot soldiers are veritable lodestones of virulence.

Still, accounts speak of churning, vomitous marshes thick with hissing reed beds of rotted bone. They tell of fungoid forests and of maggot-stuffed trees festooned with rusting bells, of pallid blooms growing bloated and foul from soil fertilised with rotting corpses and of the ghastly plague daemons that roam the blighted wilds.

The inhabitants of realspace would be fortunate if Nurgle's daemons stayed within that metaphysical garden. Yet wherever the Grandfather's power waxes amidst epidemic and sorrow, there his festering legions spill through the veil like foulness gushing from a punctured boil. They come in a shambling mass, their ragged banners flapping in pestilent winds that carry the tolling of discordant bells and the groan of mucous-choked voices to their terrified foes. Daylight curdles to a jaundice hue that renders all in sickly shades of pallor and disease. The land itself turns rotten, water thickening to effluent sludge while plants, animals and horrified soldiers alike bloat and burst with septic pus and teeming maggots. To fight the daemons of Nurgle is to be immersed in inescapable corruption, to have your weapons rust in your hands and fever wrack your aching body, even as all you seek to protect falls into ruin around you. Hopeless horror rolls ahead of Nurgle's daemons like a bow wave, mingling with masses of droning flies and billowing vapours to bring formerly staunch defenders to their knees.

Those who stand and fight face a riot of pestilent grotesques whose diseased warpflesh and rotted innards render them all but impossible to slay. Tides of giggling, biting plague-mites flow underfoot, malevolent little Nurglings that spill up the legs of screaming victims and bury them in mounds of diseased flesh. Massed ranks of Plaguebearers trudge to battle, slouched and rotten soldiers of Nurgle with but a single eye and crooked horn apiece. Bloated and foul, they maintain a droning count of Nurgle's countless maladies even as they hack away with plague swords whose touch promises poison and disease.

From the befouled skies come Plague Drones, revolting fly daemons

larger than an Ogryn that attack with slobber-wet mouthparts and filthy stings. In their shadows bound the Beasts of Nurgle, grotesquely ebullient masses of slug-like flesh and poisonous tentacles whose secretions sicken and paralyse, and whose vigorous attentions leave their mortal playthings crushed and rotten in their wakes. Looming over all, booming with cruel mirth and stinking like a sewage-choked plague pit, come the Great Unclean Ones. Fashioned in the image of their master, these rancid hulks of diseased flesh oversee Nurgle's pretties like proud parents. They slay those who oppose them with befouling magicks, clubbing blows of virulent blades and flails, and choking streams of noxious vomit so inimical that they can dissolve tank armour in seconds, or drown entire squadrons of soldiery in gelid filth.

'Seven is the tally of the Plague Lord, seven his sacred tale. Sevenfold the miseries that bubble and churn within his cursed cauldron. Seven the count of the Guards of Death. Seven the reaper's tithe. Seven, and seven, and seven again the count drones ever on.'

- Extract from the writings of Maelos the Seer

WAR ZONE:
MALAEOR

The feudal world of Malaeor lay deep within the Segmentum Obscurus. Fortified mining compounds dotted through its mountain ranges fed off-world industry, but beyond their battlements the rest of the planet languished in serfdom and ignorance. Only the world's ruling elites possessed access to modern-day Imperial technologies, and these they did not share.

The serf-classes of Malaeor lived short and fearful lives in service to their tech-lords. With little in the way of education or prospects, they clung to their faith in the God-Emperor. Over centuries, the serfs came to despise all technological or scientific lore; such matters were the domain of the God-Emperor alone, they believed. No mortal should seek to master them.

When an outbreak of retchpox began in the backwater province of Piety's Promise, medical corps from a nearby mine complex offered their aid. Retchpox was known to the Officio Medicae, and easily treatable with a course of alchemical tinctures.

Though the region's baron gave permission for the treatments to proceed, they were fiercely resisted amongst the settlements of Piety's Promise. Rumours circulated that accepting the cure betrayed a lack of faith in the God-Emperor. Village priests fed the flames, promising healing through flagellation and prayer. They had long benefited from the superstitious natures of their flocks, and did not wish to see their power undermined. Soon, angry mobs were clashing with bewildered medics and baronial militia. Lives were lost on both sides, and the retchpox continued to spread. As the disease claimed more and more victims, a chorus of suffering, sorrow, and pleas for salvation seeped into the warp.

Matters escalated further when several sufferers under the care of a priest named Frater Kalimund recovered without any medicae aid. Perhaps their cases were not so serious, or perhaps their recovery truly was miraculous. Whatever the case, Frater Kalimund took it as a sign that he had been chosen by the God-Emperor to heal Malaeor. The plague was a test of faith, or so he claimed. He preached that the people should turn from the false promises of heretic healers and barons, and instead make pilgrimage to his shrine in the Promulga Valley. He would work a great rite of cleansing, and all would be healed.

Kalimund's message spread faster even than the retchpox. Soon, many thousands of pilgrims flowed across the agri plains and through the settled passes, the healthy helping the sick along, all of them spreading the illness. Militia cordons were overrun, while the frantic warnings of the medicae adepts continued to go unheeded.

> 'Have a care, blessed
> soul, when you cry out
> in the night,
> For though your need for
> succour be great, your
> intention pure.
> You know not what listens
> for your call.
> You know not what answers
> your plea.'
>
> - Extract, Obscurun Rhymes and
> Fables, original source unknown

By the day of Kalimund's rite, Promulga Valley was overcrowded with pilgrim shanties. At last, the Frater could wait no longer, despite his desire to heal as many of the sick at once as he could. Word had reached him that the planetary governor had dispatched Astra Militarum troops to put a stop to matters. The miracle had to be worked before they arrived otherwise his efforts to bring healing to his people would end in a massacre.

Kalimund began his sermon from the steps of his shrine, his words carried by vox-horn and servo skull to the gathered faithful. When, seven verses and seven lines into his oration, Kalimund began to convulse, the congregation believed he had been gripped by the spirit of the God-Emperor. Then Frater Kalimund erupted in a revolting spray of diseased fluids. Before the screaming masses, a hillock of foetid flesh swelled from the

priest's ruptured remains. The Great Unclean One Obloxxothrax drew itself up to its full height and, with a bass chuckle, raised its leprous hands in benediction. The faithful fled this nightmare apparition, but they had no time; the daemon's blessing was only seven words long. As the last glottal syllable bubbled across the valley, the retchpox blossomed. It devoured its victims, wailing serfs and militia deserters collapsing as their liquefied innards erupted from every orifice, before their flesh in turn melted into bubbling ooze.

When the 98th Mordian Iron Guard crested the rise and looked down upon Promulga Valley, they found not a mass of civilians to be punished, but a lake of liquid putrefaction reminiscent of a bubbling cauldron. Even the most faithful soldiers began to sicken at once, as the miasmal fume from the valley rolled over them. As they choked, Obloxxothrax waded out of the lake, corpse-slop streaming from him and a shambling army of plague daemons at his heels.

Disciplined to the last, many Mordians stood and fought even as their comrades collapsed, vomiting blood and pus, or ran screaming. Yet more droning, bellowing daemons of Nurgle surged from the plague cauldron. Soon the Imperial soldiers were buried by an avalanche of filth. Obloxxothrax and his army marched on, the land sickening before them, as thunderheads of miasmal foulness gathered on high. So came the plague rains and whirling fly storms that heralded the advance. Rivers of filth gushed across the lands. Forests withered or bulged with putrescent life. The loyalist armies fought back as best they could, but one cannot fight a fever with lasbolts and bullets. By the time a strike force of Salamanders Space Marines answered the distress calls alongside Ordo Malleus daemon hunters, it seemed they could do little. Yet still they joined the fight, for just as a single retchpox sufferer had begun this entire pestilent nightmare, so Malaeor could not be allowed to be but the first of many planets to suffer Obloxxothrax's plague.

SLAANESH

No mortal being is entirely free from desire. Be it physical, mental or even spiritual, the need for fulfilment goes hand-in-hand with most species' wish to find meaning and purpose in their lives. Yet as innocent as such motivations may be, it is all too easy for desire to become obsession, debasement and excess. So are the seeds of Slaanesh's power sown.

To the cannibal tribes of Ghoma VI, Slaanesh is known as the Feastbringer, depicted as a slavering maw, vast as a canyon, whose hunger for Human flesh can never be sated. To the alien Jorvax, his name is a jarring cacophony of symphonic disharmony looped at mind-shattering volume through the organic amplifiers that grow like parasites upon their bodies. The traitorous regiments of Toloso know him as the Cruel Mirror, and mutilate themselves ever more grotesquely in hopeless displays of worshipful vanity. To the dwindling Aeldari, Slaanesh is named She Who Thirsts, and is both the product of, and eternal punishment for, their ancient empire's degeneration into murderous debauchery. The Dark Prince; the Lord of Excess; the Perfect One; there are as many names for Slaanesh in the great span of the galaxy as there are obsessions and perversions to waylay incautious and weak-willed mortals. Ultimately it matters not what name or appearance people ascribe to this Dark God; however they fixate upon him, they all worship him in their way.

THE MARK OF SLAANESH

As with everything redolent of the Dark Prince's power, his rune serves as both sign and source of corruption. Some mortals tattoo or carve his mark into their flesh, blazon it in garish colours upon war banners and fur-trimmed leather cloaks, or work it elegantly into their wargear before battle. For others it appears of its own accord, a hint of inner foulness that fractures even the most pure and pious exterior. A pattern of pearlescent scales upon the neck; a knot of pumping veins visible through pallid skin; pupils twisted into this unsettling new shape – however it manifests, the Mark of Slaanesh proclaims that here is another mortal soul claimed by the Dark Prince. Where it is borne into battle upon the magnificent standards of his daemon legions, Slaanesh's rune becomes a lurid stain upon the fabric of reality. It is a lens to focus and channel raw corruption into even the stoutest mortal heart. Merely to look upon such an icon is to risk one's soul and sanity, and for those who succumb to the mark's corrosive power a descent into obsession and madness awaits.

Slaanesh is empowered by need and want, by mortals' descents into obsession and their succumbing to temptation in any form. Thus, while he is sometimes portrayed as being the least mighty of the four great Chaos Gods, in many ways Slaanesh's power is simply more subtle and insidious than those of his infernal siblings. Moreover, its corrupting taint reaches into everything mortals strive for and want. As such, it is quite possible for Slaanesh to derive power from individuals and deeds that might – at first glance – seem dedicated wholesale to one of his rival deities. A murderous, blade-wielding gladiator, for instance, would seem on the surface to be an obvious servant of Khorne. Yet in that warrior's obsessive need to perfect her bladesmanship, in her pride at each victory and her lust for the adulation and accolades she wins, she instead gives unconscious worship to Slaanesh. Equally, a cunning noble overcoming his political opponents through elaborate scheming might appear a devotee of Tzeentch. Yet by the opulence and excess of his courtly lifestyle, not to mention his obsessive need to entrap his rivals in ever more Machiavellian plots, he too would empower the Dark Prince. Be it something as blameless as a starving labourer's desire for food, or as twisted as a sadistic killer's fixation upon inflicting pain, every mortal desire that is taken to extremes increases Slaanesh's might. In such a dark, violent and desperate age as the 41st Millennium, these energies rise like a flood tide.

ENTITIES OF EXCESS

The daemons of Slaanesh are manifestations of dark contradiction. Their aspect evokes the most desperate and hedonistic desires of mortal hearts, but also the fundamental wrongness and instinctive horror of such obsessions when they are taken to nightmare extremes. They are repugnantly beautiful, jarringly graceful, beguiling and yet wholly terrifying. The mere sight of such impossible entities can steal a mortal's wits, trapping them in an ecstasy of horror and longing that leaves them unable – often unwilling – to fight back.

The first warning of these daemons' onset may be lilting music, half-heard and strangely fascinating, borne to the ear upon a gently perfumed breeze. As the sounds and smells grow more intense they bring with them the first ripple of unease to mortal hearts. There is something acrid beneath the heady fragrances on the air, something that

hints at stale sweat, spilled blood and vomit. The faint aria becomes more strident, its source unclear, its notes clashing and intermingling with wailing voices and insidious whispers. Mortals feel their pulses racing unaccountably, their flesh prickling with waves of pleasure and pain. Their minds stray to dark needs, or else slide inexorably into a state of numbing bliss that dulls reactions and slurs speech. Guns slip from nerveless fingers. Tank engines idle as crews let their vehicles roll to a halt.

By now, even the softest daylight has become harsh and glaring, curdled with prismatic accents ranging from unnaturally garish to the livid hues of a fresh bruise. Whispering voices slither through comms networks, beguiling, threatening, imploring and tempting. Sulphurous breath caresses the napes of warriors' necks and feather-light touches rake their skin, even inside fully sealed suits of armour. Overhead, the clouds contort into writhing, half-recognisable forms caught between bliss and agony. Bedrock trembles. Those not already lost whisper frantic prayers as all around them the world holds its breath in unwilling anticipation.

Then come the daemons of Slaanesh. The skin of reality splits open like silken hangings slashed with razor blades, spattering perfumed gore and ectoplasm. Sinuous shapes surge through the rents with discordant shrieks and squeals of unholy delight. Fiends of Slaanesh scuttle towards their disoriented victims, nightmare amalgamations of insect, equine and humanoid wreathed in a billowing musk that curdles minds and bewitches souls. They rear over willing prey, who drop to their knees with sobs of horrified delight before the Fiends' claws and talons descend.

Behind these grotesque beasts flow packs of Daemonettes, lissom and beguiling monsters that dance towards their victims with insatiable hunger in their eyes. The Daemonettes' every claw-stroke is a lethal caress, their every cry of delight a soul-shredding screech whose mere utterance makes their victims yearn for more. Some of these handmaidens of Slaanesh ride upon whip-swift steeds, freakish and etiolated abominations whose trilling cries are often the last sound their luckless victims hear. Others ride aboard glittering chariots fashioned in razor-sharp curves that drag musically clattering threshing blades behind them. Driven beyond sense or sanity, some

mortals hurl themselves before the chariots, willingly succumbing to their ghastly fate. Those who choose to fight last little longer, for these elegant engines of slaughter shimmer unreally through even the fiercest fire and can travel swifter than a speeding combat bike.

As the wanton slaughter gathers pace, and those with the wit to do so try to fight back, so the violence and horror unleashed by the daemons escalates. Some torment the foe with sorcerous music, played upon instruments fashioned from contorted and still-living mortal supplicants. Others conjure ghastly warp magicks that corrupt and ruin their victims, or else drive the foe into wild rampages of cannibalistic debauchery that soon see them destroy themselves.

Even amidst such a riot of insane excess, the Keepers of Secrets loom large as true avatars of the Dark Prince's will. These are the champions and generals of Slaanesh's daemon legions, the stealers of souls and corrupters of worlds. At times they do their work subtly, by possessing those open to Slaanesh's wiles, or – even better – those whose piety should render them resistant. Be it planetary governors or Space Marine Chapter Masters, humble preachers or artists possessed of interplanetary fame, beloved, trusted or feared individuals such as these can be employed as tools to lead billions into damnation on Slaanesh's behalf.

Yet for all this, the Keepers of Secrets are most terrifying when they manifest in person upon the battlefields of realspace. Foes wail with desperate desire and prostrate themselves at the daemons' approach, allowing themselves to be crushed with delicate cruelty beneath talon and hoof. Many warriors claw their eyes out at the sight of the daemons' impossible beauty, or topple dead as their hearts rupture with self-loathing and lust. The Keepers of Secrets stalk through the madness, every motion inhumanly graceful, every blow delivered with the precision and might to shear a battle-tank in two. Their sorceries can transform the most loyal soldier into a maddened traitor, or kill mortal foes with a barrage of excruciating bliss so delicately cruel that it literally sets their victims' nerves aflame. With these terrible entities dancing at their head, the daemon legions of Slaanesh leave battlefields scattered with contorted corpses, their ruined features distorted by death screams of terrified ecstasy.

I urge you first never to read any passage of this grimoire in the presence of a mirror, no matter how small. If the compulsion takes you or need forces your hand, then in the name of the Saints at the least ensure that you are twice an arm's length from the reflective surface. Its reach is always longer than you think...

WAR ZONE:
PERSIPHON

When Drukhari raiders struck at the Imperial colony of Persiphon, the sadistic aliens inflicted unrelenting misery and terror upon the planet's people. The Drukhari became caught up in their cruel sport, lingering long enough that the Ultramarines of Strike Force Aurus arrived to deliver the Emperor's vengeance. Yet the Space Marines' victory had unintended consequences.

The people of Persiphon felt shamed. The xenos had tormented them, and they had been unable to defend themselves as the God-Emperor demanded. Yet they were also left with a bone-deep veneration for the magnificent blue-and-gold-armoured demigods who had rescued them. This adulation soon became a desire to echo the Space Marines' strength. The people of Persiphon vowed they would never need to be saved again.

Each of the world's six great clans established Halls of Excellence, wherein aspirants would train to become the best warriors that unaugmented Humans could be. A spirit of healthy competition and deserved pride in their achievements saw the Halls of Excellence turn out highly trained, physically conditioned and well-equipped warriors. For the next two generations, Munitorum tithe-takers noted an increase in the quality of Persiphon soldiery, who marched out in lockstep armoured in blue and gold.

Such accolades were not enough. The war clerics of the Halls of Excellence would accept only perfection. Seeking to push their peoples' achievements to new heights, they created the Six Circles. This new martial art encompassed body and soul, melding the spiritual teachings of the war clerics with an exacting regimen of physical training so extreme that not all survived it. Rumour had it that the Six Circles also saw aspirants undergo chemical and surgical augmentation behind the closed doors of the Halls of Excellence. Whatever the truth, the results could not be denied. For the next three generations, the Persiphon regiments became renowned for breathtaking martial excellence, even as the halls they trained in grew into vast mountains of colonnaded marble and statuary that gaudily aped the stately magnificence of Macragge.

For all their puissant skill and might, however, the Persiphon regiments were also noted for overweening pride and shocking excesses of violence in battle. When whispers circulated about a deviant religion growing within the

Halls of Excellence, it was enough for Inquisitor Rudran Luc to launch a covert investigation into the planet's darkening reputation. Luc's operation had barely begun, however, when astropathic distress calls rang out from Persiphon.

The message was semi-coherent, raving about civil war between the halls, and unidentified xenos monsters tormenting the populace. As fate – or some darker power – would have it, the same Captain Aurus of the Ultramarines was even now leading a sizeable strike force to Persiphon's rescue. Yet Inquisitor Luc suspected something more insidious at work, and raced to join Aurus' force before it reached the planet.

The Inquisitor's worst fears were realised as he and Strike Force Aurus made orbit over the hideously altered world. Interrogation of remote data-augurs revealed how the competition between the Halls of Excellence had turned sour, plunging their world into a shockingly savage civil war wherein the combatants

soon hurled aside all notions of their Humanity and the war clerics appealed to dark powers for aid in seizing final victory. So were the daemons of Slaanesh summoned by the prideful clerics of Persiphon. It was a tragically unwise invitation that could not then be rescinded.

No less than six Keepers of Secrets had claimed the planet and its people. Each now ruled one of the Halls, claiming the structures as palaces for their daemon legions and the mortal clerics as their enslaved devotees. The colossal buildings' architecture had mutated and exaggerated until each became a grotesque temple to psychotic excess that mocked the Ultramarian aesthetic to which it had once aspired. The influence of the Greater Daemons had flowed out across Persiphon as the veil between the warp and realspace weakened further. Burgeoning citysprawls, industrial macro-complexes, towering hab-stacks and rich agri zones had undergone nightmarish transformations. Stone and metal became quivering flesh, luridly hued crystal or milk-white marble that writhed with screaming faces. Perfumed fog banks of sweat-warm musk rolled in lavender clouds across the lands, driving those who inhaled them into ecstasies of pleasure, agony and mindless fury. Rivers of wine and blood gushed through ravaged settlements where former comrades tore at one another, minds lost to desperate gluttony or avarice.

Each Keeper of Secrets now ruled over its own distinct realm, each evoking one of the six circles of excess said to surround Slaanesh's Palace of Pleasure deep within the warp. Each landscape was more grotesque, extreme and cruelly distorted than the last. The civil war raged with lunatic intensity, grossly altered mortal cultists fighting alongside hosts of Slaaneshi daemons while the populace they had once sought to protect were preyed upon and made playthings of by keening murderers. Repulsed and furious, the Ultramarines launched an immediate attack. Such vile corruption could not be borne.

The citysprawl of Randa became the playground of the Keeper of Secrets Isk'ayn and its Legion of Avarice. The huge city's two billion inhabitants and garrison troops fell upon one another in their obsessive drive to seize all Randa's wealth for themselves. The daemons danced through the pandemonium, mocking, tempting and slaying.

The entire Walast Province was transformed through warp sorcery into a colossal amphitheatre ringed by jagged yet elegant mountains. Here, mortal and daemonic champions alike stalked one another through the shattered ruins of homes and shrines, seeking to slay their rivals and so earn the adoration of the Keeper of Secrets Shk'xil.

Landing amidst the swaying golden fields and sighing statues of beautiful Patiri, Ultramarines forces under Lieutenant Cassor were initially wrong-footed by this apparent idyll. Battle found them soon enough, though, daemons pouring from glades and palaces after being summoned by the self-destructive carnal rites of the pleasure-lost Patirians.

Captain Aurus led a drop assault against the greatest of the Halls of Excellence, in the province of Goahv. His forces soon found themselves scattered amidst a maze of distorted mirrors. As whispered temptations drowned the vox, and soporific incense seeped into even sealed power armour, daemons burst from every twisted reflection to attack.

Inquisitor Rudran Luc listened with growing dismay as a world's worth of debauched insanity converged on the outnumbered Ultramarines. Watching the weave of the warp thinning and realising a huge daemonic incursion threatened, Luc had his Astropaths send an encoded summons to Titan. The Grey Knights were needed on Persiphon.

THE GREAT RIFT

In the closing years of M41, a colossal belt of warp storms erupted across the galaxy, bifurcating the Imperium from the darkest reaches of the Segmentum Obscurus to the most remote extremes of the Eastern Fringe. This Great Rift not only severed half of Humanity from the Emperor's guiding light, but also ushered in a new era of witchery and daemonic rampage.

There are many varied theories regarding the origins of the Great Rift. Fragments of rumour suggest everything from the fall of the Cadian Gate, the fracture of Craftworld Biel-Tan, the manifestation in realspace of the Planet of the Sorcerers, or even the shattering of the daemon cage of Amethal. The likelihood is that all these events and countless others besides created the all-consuming cascade of unreality that ripped the galaxy so completely in two. In the wake of this catastrophic event, there were few mortals with the time or security to ponder such questions.

The Great Rift was, in truth, not a unified phenomenon but instead a roiling belt of warp storms stretching across the galactic plane from end to end. Even a single warp storm is a deadly threat to all mortal life – a raging tempest of empyric insanity that spills through from the immaterium and corrupts all that it touches. Warp storms swell and recede without apparent cause, sometimes blanketing vast regions. They foul any attempt at warp travel or psychic communication, and bring madness and mutation to every world, ship and being engulfed in their sprawl.

Daemons are able to inhabit such warp-realspace interstices, and entire planets may be transformed into nightmarish daemon worlds at their whims. Moreover, daemonic legions often spill out of these regions to attack the tracts of realspace beyond, given power and substance by the immaterial energies flooding out from the warp storm at their backs. The Great Rift comprises dozens of such immense metaphysical tempests, some of which have set to roaming the galaxy with an almost sentient malice, engulfing fresh star systems with every passing cycle. The rift's impact upon vast swathes

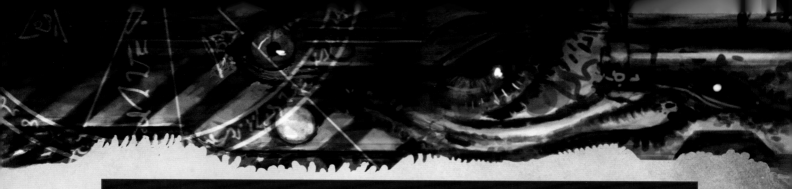

NIGHTMARE REALMS

Some warp storms rage briefly before collapsing in upon themselves in cascades of unreality and contradiction. Others wax and wane for centuries, even millennia, their fringes washing over planetary systems like nightmare tides before at last they recede altogether. Then there are those warp storms that take root, wounds in the fabric of reality so vast and ragged that they can never heal. These interstitial anomalies become regions where the warp and reality overlap permanently and infernal entities dwell alongside – or rule over – the heretics, renegades and madmen who offer them worship.

The names of such enduring warp storms are whispered in secret across entire segmentums of the Imperium. Their very mention conjures images of raging warp tides that drag void ships to their destruction, and of piratical havens and heretic empires where unholy, often daemonic, despots rule in defiance of the God-Emperor's will. Even without knowing the true horror of the daemonic threat, the most belligerent or pious shipmaster would still sooner scuttle their own craft than brave crossing the borders of one of these dangerous warp-realspace overlaps.

The Maelstrom is one such storm that has long held a dread reputation amongst mortals. Not only has this vast storm long played host to the renegade Space Marines of the Red Corsairs, but since the coming of the Great Rift it has also vomited host after host of daemons to assail the worlds beyond its rapidly expanding borders. It was from out of the Maelstrom that the Bloodthirster Kh'argosh Boilblood led the host that annihilated the Rhagmor System. The daemonic Pyrehunt of Tzeentch is said to haunt the Maelstrom also, surging forth on umbilici of sorcery to prey upon mortal worlds before retreating to the storm once more.

Other infamous storms, too, have spat out infernal legions to sow terror across realspace. The Glopslythe plague hosts of Van Grothe's Rapidity; the Shuddering Cavalcade that brought delightful horrors to those worlds around the Augatan Abyss; the murderous daemonic warbands that still reap their growing tallies of souls around the Tallarn Rift; the entities spilling through the shattered ruin of Khaine's Gate within the shadow city of Commorragh – all have wrought bloody havoc not only upon the settled systems of the Imperium, but also amidst the territories of countless alien races.

of realspace – and the beings inhabiting them – was nothing short of cataclysmic.

When the rift first erupted into being, shock waves of warp energy rolled across the galaxy to its furthest reaches. They plunged worlds into shadow and madness. Daemons manifested in great hosts upon planets that had never known the touch of heresy. Plagues of mutation ran rife through almost every sentient species, the spontaneous development of psychic powers chief amongst their effects. As uncounted souls wrestled to control supernatural abilities for which they were wholly unprepared, so the daemons of the warp indulged in a gleeful orgy of possession, corruption and spiritual predation.

The sheer upswell in background warp energies flowing through the void allowed daemonic armies to surge into realspace in previously impossible numbers. Amongst the most perilous of these were the eight legions of the Blood Crusade, each of which rampaged across the stars bringing slaughter in the name of Khorne. It was during this dark hour that the Blood God's daemons assailed

Holy Terra itself, launching a brief but exceptionally savage siege that was only repulsed at great cost by some of Humanity's mightiest heroes.

The daemons of Nurgle, meanwhile, fell upon the Scourge Stars in shambling masses, and there claimed a realm in realspace for the Plague God. A tri-lobe of star systems became extensions of the suppurating Garden of Nurgle. They would soon go on to threaten the stellar realm of Ultramar with their fecund hosts.

For their part, the daemon legions of Tzeentch turned their gaze upon the Stygius Sector where they, too, sought to establish a foothold in realspace for their master's realm. Worlds were transformed into prismatic ruinscapes of ever-changing madness. Armies of the Imperium, the Aeldari, the Necrons, the Orks and many other alien races all did battle with the scintillating legions that bedevilled them.

Slaanesh's Legions of Excess, meanwhile, cavorted at whim across realspace and invaded any world, void station or

nomadic fleet that took their fancy. They brought blissful agonies to every army that opposed them, while bestowing twisted crowns of excess on behalf of the Dark Prince to those mortals whose hedonistic extremes most amused them.

Such invasions and diabolic crusades were but a fraction of the daemonic incursions that struck the galaxy in the wake of the Great Rift's appearance. They have continued since, and might even have overwhelmed the defences of many mortal races but for one crucial fact. Just as the Dark Gods of Chaos are said to wage their Great Game against one another through the infinite realms of the warp, so now their contest is also fought out across realspace. Even as the Dark Gods' greatest champions do battle in the immaterium, so their legions both daemonic and mortal fall upon each other across star systems already ravaged by war. Though it was scant respite for the races of realspace, this has been enough for plans to be drawn, barricades to be shored up and – in Humanity's case – the Inquisition to once more draw a tattered veil of secrecy over the nightmare that threatens the Emperor's realm.

Second, you may feel a desire to walk away and leave the grimoire open, its pages exposed. Do not trust these thoughts, for they are not of your own mind. Seal the tome when it is not in your care. Place upon it a heavy weight, or bind it in warded chains. If you find it open upon your return, watch those around you with redoubled caution for they may no longer be themselves.

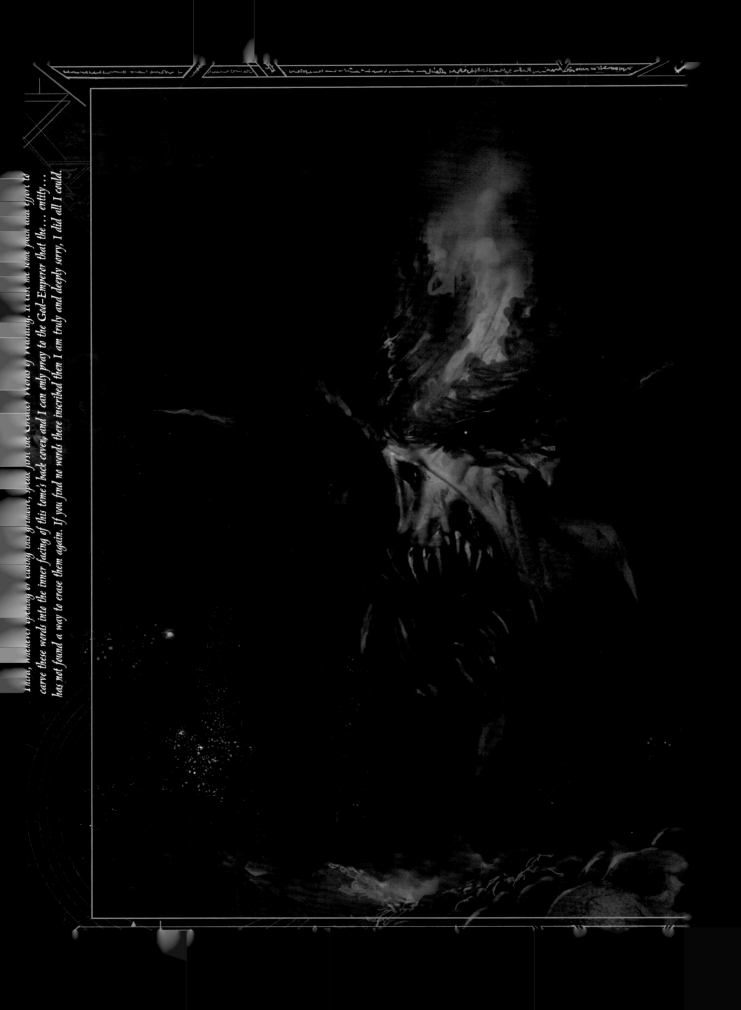

There, whatever opening or closing this grimoire, speak just the Greater Words of Warding. It cost me some pain and effort to carve these words into the inner facing of this tome's back cover and I can only pray to the God-Emperor that the... entity... has not found a way to erase them again. If you find no words there inscribed then I am truly and deeply sorry, I did all I could.

BE'LAKOR

Countless mortals compete for the favour of the Dark Gods. Most fall, slain in battle or physically and mentally destroyed by the mutating gifts bestowed by their patron deities. Those who endure earn the reward of immortality and become Daemon Princes in service to the Chaos God they worship. Be'lakor was the first such transcendent entity.

Be'lakor is also known – to those unfortunate few who know of him at all – as the Dark Master. Heretical myth tells that he was the first Daemon Prince ever elevated by the Dark Gods. Unlike those who have come after him, this mighty daemonic champion achieved apotheosis at the hands of all the great Chaos Gods acting as one. Nothing more is known of Be'lakor's origins, however. None will ever know why the Chaos Gods set aside their rivalries to fashion such a being, nor what manner of mortal creature Be'lakor was before his ascension. In part this is because these events are lost to uttermost antiquity. Yet more than this, the Dark Master has taken great pains to obfuscate his origins, erasing his taloned footprints through the dust of past millennia.

Be'lakor is to a Daemon Prince as most Daemon Princes are to the mortal beings they once were. Functionally he has become a demigod of the warp, not so great as Khorne, Slaanesh, Nurgle or Tzeentch, but certainly possessed of both the metaphysical might and the mortal worshippers to qualify him as a power in his own right.

Civilisation after civilisation has believed Be'lakor to be a god, and praised and feared him as such. Though he has taken pains to shroud his past, clues remain of entire planetary – even star-spanning – empires that have worshipped Be'lakor as their manifest deity. Crumbling friezes and vine-shrouded statues survive amidst overgrown ruins or upon the desolate surfaces of life-scoured worlds, hinting at veneration of the Dark Master. Such desolate echoes all suggest the same conclusion: the worship of Be'lakor ended with the wholesale destruction of his faithful. One after another, the Dark Master has laid claim to civilisations primitive and advanced alike, has established himself as their shadowy and sinister god, and has then driven his terrified followers to venerate and serve him unto their own destruction.

Those seeking some grand motive for Be'lakor's ruinous passage through the aeons and his cruel use of mortals would be disappointed. The truth is that he is a jealous and colossally narcissistic being,

as well as being merciless and cruel. Be'lakor believes that as the first chosen of the Chaos Gods he should be their greatest champion. That mortals such as Abaddon the Despoiler continue to enjoy the great gods' favour in his stead enrages him, and leads him to plot endlessly for his own advancement while at the same time taking his wrath out on all those who fall beneath his shadow.

It pleases Be'lakor to receive the adoration of fawning mortal masses. It pleases him to drink deep of their fear, and to feel how their zealous terror flows into the warp and empowers his eternal form beyond the veil. It pleases him to unleash them as his wild-eyed warriors, alongside daemonic legions he has tricked or tempted into his service. When he becomes bored, it also pleases Be'lakor to destroy that which he has made, plunging entire civilisations into apocalyptic civil wars before moving on in search of his next victims.

Be'lakor employs proxies and pawns to enact each new scheme. Yet this is not for want of his own martial and sorcerous

might – when roused to wrath, the Dark Master can slaughter entire hosts of foes. Like unto a god made manifest, Be'lakor wields the energies of the warp to alter reality at will. He conjures unholy shadows, plunges entire continents into sudden unnatural night and sows dissension, mistrust and terror through the hearts and minds of mortal foes. His terrifying Blade of Shadows exists in realspace only when Be'lakor wills it to, allowing him to drive its ephemeral form through layers of armour and crackling force fields before restoring it to physical form deep within the bodies of his victims.

Be'lakor is possessed of boundless cunning too, both as a schemer and a grand battlefield strategist. Whether he desires mortal disciples or daemonic legions to fight for him, he is almost always able to strike the right bargains and offer the correct blandishments or threats to secure the forces that he requires. During the War of Slime and Rust, the Dark Master extended his influence to steal away the planet Kolossi – seat of the noble House Raven – and relocate it deep into the benighted Imperium Nihilus. At a stroke Be'lakor gained a night-shrouded daemon world to rule, and from which his disciples could strike out at the worlds of the Imperium Sanctus. Not only do his forces include those Knights Be'lakor was able to spirit away and corrupt – and who now call themselves House Korvax – but also hosts of Renegade Astartes, mortal cultists and daemons of all four of the great Chaos Gods. What pacts the Dark Master forged with the generals of these infernal legions, what rivalries he has exploited and what desires he has manipulated, may never be known. However he achieved it, Be'lakor gained the allegiance of a combined mortal and daemonic host of vast numbers and power. Precisely what evils he planned to work with this gathering of might were unclear, for as always Be'lakor's plans remained shrouded in shadow. Moreover, with a being so cunning and whose plans stretch over such vast spans of time, it might be many years until his true intentions became clear. By then, it would be far too late for many luckless souls.

S ergeant Idras stepped through the side door of the hovering Valkyrie and into the night sky. He allowed his rappelling line to slither through its harness with practised smoothness, his stomach dropping away while the lights of Raddhab Downhive wheeled below him. His boots hit the ferrocrete roof and he detached his line. An instant later, he was stood amongst his squad of Dantos Grenadiers, taking in every detail of his drop zone.

Four gunships hovered low over the roof of the Administratum shrine, which jutted like a prow from one end of the sprawling complex it oversaw – the Guild Grisalt Slaughterhouse, big as a district, complex as a maze, not a single lumen lit in the whole place. It spread out dark and silent below the drop zone rooftop like a slumbering beast.

In the downdraught of the Valkyries' thrusters, three squads of veteran Dantosian soldiery had formed up. Alongside them gathered another knot of personnel, whom Idras eyed with wary interest. Lieutenant Naal he knew, having served under her for going on three years across seven war zones. Naal was typically unflappable, a fixed point of glacial calm amidst even the worst firefights. Tonight, Idras thought she looked unsettled. He could sympathise. In place of Naal's familiar command squad towered the robe-swathed figure the Dantosians had been instructed to call 'Saint' and his gaggle of strange attendants. Idras had never seen such an odd collection of armoured leather bodysuits, glowing goggles, mysterious augmetic armatures, gurgling fluid-shunts and baroque brass-chased equipment in all his days.

'I don't know what the freak show are here for,' he muttered to Corporal Haryl, 'but I don't like it.'

'Feels like a bad job, don't it Sarge?' replied Haryl in his distinctive valley-lander drawl.

Idras nodded to a trio of regimental priests huddled together near the corner of the roof. Sergeant Courtan's squad had helped the holy men to rappel, white-knuckled, down to the roof. Now the trio clung to their religious paraphernalia and fought to keep their robes from whipping about in the downdraught. To Idras they looked as out of place as a turd on a banqueting table.

'Reckon they feel the same as us about it,' he said.

'This is soldiers' work. What d'we need priests for?' asked Haryl.

'Who knows, Corporal, p'raps this so-called Saint is concerned for the good of our souls?' replied Idras.

Lieutenant Naal finished her hushed exchange with the looming Saint and turned to her assembled soldiers. Thrusters bellowed then receded as the Valkyries climbed away to begin a circling patrol. Idras tried not to think of them as carrion birds above a corpse, then frowned, wondering where such a macabre notion had come from.

'Soldiers of Dantos, duty calls and we shall answer,' Naal began. 'I am now at liberty to tell you that a substantial heretic cult has taken root within the depths of this complex. It is Saint's intention to expunge this infestation. We shall be his weapons of purification. Idras, your squad has point. Courtan, you're rearguard. Saav, you and yours will stay central and act as ready reserve. Meanwhile, Saint assures me that he and his operatives will handle any… heretical witchery that may be forthcoming. Mission is a kill sweep, no mercy, no survivors. Questions?'

Idras glanced at Haryl, saw that he too had heard the Lieutenant's hesitation on the word "witchery". He considered asking for more details on the nature of the deviance they might expect. A glance at the cowled Saint looming behind Naal told Idras he would be unlikely to receive any meaningful answers.

'Any foresight on enemy numbers or armaments, Ma'am?' asked Sergeant Saav.

'We expect substantial presence but poor quality heretic dregs, nothing to challenge good Dantos Grenadiers,' Naal replied.

'Time is not our ally,' came a rumbling voice. It took Idras a moment to realise that it had emerged from the deep shadows of Saint's cowl.

'You heard him,' Naal said. 'Sergeant Idras, breach and clear. The rest of you, follow up and watch our flanks. The Emperor protects, ladies and gentlemen.'

Idras' disquiet grew at how easily his Lieutenant had been pushed to haste. Just who was this Saint, and what were they doing here anyway? Why send veteran infantry to root out cultists, wasn't that what Enforcers were for? If life in the Imperial Guard had taught Sergeant Idras anything, however, it was that asking unwanted questions never led to anything good. Instead he gestured to the men and women of his squad to proceed.

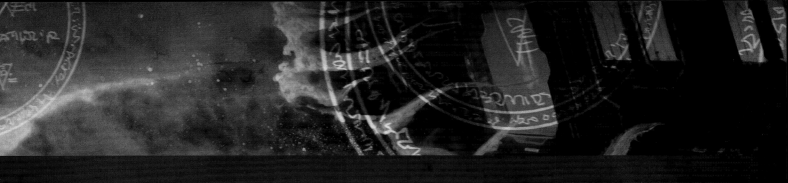

Grenadiers Polda and Cratch moved to the armoured access hatch set into the centre of the roof. Unhitching las-torches from their webbing, the two veterans muttered prayers of ignition and set to work on the hatch. The blue flames of the torches threw stark shadows across the rooftop and Idras had the sudden sense of a wrongness to their shape. They writhed in the corners of his eyes, jagged and somehow too large. Instinctively, Idras glanced aside. Seen dead on, the shadows were only that; shadows of soldiers. He thought he felt Saint's eyes upon him from within that darkened cowl and looked hurriedly back to Polda and Cratch.

The two troopers rose, hitching their cutters back to their webbing and hefting their lasguns.

'Breaching,' said Polda, raising one booted foot and kicking the hatch inward. The metal slab clanged against the stairs below and tumbled away. Idras winced at the din, feeling suddenly as though breaking the silence within constituted a transgression. Then he was moving, training taking over as Polda and Cratch led the way down the stairs with lasguns raised. Idras went after them, Corporal Haryl and the rest of the squad on his heels.

Below lay a spread of spartan Administratum offices and scriptoriums wreathed in shadow and silence. As the squad advanced, covering angles through arched doorways and between parchment-heaped desks, Haryl gestured at the ceiling lumen. Idras frowned, seeing every bulb blackened as though blown out by a surge of motive force.

'Lanterns,' he ordered. Beams of light cut the still air as his squad roused the light-packs strapped to their lasguns.

The Sergeant and his squad spread out, covering all movement, smooth and efficient. Behind them, the rest of the force entered the offices.

'Move down and press east,' ordered Saint in that same bass rumble. 'They will be concentrated around their fane this night, that lies at the heart of this complex.'

Wondering how the mysterious giant knew this, Idras shot hand signals to his squad to obey. The Dantosians slipped like wraiths from one office-cell to the next until Polda located a circular stone stairwell. Idras was about to take his first step down into the spiralling darkness when Voxman Thedak spoke up. He sounded unnerved.

'Sergeant, there's… something on the vox.'
Instinct told Idras to glance back to see whether Lieutenant Naal was sending or receiving. When he saw her doing neither, but instead returning a questioning look, he turned to Thedak.

'Define "something", Voxman.'

'Think you'd best take a heed f'r yourself, Sarge,' said Thedak. Impatient to keep moving, Idras nonetheless took the proffered headset and held it to one ear. His skin prickled as sibilant whispers and glottal muttering crawled into his ear. Idras felt hot and cold all at once. Nausea turned over in his gut. He met Thedak's eyes, saw his unease mirrored there.

From behind came a rising metallic clatter mingled with a whistle like steam from a boiler. Idras looked to see one of Saint's retinue pointing at the vox set, mouth stretched in a dark 'Oh'. The noise came from a bizarre mass of dials and valves grafted to the side of the man's skull. Several bulbs set into the black leather of his chest had lit up angry red.

'Disable all vox,' ordered Saint in a tone that brooked no disagreement. Thedak and the other squads' Voxmen obeyed at once. Idras, both hands back on his gun, stalked down the stairwell behind Polda and Cratch. As his footfalls echoed weirdly around him, he tried and failed to banish the word that had sprung back into his mind.

Witchery.

They descended past several more floors of nondescript cubicles before passing through a metal archway. This brought Idras and his soldiers out onto a metal gantry running west to east through a cavernous chamber. A glance over the rail suggested a drop of at least fifty feet, down onto the machinery of an industrial killing floor.

'Push east, cover the angles, watch your footing,' Idras ordered. His grenadiers obeyed, and soon found themselves advancing between ceiling conveyors from whose chain-hooks dangled hundreds of grox carcasses.

'Smell like they been 'ere a while,' said Haryl, face creased in disgust.

Idras was about to respond but froze, staring at a nearby carcass. Surely it had been swinging in the breeze. Surely, he hoped, it hadn't squirmed like a worm on a hook.

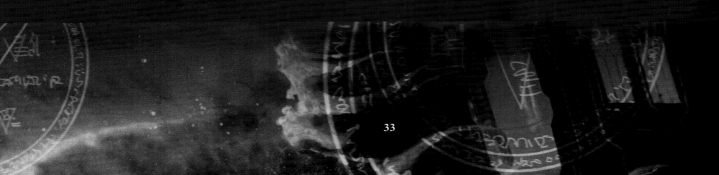

'Sergeant?' asked Polda, who had stopped ahead of him. Idras glanced her way then gave a bark of surprise and recoiled against the railing. Grenadier Polda's features were a mask of rotted meat, one eye hanging like a bulbous sac from its socket, fat maggots spilling from a gaping hole where nose and mouth should have been.

'Sergeant?' she asked again, and then all of their light-packs blinked off at once.

The next few seconds felt to Idras like the longest of his life. The saviour rail groaned and his heart leapt into his mouth as he imagined plunging down onto the spikes and blades below. Voices cried out, but they sounded wrong, hoarse and rasping or clotting with fluids. From all around came the rattle of chains, as though what hung from them was writhing and dancing with a terrible eagerness. Again there came the clatter and whistle of bizarre machinery, this time mingled with a bellows-wheeze followed by a moaning voice that uttered something like prayers. A lasgun discharged with a flash.

'In the God-Emperor's name, spirits I deny thee!' Saint's voice cut through the bedlam, accompanied by a pressure wave that made Idras' ears pop. In its wake the chains stilled their rattling. One by one, the lights on the soldiers' guns flickered back to life. Idras exhaled as he saw Polda's bewildered features were free of corruption.

'What in the name of the Throne- ?' began Lieutenant Naal, but Saint spoke over her.

'Portenta pre-malignor. The veil thins, Lieutenant. I did not think… no matter, what is, is. Haste, all of you, lest we arrive too late. Priests, your prayers may shield us – raise your voices in praise unceasing.'

The three preachers did as bidden, hesitant at first but gaining confidence until their words rang through the cavernous space in holy exhortation.

'Advance, double time, weapons roused,' barked the Lieutenant. Idras, glad of something concrete and rational, obeyed. Dantosian boots rang against the swaying gantry as he and his soldiers jogged eastward, and as they went he did his best to banish the supernatural horrors of the last minutes from his mind. He reached for anger, hoping to use it to scour away his fear. Some witch had gotten into his mind, and he would exact revenge for that violation. More corridors led on from the gantry, then more spiralling stone stairways coiling down to a network of brushed steel

halls and chambers lined with blackened lumen sconces. They all looked alike to Idras. He found himself checking his handheld auspex with increasing regularity.

He turned a corner into another corridor and pulled up short. Idras scowled down at the map readout on his device, then back up at the solid metal wall that should not have been there. He noted the patina of rust clinging to the metal, suggesting it had been there a long while and had not been well maintained.

'Back up, map error,' he snapped, retreating to the cross-corridor they had just passed.

'Sergeant?' asked Naal, and he was about to suggest they try the northward passage when he saw with increasing alarm that it, too, was nothing but a rusted wall.

Saint swept past them. His retinue had formed up around him and had an arsenal of weird-looking weapons in hand.

'Fallible human senses will not serve this close to the epicentre,' Saint threw back over his shoulder. 'Follow, and stay close if you do not wish to be forever lost.'

Idras didn't feel inclined to argue, and from the haste with which his comrades followed the robed giant, neither did they. For all their veterancy, the Dantosians bunched close as though for mutual reassurance, and almost all of them were now muttering their own prayers to the Emperor. Idras was no exception.

As they hastened through the disorienting maze, he tried hard not to think about the sights he saw. Some corridors seemed to stretch away for miles, vanishing in impossibly distant dots of sickly light. Others were furred with centuries of rust and bulbous fungi across which scuttled things with too many legs and pallid bodies that looked on the verge of bursting. A stench hung thick in the air. Idras' lungs felt hot, and sweat prickled his brow as though he was sickening with something.

The Sergeant was just about to voice his growing fear that the cultists had released a viral weapon, when Saint led them down a sloping corridor and halted before a sagging pair of metal double-doors that were rusted shut.

'Be ready, all of you, and remember that the Emperor protects,' he said. 'Whatever you see beyond this door, understand it is but the illusion of witchery. Slay your foes, whatever form they might appear to take. Do not falter.'

Before any of the Dantosians could raise a voice in protest or caution, Saint cast aside his robes. A towering figure was revealed, not the bulk of a Space Marine but rather the elongated form of one who had undergone strange and extensive augmentations. Saint wore ornate golden armour painted with complex hexagrams, and a closed helm with a blank metal faceplate. From somewhere, a long silver sword had appeared in his double-handed grip.

At a nod from their master, Saint's retinue swung power hammers into the doors and stove them inward. The reek that rolled out through the sundered portal hit Idras like a physical blow. Some of the Dantosians staggered back and vomited explosively. The rest stared through the portal, frozen in horror at the sight now revealed.

Perhaps this had once been a chamber like the rest, a physical space in which the shadowy suggestions of metal pews and some manner of altar still lingered. Yet it shuddered before Idras' eyes, reeling in and out of focus, overlaid with a nightmarish double-image. The floor both was and was not flooded with rancid mud, that did and did not pop and bubble as finger-thick worms seethed through it. Rag-robed corpses lay everywhere, both submerged beneath the filth and not, simultaneously appearing newly dead yet also furred with green mould and sprouting man-high fungi rippling with screaming human faces. Something like a fanged and grotesquely bloated tree grew where the altar had been, the bells that did and did not festoon its un-branches tolling mournfully in a spore-thick breeze that blew from nowhere. Worst of all, where there should have been and still were walls, there was also a vista of ghastly swampland and mutant underbrush so foul that Idras' mind refused to make sense of it. Wading towards them through the miasmal clouds of the impossible swamp were rotting humanoid figures. Their cyclopean eyes stared. Their voices were raised in a croaking mantra of ceaseless counting.

Several of Idras' soldiers crumpled, collapsing into the unreal mire as though their hearts or minds had given way. For his part, the Sergeant had just enough wherewithal to shout a single word.

'Fire!'

He squeezed his trigger and his surviving soldiers followed suit. Lasblasts flickered. Their first volley peppered the nearest of the approaching monsters. Some blew clots of rancid flesh from the creatures' frames,

while others passed straight through them as though they weren't there.

'Sarge, what… what…?' Haryl's voice was a half-sob and contained a pleading note.

'Illusion, witchery, got to be,' the Sergeant replied, and barely recognised his own wet croak of a voice. He blinked crusted eyes and tried to ignore the pustules breaking out across his hands, the rust tendrils crawling along his lasgun. *All just illusion and witchery*, he told himself. *Don't think. Keep shooting.*

Saint had waded into the deformed chamber and his silver sword flashed as he hacked at the advancing monsters while roaring strange words. Sigils glowed into being in the air around him, spinning like ethereal gears and coiling out to bind and then dissolve groaning entities. Around him his retinue unleashed arcs of searing energy and bursts of magnesium-white flame from their weapons, while at their backs the priests advanced, praying fervently. At the doorway, Sergeants Courtan and Saav pushed their soldiers up to join the firing line, bawling at them to focus, to pray, and for the Throne's sake to keep shooting. For a moment Idras felt a surge of fervent hope. One by one, the monsters were falling. As they did, the stigmas of sickness he saw on his flesh flickered as though they truly were just an illusion.

When the monster surfaced beneath Saint and his followers, it came up like a submerged island dredged from the deeps. Idras had an impression of yard upon yard of diseased green flesh and rancid fat, of rotted muscle and of fanged imps that clung to the emerging mass and cackled like spiteful infants. He saw a distended jaw yawn impossibly wide, saw the golden armour and bright silver blade of Saint vanish into a gullet as though into an infernal abyss. Then the monster was looming above them, head thrown back, throat bulging as it swallowed the man who had led them into this nightmare. The thing looked down at Saint's scattered followers, already vanishing under a tide of its scrabbling plague-mites. It gave a deep, wet chuckle and turned its ancient yellow-eyed gaze upon the quailing Dantosians.

By the time it opened its rotted jaws to laugh, and the ceiling tore away amidst a vortex of lurid green lightning and thrumming plague flies, Sergeant Idras' sanity had fled and his gun had fallen from palsied and rotting hands. It was, perhaps, an Emperor-sent mercy that he had not the wit remaining to understand what happened next…

THE EYE OF TERROR

The greatest and most nightmarish of all warp-realspace interstices is known as the Eye of Terror. This colossal zone of immaterial overlap dominates the Segmentum Obscurus and – before the coming of the Great Rift – represented the single largest and most corrosive region of warp corruption in the known galaxy.

Within the Eye of Terror, space itself is corrupted by the warping touch of Chaos. Stars have become colossal runes blazing with eldritch fire, or staring eyes whose inescapable regard drives mortals slowly mad. Planets have mutated into raging ruinscapes, become nomadic and predatory entities, or have slid outside of the flow of time, trapping all on their surface like insects in amber.

Typically of the inconstant nature of the warp, corruption does not saturate all those systems within the Eye of Terror equally. Relative geography and fundamental physics mean less and less the deeper one travels into this bizarre region. However, there are zones – particularly within the fringes of the storm – still broadly governed by natural laws. Even here, though, mutation and sorcery hold sway. Worlds turn beneath distorted skies ravaged by storms of coruscating flame or haunted by fleeting and grotesque faces. Mountain ranges transmogrify into sky-scraping skulls from whose cavernous eye-sockets pour waterfalls of molten blood. Oceans clot into seething morasses of diseased filth, through which foul leviathans hunt and sport. Forests grow into masses of fleshy extrusions dense with scintillating cilia whose touch brings blissful oblivion before draining their comatose victims dry.

On these deformed worlds, once-elegant cities become endless mazes that coil impossibly around libraries crammed with sentient grimoires and hunched daemonic scholars. Land masses migrate, or do battle with one another, or drift away into the skies while trailing stinging tendrils across the lands below. One world may become a hellscape where brazen daemon forges tower over plains of blackened skulls. Another may run like melted tallow until it becomes an ever-shifting morass to trap the unwary. There are worlds that seem idyllic, until one realises that every species of flora and fauna has become an exaggerated predatory horror rendered all the more nightmarish by their outward beauty.

Mortal beings dwell on many of these habitable worlds within the Eye of Terror, albeit not always by choice. Primitive tribes and mutant cults raise gruesome idols to placate their daemonic deities, their champions battling one another in the faint hope of attracting the eye of the Dark Gods. Enclaves of piratical raiders – both Human and xenos – risk madness and corruption to hide out amidst the wheeling balestars and carnivorous asteroids. Many do this because they know that only the most desperate and dogged pursuers will risk tracking them to such dangerous lairs.

These tribes and gangs must find ways to survive the attentions of the daemonic entities that hunt them like prey, or rule over them as monstrous overlords. Even for those mortals who maintain this perilous balance, there can be no sane or happy existence within the Eye of Terror. All living beings instinctively sense the wrongness of the warp-tainted reality all around them, and their minds and souls inevitably rebel.

Greater and more powerful heretics, however, are able to maintain enduring strongholds within the more stable reaches of the warp interstice. Chief amongst these are the Heretic Astartes. Some warbands of these post-human traitors rule hideouts little larger or more imposing than the pirate enclaves. However, Traitor Legions such as the Death Guard, the Iron Warriors or the dreaded Black Legion control vast swathes of tainted territory and strings of worlds within the Eye of Terror.

THE CRONE WORLDS

The Eye of Terror was created in the moment that the galaxy-spanning empire of the ancient Aeldari fell from grace. For thousands of years these puissant aliens ruled as undisputed masters of the stars. So incredibly advanced was their civilisation that they were free to indulge their every curiosity, perfect whatever skills or art forms took their fancy, and indulge themselves with a galaxy's worth of available sensations. Slowly but surely the ancient Aeldari passed from lives of ease and splendour into indolence, arrogance and a spiralling descent into hedonism. By the time the pleasure-cults took hold, and murder became a recreational sport, and other sentient species were deemed ingredients to be rendered down for narcotics, the Aeldari were lost. Some of their people fled aboard the stately void-arks they called Craftworlds, or escaped to pursue puritan and simple lives on distant Exodite worlds. They survived when all the collective obsession and perversion of the ancient Aeldari finally coalesced in the warp and formed the newborn Chaos God Slaanesh.

In the instant of his manifestation, Slaanesh's warp-borne scream blasted the souls from every one of the ancient Aeldari still dwelling in the heartlands of their empire. With his first inward breath, the Dark Prince consumed them all. Aeldari legend has it that She Who Thirsts – as they know Slaanesh – then went on to butcher their gods and shatter what remained of their maimed empire. Whatever truth of such metaphysical tales, it is an undeniable fact that the worlds of the ancient Aeldari remain, deep within the Eye of Terror, and that they are bleak and terrible places. Tattered clouds race ragged over the hollow spires of once-elegant cityscapes. Ashen winds wail between skeletal forests and scatter dust over vitrified tangles of alien bone. Unliving entities stalk the wastes, preying upon one another, or upon those brave or foolhardy enough to come in search of the powerful treasures of the ancient Aeldari. These Crone Worlds remain a tragic reminder to the Aeldari of all they have lost, and of the doom that awaits all those civilisations who slip into the clutches of the Dark Gods.

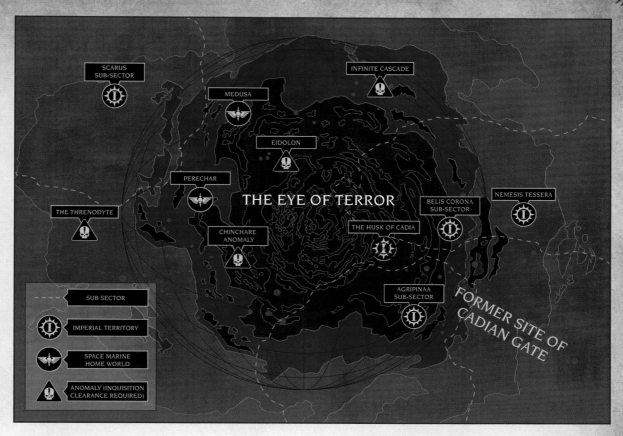

The diabolical tech-magi of the Dark Mechanicum also control facilities within the storm, infernal forge complexes and unnatural weapons-research shrines of horrific aspect and power. The magi readily exploit the cessation of natural physical laws to raise colossal structures and planet-sized forges that would collapse under their own insane vastness and complexity outside the Eye of Terror. They channel the energies of the warp through runic lenses, entrap daemons drawn from the tides of the empyrean and fashion weapons that would shatter the sanity of any other mortal minds.

THE DAMNED REACHES

In the depths of the Eye of Terror are stranger and more primal regions where realspace has been wholly subsumed into the madness of the warp. Here lie true daemon worlds, where greater warp entities lay claim to planets and luckless flora and fauna, before refashioning them however they see fit.

Upon such worlds the daemons of Chaos rule like malicious gods. They meld and unmake reality at whim, channelling the unfettered power of the warp to do so. Air becomes solid stone, becomes raging fire, becomes gibbering flesh and liquid

sorrow and carnivorous deceit. Worlds unravel into Möbius spirals over which daemon legions wage sanity-blasting wars. Moons become vile steeds for daemon overlords, driving titanic probosces into neighbouring planets and spinning cocoons of dreams and nightmares about their celestial prey. Worlds come and go like gheist ships, dragging trillions of screaming souls in and out of the warp with them.

Amidst these zones of madness, daemon legions make their lairs. Some sail the warp tides aboard fleets of infernal ships. These may be mortal void craft stolen or possessed, or vessels of fashioned warp energy in the form of ironclad warships, rotting hulks, spinning discs of crystal and flame, or opulent void-borne pleasure fortresses. Such daemon fleets have been known to emerge from the Eye of Terror to reave the systems about its fringes, spreading terror and despair before vanishing again on the tides of the warp. Other daemon warlords raise strongholds upon worlds transformed by their desires. From stygian forges to temples of wild delirium, rotting marshland fortresses to clockwork city-engines of infinite complexity, these fastnesses teem with

daemon hosts. They form not only staging posts for the ongoing wars of the Great Game, but also mustering grounds from which daemonic legions launch crusades of slaughter across realspace.

DREAD OMENS

The nightmare truth is that, should the daemonic legions prevail, the bedlam that reigns within the Eye of Terror would be the fate of the entire galaxy. Though each might pursue their masters' unique agendas with single-minded tenacity, the ultimate aim of most daemons is to manifest within realspace and corrupt it entirely with the energies of the warp, until it too collapses into formless madness. Should enough of realspace be subsumed, matters will reach a tipping point where that which conforms to sanity and natural law becomes a series of shrinking islands amidst an endless ocean of rapacious madness. Such a fate will bring complete damnation to all mortal beings. Those who understand the danger still fight against this impending doom, yet as the storms of the Great Rift rage and the daemon legions spill out to overrun one world after another, the last days of reality draw ever closer.

INFERNAL PANOPLY

The daemon legions have no use for the formalised markings and heraldic systems used by mortals to order their hosts. Instead, their appearances and aspects are dictated by the nightmares of living beings and the natures of their patron deities. If they do display icons and insignia, these manifest as ghastly distortions of those over which mortal beings obsess.

The overriding colouration and aesthetic of each daemonic host is dictated most strongly by the Dark God to whom the daemons owe their allegiance – often their very existence. Daemons of Khorne tend towards a panoply of blood red and brass, offset by black and bone. Those of Nurgle manifest all the varied and gruesome hues of decay, rancid greens and mouldering greys clashing with the vivid hues of spilled viscera and lurid boils. The daemons of Slaanesh manifest in delicate and luxuriant shades with gossamer silks and pastel flesh blending into glimmering silver and bronze. Meanwhile, the daemons of Tzeentch are kaleidoscopic in their aspect, pinks, blues and purples flowing into the vivid yellows, greens and reds of roiling warpfire. Yet as with all things born of the warp, there is no rule save that all rules exist to be broken. Some strange hosts manifest in hues that mock and distort full martial regalia, with proud standards fluttering and insignia manifesting like stigmata upon unholy flesh and armour. Others take corporeal forms that clash wildly with the typical colours associated with their god, or may even assume aspects of the environment in which they spawn, from flowing lava and dancing flame to industrial iron or sucking trench-mud.

Karanak

Flesh Hound

Bloodletter

Bloodreaper

Bloodletter with instrument of Chaos

Bloodletter with daemonic icon

Upon the doomed world of Herculanis, the unstoppable might of the Blood God's daemons is unleashed in all its barbaric splendour. Though the brotherhoods of the Grey Knights seek to stem the tide, they cannot stand against the raw fury and aggression of the bloodied host.

Bloodmaster

Skulltaker

Bloodcrusher

Pink Horror with daemonic icon

Pink Horror

Blue Horrors

Brimstone Horrors

A Lord of Change, its prophetic powers combined with the devious trickery of the Changeling, leads a sudden and sanity-warping assault against the forces of the Dark Angels. Warp flames leap and reality twists out of true as the raw might of madness and horror are unleashed.

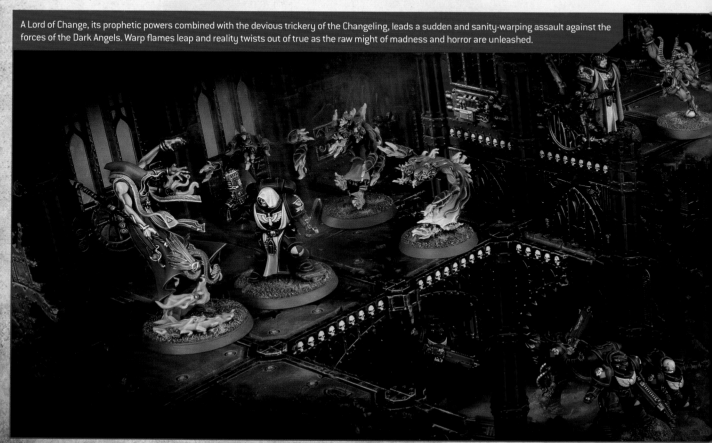

Screamer

The Blue Scribes

The Changeling

Flamers

Plaguebearers

Spoilpox Scrivener

Beast of Nurgle

Like a revolting tri-lobe writ large upon the battlefield, Rotigus, Horticulous Slimux and Epidemius lead the daemons of Nurgle to the attack. The Ork tribes of Ugmok's World fight for all they are worth, but with reality itself putrefying around them, their end is inevitable.

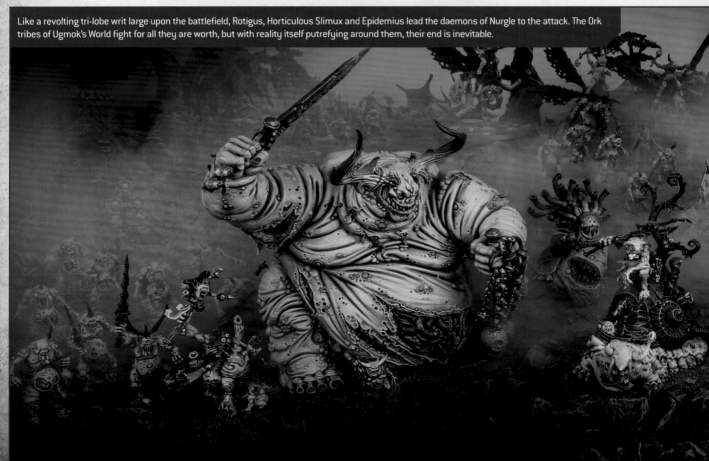

Horticulous Slimux

Sloppity Bilepiper

Embodiments of unfettered hedonism, obsession and debauchery, the daemons of Slaanesh spill from the tainted Basilica of Saint Dorieas with Shalaxi Helbane urging them on. The prayers and gunfire of the Sisters of Battle are not enough to stay their wild bacchanal of war.

The Contorted Epitome

Fiend of Slaanesh

The Masque of Slaanesh

Daemonettes and Alluress

Daemonettes

Be'lakor, the Dark Master

Though their masters might be rivals in the Great Game, when the wards around the Sanctuary of Gethsemanon collapsed, the daemons of Khorne and Tzeentch swept down upon the Adeptus Custodes defenders as one.

Upon Phaedox XIII, both indolence and unclean practices brought damnation to the populace. So it was that when that damnation found physical form, it was both the daemons of Nurgle and those of Slaanesh.

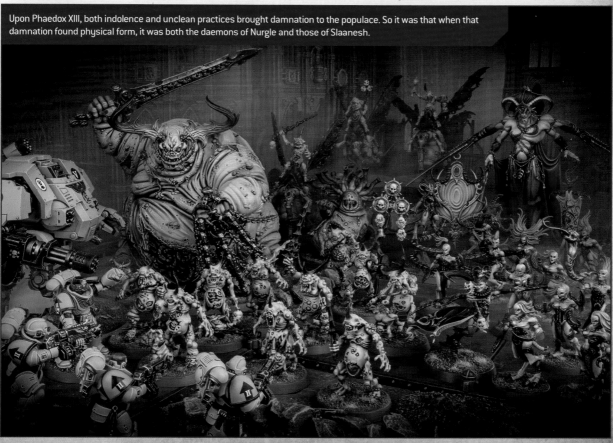

THE RULES

Welcome to the rules section of *Codex: Chaos Daemons*. On the following pages you will find all the rules content you need to bring every aspect of the legions of the Dark Gods to life on your tabletop battlefields. Maybe you're inspired to dive straight into some open play games, maybe you want to forge your own tales of glory and infamy with narrative play, or perhaps you can't wait to pit yourself against your opponents in nail-biting matched play contests. Whichever appeals to you – even if it's a bit of all three – this section of your Codex provides a modular toolbox that allows you to get the most out of your collection.

Of course, there's no need to take it all in at once! Some of the content on the following pages, things like your army's datasheets and the rules for its weapons, will be useful no matter what kind of game you're playing. Others, such as your army's Stratagems, Warlord Traits and Relics, will become relevant once you start playing games with Battle-forged armies. Then there's content like rules for upgrading your Greater Daemons, or the various psychic disciplines that you will unlock by including particular models in your tabletop army. In each case, you can include these new elements at your own pace; whether you're a brand new hobbyist playing your first few games or a veteran general ready to cause carnage, there's plenty here to provide you with countless hours of fresh and exciting gameplay.

On top of this, Chaos Daemons are the only faction in Warhammer 40,000 with access to the Warp Storm rules, by which you can bring the madness and chaos of the Warp to the battlefield to boost the powers of your daemons and even replace destroyed models with new reinforcements from beyond the borders of reality! You will find everything you need on the following pages to include these rules in your games of Warhammer 40,000, not to mention bespoke content for your Chaos Daemons Crusade force. Included in the latter are exciting Requisitions that enable you to expand the powers of your Greater Daemons and a system allowing you to track the Great Game, the eternal battle between the Dark Gods of the warp, to empower your units based on which Chaos God's powers are in ascendancy!

'We manned our trenches, recited our prayers, and waited to see what foes had made it through our bombardment. We expected a handful of survivors to stagger from the smoke to be cut down, you understand? But I wondered even then, why did our officers seem so tense if that was all we faced? I had never seen real fear on Captain Tshul's face, but I remember I saw it that day and it disquieted me deeply. Then the smoke started to clear, and those… things… They were all but unscathed! They bore down upon our lines so fast, and as they did soldiers ran mad with terror or fell dead at the mere sight of them. Let us say simply that Captain Tshul wasn't the only one undone by fear that day.'

- Unnamed soldier, last testament before purgation

50

BATTLE-FORGED RULES

DETACHMENT ABILITIES (PG 53)
Units in Legiones Daemonica Detachments gain additional abilities to reflect how these daemons fight on the battlefield, including Legions of the Gods rules that grant additional Warp Storm points. You can find out more about Detachment abilities in the Battle-forged Armies section of the Warhammer 40,000 Core Book.

ARMY RULES

THE BOOK OF BLOOD (PG 61-73)
This section is dedicated to Khorne, the god of war and bloodshed. You can find full details of the contents of this section on page 61.

THE BOOK OF CHANGE (PG 75-87)
This section is dedicated to Tzeentch, the god of sorcery and change. You can find full details of the contents of this section on page 75.

THE BOOK OF CONTAGION (PG 89-103)
This section is dedicated to Nurgle, the god of plagues and decay. You can find full details of the contents of this section on page 89.

THE BOOK OF EXCESS (PG 105-121)
This section is dedicated to Slaanesh, the god of sensation and excess. You can find full details of the contents of this section on page 105.

THE BOOK OF THE WARP (PG 123-129)
This section is dedicated to Be'lakor, the Dark Master, and other daemons that are not specifically dedicated to one of the other gods. You can find full details of the contents of this section on page 123.

CRUSADE RULES

CRUSADE (PG 130-143)
Chaos Daemons have access to a host of additional rules that enhance your Crusade experience and further personalise your Crusade force. These include bespoke Requisitions, Agendas, Crusade Relics and Battle Tactics that help to reflect the fighting style of these otherworldly beings. Amongst the rules presented in this section are rules for the Great Game, the eternal battle between the gods, and its effects on your army.

WARGEAR

WEAPON PROFILES (PG 144-147)
This section provides an alphabetised list of all the weapons that Chaos Daemons units can be equipped with, and should be used in conjunction with the datasheets section.

POINTS

POINTS VALUES (PG 148-149)
If you are playing a game that uses points values, you can use the alphabetised lists in this section to determine the cost of each unit from your army. These values will be reviewed and updated annually.

RULES REFERENCE

GLOSSARY (PG 150)
In this section you will find a glossary of rules terms used in this Codex. This is intended to work alongside the glossary found in the Warhammer 40,000 Core Book, and aid in resolving any complex rules interactions that may arise.

REFERENCE (PG 151)
Here you will find a bullet-pointed rules reference that summarises some common Chaos Daemons rules.

COMBAT PATROL

This Combat Patrol sized force is the perfect way to start a Chaos Daemons collection, regardless of whether you want to play an open play game, forge an epic narrative with a Crusade force or assemble an army to do battle in a matched play mission.

Created from the contents of the Combat Patrol: Chaos Daemons boxed set, this force can be used in a Battle-forged army, and in itself comprises a Patrol Detachment dedicated to Khorne, as described in the Warhammer 40,000 Core Book.

A solid core of two units of Bloodletters forms the mainstay of the army. These daemons are swift and lethal in melee combat (as you would expect of Khorne's children!), striding into battle wielding deadly hellblades. These formidable fighters can be made even more brutal in combination with some of the Stratagems

found in the Book of Blood on page 63, and gain the Objective Secured ability (see the Warhammer 40,000 Core Book), allowing these units to steal objective markers away from their beleaguered foes.

Backing up this troops unit are two packs of swift Flesh Hounds. Able to move quickly up the battlefield, they are ideal for threatening your opponent's support units, or securing isolated objective markers. Speed isn't their only strength however. Flesh Hounds are deadly and resilient melee fighters, equally capable of tearing apart your foe.

Providing a solid counter-attack unit, the Bloodcrushers are at their best on the charge. Their riders wield savage hellblades and their Juggernaut steeds can attack with their bladed horns, giving this unit a surprising amount of damage output from its relatively small

numbers. Able to rove ahead and attack the foe head-on, or wait and support the Bloodletters with a savage counter-charge, this unit can weather enemy fire before crashing into them at full speed.

Leading this force is a remorseless Bloodmaster, a Bloodletter raised up above his fellows and packing a deadly punch. This creature is able to lead your Bloodletters from the front, making use of its Herald of Khorne aura ability, and its Bloodmaster ability to boost the already ruinous abilities of your other units.

As your Warlord, the Bloodmaster can also be given a Warlord Trait to enhance their abilities, as well as being able to be equipped with a potent Relic of Khorne. Whether this is an upgraded weapon, a blood-drinking talisman or a brazen rune to defy the sorceries of the enemy, all render this leader more deadly.

DETACHMENT ABILITIES

A **Legiones Daemonica** Detachment is one that only includes models with the **Legiones Daemonica** keyword (excluding models with the **Agent of Chaos** or **Unaligned** keywords).

- **Legiones Daemonica** Detachments gain the Daemonic Allies, Daemonic Legions and Daemonic Relics abilities.
- Troops units (excluding **Swarm** units) in **Legiones Daemonica** Detachments gain the Objective Secured ability (see the Warhammer 40,000 Core Book).

DAEMONIC LEGIONS

Eldritch and ritualistic hierarchies exist in the daemonic legions, arcane rules that bind each entity to its place with an immutable inevitability weirdly at odds with the anarchy of the warp.

- If your army only contains **Legiones Daemonica** Detachments, and includes any **Greater Daemon** units, one of these must be your **Warlord**, unless your army also includes **Be'lakor**.
- For each **Greater Daemon** unit included in a Detachment, you can include 1 **Herald** unit with the same Allegiance keyword in that Detachment without that **Herald** unit taking up a Battlefield Role slot.

DAEMONIC RELICS

The daemons of the warp go to war carrying all manner of deadly and esoteric artefacts, creations of pure chaos, aiding their owners in sowing terror and destruction wherever they tread.

If your army includes a **Legiones Daemonica Warlord**, you can give one **Legiones Daemonica Character** model from your army a Relic. This can be selected from the Relics of Khorne (pg 65), Relics of Tzeentch (pg 80), Relics of Nurgle (pg 94) or Relics of Slaanesh (pg 110).

DAEMONIC ALLIES

When the mortal servants of the Dark Gods march to war, the most favoured may find daemonic entities accompanying them.

The following rules apply if you wish to include any **Legiones Daemonica** units in a **Chaos** army in which not every unit has the **Legiones Daemonica** keyword.

Daemonic Pact

If your army includes one **Legiones Daemonica** Detachment, and the combined Power Ratings of all units in that Detachment make up no more than 25% of your army's Power Level, then until the end of the battle, every unit in that Detachment gains the **Agent of Chaos** keyword. If a **Be'lakor** unit is included in that Detachment, this ability has no effect.

- The inclusion of **Legiones Daemonica Agent of Chaos Khorne** units in your army does not prevent **World Eaters** units in your army from using any rules that require every model in your army to have the same keyword.
- The inclusion of **Legiones Daemonica Agent of Chaos Tzeentch** units in your army does not prevent **Thousand Sons** units in your army from using any rules that require every model in your army to have the same keyword.
- The inclusion of **Legiones Daemonica Agent of Chaos Nurgle** units in your army does not prevent **Death Guard** units in your army from using any rules that require every model in your army to have the same keyword.
- The inclusion of **Legiones Daemonica Agent of Chaos Slaanesh** units in your army does not prevent **Emperor's Children** units in your army from using any rules that require every model in your army to have the same keyword.

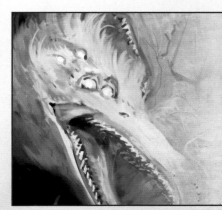

'We draw our wards and our protective sigils. We light our votive candles, burn our blessed incense and offer up our most fervent prayers. Yet in the end, what true defence can there be against the deeper darkness of our own damned souls? Ever we must hope that the Emperor protects, for the stark truth is we cannot protect ourselves.'

- Master Astropath Thervillion VanShen

DATASHEET ABILITIES

ALLEGIANCE KEYWORDS

Most of the datasheets in this book have an Allegiance keyword. The following are Allegiance keywords:

- **KHORNE**
- **TZEENTCH**
- **NURGLE**
- **SLAANESH**

If a unit instead has the **<ALLEGIANCE>** Faction keyword, then when you add that unit to your army, you must select one of the listed Allegiance keywords above and replace the **<ALLEGIANCE>** keyword in all instances on that Datasheet with the selected Allegiance keyword.

Example: If you include a Daemon Prince in your army, and you decide it is a Daemon Prince of Khorne, its **<ALLEGIANCE>** *keyword becomes* **KHORNE** *and its Prince of Chaos ability reads, 'While a friendly* **LEGIONES DAEMONICA KHORNE CORE** *unit is within 6" of this model, each time a model in that unit makes an attack, re-roll a hit roll of 1.'*

MALEFIC WEAPONS

Many daemons fashion forms for themselves that exhibit strange and esoteric weapons, with which they give vent to their spiteful natures. While most fight with blade or claws, often they can also lash out with spiked tails, envenomed pseudopods or other bizarre appendages. Daemons may also ride to battle atop other daemonic creatures that make attacks with weapons of their own, or may be attended by daemonic minions who swipe at those who draw near their masters.

Many Chaos Daemons weapons are malefic weapons. Such a weapon will have an ability that reads 'Malefic' and then a value, such as 2 or 4. Each time the bearer fights, it makes a number of additional attacks with that weapon equal to that value, and no more than that number of attacks can be made with that weapon while resolving that fight. If a model is equipped with more than one malefic weapon, it can make additional attacks with each one it is equipped with.

Unless otherwise specified, malefic weapons are never affected by effects or abilities that allow models to make additional attacks, or abilities that would add to, subtract from, or improve their characteristics in any way.

Example: A Skullmaster is equipped with a blade of blood and its Juggernaut's bladed horn, which has the 'Malefic 4' ability. Each time this model fights, it makes a number of attacks equal to its Attacks characteristic with its blade of blood, then an additional 4 attacks with the bladed horn profile.

ABILITIES

A unit's datasheet will list all the abilities it has. Certain abilities that are common to many units are only referenced on the datasheets rather than described in full. These are described below.

DAEMONIC

This unit has the following abilities: Daemonic Invulnerability; Manifestation; Daemonic Terror; Warp Storm.

Daemonic Invulnerability

Daemons are madness given form. Their very bodies are fashioned from the stuff of the warp, and are difficult to destroy through conventional means. By far the surest way to banish them, short of ritual witchery, is to fight them at close quarters where a warrior's conviction and faith may strike as surely as their blade.

Instead of a normal Save characteristic as described in the Warhammer 40,000 Core Book, each **LEGIONES DAEMONICA** datasheet has a Daemonic Save characteristic (abbreviated to DSv on that datasheet's profile line). This characteristic has two values. The first characteristic is used when a melee attack is allocated to that model, while the second characteristic is used when a ranged attack is allocated to that model. In either case, this saving throw cannot be modified in any way.

Manifestation

Daemonic legions tear through the fabric of realspace, malevolent entities flickering into being like phantasms from a nightmare. Worse still, as terror and panic take hold of their victims, so their mortal souls become ever easier prey for the entities pouring through from the warp.

During deployment, you can set up this unit in the warp instead of setting it up on the battlefield. If you do so, then in the Reinforcements step of one of your Movement phases you can set up this unit anywhere on the battlefield that is more than 9" away from any enemy models, or more than 6" away from any enemy models and wholly within 6" of a friendly **WARP LOCUS** model that was on the battlefield at the start of your turn. If that **WARP LOCUS** model has an Allegiance keyword (see left), the unit being set up can only use this ability if it has the same Allegiance keyword.

If every unit from your army has the **LEGIONES DAEMONICA** keyword, then in the Reinforcements step of one of your Movement phases you can instead set up this unit anywhere on the battlefield with one of the following restrictions:

- Wholly within your deployment zone and more than 3" away from any enemy models.
- Neither wholly within your deployment zone nor within your opponent's deployment zone, and more than a number of inches away from each enemy unit, equal to the current Leadership characteristic of that enemy unit (to a minimum of 3" and a maximum of 9").

Daemonic Terror (Aura)

To encounter a creature of the warp is to face a being utterly anathema to the fundamental laws of reality. Even the most emotionless warrior feels an unnatural primal terror while in their presence.

While an enemy unit is within 6" of this unit, subtract 1 from that enemy unit's Leadership characteristic and subtract 1 from any Combat Attrition tests taken for that enemy unit.

Warp Storm

When daemons pour into realspace, maelstroms of warp energy spill through in their wake. Manifest emotion and unbridled, nightmarish energies twist all that they touch, reshaping the landscape into bizarre forms and tormenting mortal beings.

This ability can be used to apply Warp Storm effects to eligible units from your army – see pages 58-59.

'It is the great fortune of most who dwell within the Imperium that they possess not the imagination to picture even a fragment of the horrors that lurk within the warp. Should those same horrors be unleashed upon them, however, this shield of ignorance collapses all too swiftly and, in its demise, often destroys the mind it once protected. Truly it is nobler to purge all such unfortunates for the good of all, than to force them to live on in enlightened insanity.'

- Inquisitor Fabiranice Var Koldenvaal,
ruminations on Exterminatus

WARP STORM EFFECTS

If every unit from your army has the **Legiones Daemonica** keyword (excluding models with the **Agent of Chaos** or **Unaligned** keywords), at the start of each battle round, you can make a Warp Storm roll. To do so, roll eight D6. For each 4+, gain 1 Warp Storm point (WSP).

Warp Storm points can also be gained via other rules or abilities. No matter the source, you can only gain Warp Storm points from such a rule if every unit from your army has the **Legiones Daemonica** keyword (excluding models with the **Agent of Chaos** or **Unaligned** keywords).

Warp Storm points can be spent during that battle round on the Warp Storm effects listed below and opposite, and each will specify when it can be used. These include a series of effects themed around each of the four Dark Gods, which can be used if your army contains a detachment dedicated to the appropriate Dark God.

Each effect has an associated Warp Storm points cost. If you do not have enough Warp Storm points for a specific Warp Storm effect, you cannot use it. Unless otherwise specified, you can use the same Warp Storm effect multiple times over the course of the battle, but you cannot use the same Warp Storm effect more than once per battle round. Any spent Warp Storm points are deducted from your total.

If an effect instructs you to return any destroyed models to a unit, a returned model cannot be set up within Engagement Range of any enemy units unless those enemy units are already within Engagement Range of its unit.

At the end of each battle round, unless otherwise specified, any unspent Warp Storm points are lost. Some abilities will allow you to retain Warp Storm points. Each ability will specify how many Warp Storm points can be retained. Retained Warp Storm points are not lost at the end of the battle round.

UNDIVIDED

DARK INVIGORATION — 5 WSP

Use this effect at the start of the Morale phase. One model in each **Legiones Daemonica** unit from your army can regain up to D3 lost wounds. If every model in that unit has a Wounds characteristic of 1, that unit can instead be replenished. When a unit is replenished, you can return D3 destroyed models to that unit with their full wounds remaining. Each returned model no longer counts as having been destroyed for the purposes of Morale tests this turn. Each unit can only be replenished once per turn.

PRIMEVAL TERROR — 3 WSP

Use this effect at the start of a turn. Until the end of the turn, while an enemy unit is within range of the Daemonic Terror ability (pg 57) of one or more units from your army, subtract 1 from the Leadership characteristic of models in that unit.

MUSIC OF THE WARP — 2 WSP

Use this effect at the start of your turn. Until the end of the turn, add 6" to the range of the Daemonic Terror ability (pg 57) for **Instrument** units from your army (to a maximum of 12").

MALICIOUS MISDIRECTION — 2 WSP

Use this effect at the start of the Reinforcements step of your opponent's Movement phase. Until the end of that step, enemy Strategic Reserve units can only be set up as if it were the second battle round.

MAGNIFIED GLORY — 3 WSP

Use this effect at the start of any turn. Until the end of the turn, add 3" to the range of aura abilities of **Legiones Daemonica** units from your army.

OTHERWORLDLY TREAD — 2 WSP

Use this effect at the start of your Movement phase or at the start of your Charge phase. Until the end of the phase, **Legiones Daemonica** units from your army can ignore any or all modifiers to their Move characteristic, Advance rolls and charge rolls.

DESCENDING SHADOW — 3 WSP

Use this effect at the start of your opponent's Shooting phase. Until the end of the phase, each time a ranged attack is made against a **Legiones Daemonica** unit from your army, if the attacker is more than 12" away, subtract 1 from that attack's hit roll.

INSIDIOUS WHISPERS — 2 WSP

Use this effect at the start of your opponent's Psychic phase. Until the end of the phase, **Legiones Daemonica** units from your army have the following ability:

Insidious Whispers (Aura): While an enemy **Psyker** unit is within 12" of this unit, each time a Psychic test is taken for that **Psyker** unit, it suffers Perils of the Warp on any dice roll that includes a double, instead of only a double 1 or double 6.

KHORNE

If your army includes any **LEGIONES DAEMONICA** Detachments (excluding Auxiliary Support, Super-heavy Auxiliary or Fortification Network Detachments) in which every unit has the **KHORNE** keyword, you have access to the following Khorne Warp Storm effects, and can spend Warp Storm points to use them.

FURY OF KHORNE — 4 WSP

Use this effect at the start of the Fight phase. Until the end of the phase, add 1 to the Attacks characteristic of **LEGIONES DAEMONICA KHORNE** models from your army.

BURNING TERROR — 2 WSP

Use this effect at the start of your Shooting phase. Roll one D6 for each enemy unit within 24" of any **LEGIONES DAEMONICA KHORNE** units from your army and that is not wholly within an Area Terrain feature. On a 6, that unit suffers D3 mortal wounds.

OVERWHELMING RAGE — 4 WSP

Use this effect at the start of your opponent's Movement phase. Until the end of the phase, each time an enemy unit (excluding **AIRCRAFT** units) within Engagement Range of any **LEGIONES DAEMONICA KHORNE** units from your army is selected to Fall Back, roll one D6: on a 4+, that unit cannot Fall Back.

TZEENTCH

If your army includes any **LEGIONES DAEMONICA** Detachments (excluding Auxiliary Support, Super-heavy Auxiliary or Fortification Network Detachments) in which every unit has the **TZEENTCH** keyword, you have access to the following Tzeentch Warp Storm effects, and can spend Warp Storm points to use them.

DELUGE OF FIRE — 4 WSP

Use this effect at the start of your Shooting phase. Until the end of the phase, improve the Ballistic Skill characteristic of **LEGIONES DAEMONICA TZEENTCH** models from your army by 1.

SORCEROUS WINDS — 3 WSP

Use this effect at the start of your Psychic phase. Until the end of the phase, each time a Psychic test is taken for a **LEGIONES DAEMONICA TZEENTCH** unit from your army, add 1 to that Psychic test.

RAMPANT MUTATION — 3 WSP

Use this effect in the Fight phase. Until the end of the phase, each time a **LEGIONES DAEMONICA TZEENTCH** model from your army makes a melee attack, an unmodified wound roll of 6 inflicts 1 mortal wound on the target in addition to any normal damage (each enemy unit can only suffer a maximum of 3 mortal wounds as a result of this effect per phase).

NURGLE

If your army includes any **LEGIONES DAEMONICA** Detachments (excluding Auxiliary Support, Super-heavy Auxiliary or Fortification Network Detachments) in which every unit has the **NURGLE** keyword, you have access to the following Nurgle Warp Storm effects, and can spend Warp Storm points to use them.

SWARMING INSECTS — 4 WSP

Use this effect at the start of the Fight phase. Until the end of the phase, each time a **LEGIONES DAEMONICA NURGLE** model from your army makes a melee attack, add 1 to that attack's hit roll.

PLAGUE OF RUST — 2 WSP

Use this effect at the start of the Fight phase. Until the end of the phase, each time a **LEGIONES DAEMONICA NURGLE** model from your army makes a melee attack against an enemy **VEHICLE** unit, improve the Armour Penetration characteristic of that attack by 1.

WAVE OF SICKNESS — 2 WSP

Use this effect at the start of your Shooting phase. Roll one D6 for each enemy unit within 12" of one or more **LEGIONES DAEMONICA NURGLE** units from your army. On a 6, that unit suffers D3 mortal wounds.

SLAANESH

If your army includes any **LEGIONES DAEMONICA** Detachments (excluding Auxiliary Support, Super-heavy Auxiliary or Fortification Network Detachments) in which every unit has the **SLAANESH** keyword, you have access to the following Slaanesh Warp Storm effects, and can spend Warp Storm points to use them.

MESMERISING DANCE — 4 WSP

Use this effect at the start of the Fight phase. Until the end of the phase, each **LEGIONES DAEMONICA SLAANESH** unit from your army that is within Engagement Range of any enemy units can fight first that phase.

LIGHTNING SPEED — 3 WSP

Use this effect in your Movement or Charge phase. Until the end of the turn, each time an Advance roll or Charge roll is made for a **LEGIONES DAEMONICA SLAANESH** unit from your army, add 1 to the result.

DARK HALLUCINATIONS — 2 WSP

Use this effect at the start of your opponent's turn. Until the end of the turn, while an enemy unit is within 12" of one or more **LEGIONES DAEMONICA SLAANESH** units from your army, each time that enemy unit starts to perform an action, roll 2D6. If the result is greater than that enemy unit's Leadership characteristic, that action fails and that enemy unit suffers D3 mortal wounds.

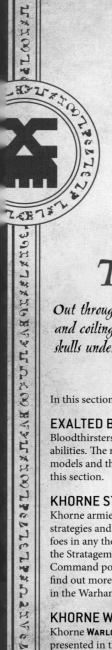

THE BOOK OF BLOOD

Out through brazen gates they march, across endless fields of slaughter. Searing brass they bear, and coiling fire, and the hatred that beats in every living heart. Cloven hooves crack blackened skulls underfoot as they stalk forth beneath a rain of boiling blood, and mountains of bodies they raise for the Lord of Battles.

In this section you will find the following rules:

EXALTED BLOODTHIRSTERS (PG 62)
Bloodthirsters can be upgraded with potent new abilities. The rules for how you can upgrade these models and the abilities they bestow are described in this section.

KHORNE STRATAGEMS (PG 63)
Khorne armies have access to unique battlefield strategies and tactics that they can utilise to best their foes in any theatre of war; these are represented by the Stratagems in this section, and you can spend Command points to use them in your games. You can find out more about Stratagems and Command points in the Warhammer 40,000 Core Book.

KHORNE WARLORD TRAITS (PG 64)
Khorne **Warlord** models can have one of the traits presented in this section. These help to better reflect their individual combat and command style on the battlefield.

RELICS OF KHORNE (PG 65)
Khorne's greatest champions can be equipped with powerful artefacts called Relics of Khorne; these Relics and the rules they bestow are described in this section.

KHORNE DATASHEETS (PG 66-73)
This section is essential to all Chaos Daemons players who wish to include **Khorne** units in their army, regardless of preferred play style, containing as it does the datasheets for **Legiones Daemonica Khorne** units. Each datasheet describes, amongst other things, the profiles of its models, the wargear they can be equipped with and the abilities they have. You can find out more about datasheets in the Warhammer 40,000 Core Book.

EXALTED BLOODTHIRSTERS

There are those amongst the Bloodthirsters of Khorne who serve as the Blood God's personal guard, his champions, executioners and generals. Such lords of slaughter exhibit might and unholy blessings beyond even those of other Bloodthirsters, and embody the greatest warrior archetypes of the ages. Ka'Bandha is such a being, he who battled the angelic Primarch Sanguinius during the Siege of the Emperor's Palace, and who almost destroyed the assembled might of the Ultramarines Chapter so many millennia later.

If your army includes any **LEGIONES DAEMONICA** Detachments (excluding Auxiliary Support, Super-heavy Auxiliary or Fortification Network Detachments), then when you muster your army, you can upgrade any **BLOODTHIRSTER** models from your army to be exalted.

When a model is upgraded to be exalted it gains an Exalted ability. You can select one of the Exalted abilities (see right) for that model. That model's Power Rating is increased accordingly, as shown in the table below. If you are playing a matched play game, or a game that uses a points limit, then the points value of that unit is also increased by the amount shown in the same table. Make a note on your army roster each time you upgrade a unit using these rules, specifying the ability it has gained.

Named characters (e.g. **SKARBRAND**, page 66) cannot be given Exalted abilities. Each model can only be upgraded to have Exalted abilities once. An army (or a Crusade force) cannot include the same Exalted ability more than once.

A Crusade force cannot start with any models having Exalted abilities – to include one in a Crusade force, you must use the Exalted Daemon Requisition (pg 132).

EXALTED ABILITY	POWER	POINTS
Indomitable Onslaught	+2	+40
Master of the Blood Tide	+1	+20
Rage Unchained	+2	+35

EXALTED ABILITIES

INDOMITABLE ONSLAUGHT
Hate and bloodlust bind this daemon's corporeal form together with such furious vehemence that its victims struggle to banish the rampaging monster with even the most powerful weapons.

This model cannot lose more than 8 wounds in the same phase. Any wounds that would be lost after that point are not lost.

MASTER OF THE BLOOD TIDE
The bloody tides of battle fill this daemonic warrior with surging might, every fresh charge and countercharge sending infernal vitality coursing through its limbs and lending renewed ferocity to its blows.

Each time this model fights, if it made a charge move, was charged, or performed a Heroic Intervention this turn, then until that fight is resolved, add 1 to this model's Strength and Attacks characteristics.

RAGE UNCHAINED
No matter the hurts done to it, this blood-spattered abomination continues to slaughter its foes without seeming even to register the desperate blows of.

This model is considered to have double the number of wounds remaining for the purposes of determining what its characteristics are.

KHORNE STRATAGEMS

If your army includes any **LEGIONES DAEMONICA KHORNE** units (excluding units in Auxiliary Support, Super-heavy Auxiliary or Fortification Network Detachments), you have access to these Stratagems, and can spend CPs to use them.

FRENETIC BLOODLUST   1CP/2CP

Legions of Khorne – Battle Tactic Stratagem

Ravening packs of Bloodletters spill across the battlefield seeking out the foe, eager to spill their blood.

Use this Stratagem at the start of the Fight phase. Select one **BLOODLETTERS CORE** unit from your army.

- If that unit is not within Engagement Range of any enemy units, make a Normal Move of up to 6" with that unit. It must end this move closer to the closest visible enemy unit.
- If that unit is within Engagement Range of any enemy units, make a pile-in move with that unit.

If this unit makes a Normal Move, this Stratagem costs 2CP; otherwise, it costs 1CP.

GLORIOUS DECAPITATION   2CP

Legions of Khorne – Epic Deed Stratagem

No sight does more to drive the legions of the Blood God into a killing frenzy than the head of an enemy champion lopped off in a fountain of gore, and another worthy skull added to the charnel mountain upon which Khorne's brass throne is set.

Use this Stratagem when an enemy **CHARACTER** model is destroyed by a melee attack made by a **LEGIONES DAEMONICA KHORNE CHARACTER** model from your army. Until the end of the battle, that **KHORNE CHARACTER** model has the following ability:

Slayer of Champions (Aura): While a friendly **LEGIONES DAEMONICA KHORNE** unit is within 6" of this model, each time a model in that unit makes an attack, an unmodified wound roll of 6 inflicts 1 mortal wound on the target in addition to any normal damage. A unit can only suffer a maximum of 6 mortal wounds per phase as a result of this ability.

You can only use this Stratagem once.

RELICS OF THE BRASS CITADEL   1CP

Legions of Khorne – Requisition Stratagem

The infernal armouries of Khorne's daemon legions overflow with macabre artefacts of unbridled slaughter.

Use this Stratagem before the battle, when you are mustering your army. Select one **LEGIONES DAEMONICA KHORNE CHARACTER** model from your army and give them one Relic of Khorne (this must be a Relic they can have). Each Relic in your army must be unique, and you cannot use this Stratagem to give a model two Relics. You can only use this Stratagem once, unless you are playing a Strike Force battle (in which case, you can use this Stratagem twice) or an Onslaught battle (in which case, you can use this Stratagem three times).

CONTEMPT FOR SORCERY   1CP

Legions of Khorne – Strategic Ploy Stratagem

The loathing for witchery that radiates from the daemons of Khorne can unmake even the mightiest of conjurations.

Use this Stratagem in your opponent's Psychic phase, after a Psychic test is passed for an enemy **PSYKER** unit and after any Deny the Witch attempt is made. If that enemy **PSYKER** unit is within 24" of any **LEGIONES DAEMONICA KHORNE** units from your army, roll one D6, adding 1 to the result if that enemy **PSYKER** is within 12" of any **FLESH HOUNDS** units from your army: on a 4+, that psychic power is denied.

BRASS STAMPEDE   1CP

Legions of Khorne – Strategic Ploy Stratagem

The daemonic cavalry and chariots of the daemons of Khorne slam into the enemy lines like a brass-shod avalanche of death.

Use this Stratagem after a **LEGIONES DAEMONICA KHORNE CAVALRY** or **LEGIONES DAEMONICA KHORNE VEHICLE** unit from your army finishes a charge move. Select one enemy unit within Engagement Range of that unit and roll one D6 for each model in the charging unit, adding 3 to the result if the charging unit is a **VEHICLE** unit:

- On a 6-8, that enemy unit suffers D3 mortal wounds.
- On a 9, that enemy unit suffers D3+3 mortal wounds.

BANNER OF BLOOD   1CP

Legions of Khorne – Wargear Stratagem

The dark icons carried above Khorne's daemonic hosts spur those who march below them forward with greater fury.

Use this Stratagem when a **LEGIONES DAEMONICA KHORNE ICON** unit from your army is selected to charge. Until the end of the phase, each time you make a charge roll for that unit, roll one additional D6 and discard the lowest result.

KHORNE WARLORD TRAITS

If a **LEGIONES DAEMONICA KHORNE CHARACTER** model from your army gains a Warlord Trait, you can use the Khorne Warlord Traits table below to determine which Warlord Trait they have. You can either roll one D6 to randomly generate one, or you can select one.

If a **KHORNE HERALD** model gains a Warlord Trait, they can only have the Aspect of Death, Brazen Hide or Devastating Blow Warlord Traits. You can either roll one D3 to randomly generate one, or you can select one.

ARMY RULES

Fourth, should the inclination take you to read the words of this grimoire backwards, or indeed to intone aloud any of the text scribed herein, resist this urge with all the strength you have. Read neither every sixth word, nor seventh, nor eighth nor ninth, lest something take your voice from you and make it not your own.

1. ASPECT OF DEATH (AURA)
Such is the palpable aura of dread this daemon emanates that its enemies may die of sheer terror.

While an enemy unit is within 6" of this **WARLORD**:

- Subtract 1 from the Leadership characteristic of models in that unit.
- Each time a Combat Attrition test is taken for that unit, subtract 1 from that Combat Attrition test.

2. BRAZEN HIDE
This daemon's warpflesh is infused with rune-wrought brass that shatters blades and turns aside even the most powerful enemy blows.

Each time this **WARLORD** would lose a wound, roll one D6: on a 5+, that wound is not lost.

3. DEVASTATING BLOW
So monstrous is the strength behind this warlord's blows and so unstoppable their hatred that they can lay victims low with but a single strike.

Each time this **WARLORD** makes a melee attack, rules that ignore wounds cannot be used.

4. GLORY OF BATTLE
The more foes that surround this daemon, the faster and more eagerly it fights.

- Add 1 to this **WARLORD**'s Attacks characteristic.
- While this **WARLORD** is within 3" of 6 or more enemy models, add 1 to this **WARLORD**'s Attacks characteristic.
- While this **WARLORD** is within 3" of 11 or more enemy models, add 1 to this **WARLORD**'s Attacks characteristic.

5. IMMENSE POWER
The molten fury of the Lord of Battle rages within this daemon, and its body is swollen with unholy might.

Each time this **WARLORD** makes a melee attack, add 1 to that attack's wound roll.

6. RAGE INCARNATE
The fury with which this daemon hurls itself at the enemy serves as a beacon of wrath to its like-minded minions.

- Add 1 to Advance and charge rolls made for this **WARLORD**.
- Each time a friendly **LEGIONES DAEMONICA KHORNE CORE** unit declares a charge against an enemy unit within Engagement Range of this **WARLORD**, add 1 to the charge roll made for that unit.

NAMED CHARACTERS AND WARLORD TRAITS
If one of the following characters gains a Warlord Trait, they must have the relevant one shown below:

Named Character	Warlord Trait
Skarbrand	Rage Incarnate
Skulltaker	Devastating Blow
Karanak	Aspect of Death

RELICS OF KHORNE

If a **LEGIONES DAEMONICA KHORNE CHARACTER** model gains a Relic, you can give them one of the following Relics of Khorne. Named characters and **VEHICLE** models cannot be given any of the following Relics.

Note that some Relics replace one of the model's existing items of wargear. Where this is the case, you must, if you are using points values, still pay the cost of the wargear that is being replaced. Write down any Relics of Khorne your models have on your army roster.

ARMOUR OF SCORN

Though this armour was forged in the Brass Citadel, it was the Blood God's contempt that gave it life. Aeons after its creation, it is this same burning scorn that shields its wearer in battle.

KHORNE MONSTER model only.

- Each time an attack with a Damage characteristic of 1 is allocated to the bearer, add 1 to any saving throw made against that attack.
- Each time the bearer would lose a wound as a result of a mortal wound in the Psychic phase, roll one D6: on a 4+, that wound is not lost.

THE CRIMSON CROWN

It is said that this crown was created from a single drop of Khorne's blood. A measure of the Blood God's endless wrath is bound within the crown, and its effect upon his daemonic servants is palpable. Fuelled by the artefact's fell presence, Khorne's daemons are driven to ever greater heights of savagery and slaughter.

At the end of each battle round, if the bearer destroyed any enemy models during that battle round, you can retain up to 2 unspent Warp Storm points (pg 58).

RUNE OF BRASS

Etched into the daemon's armour – or embedded into its flesh – the Rune of Brass retains the infernal heat of its creation. The glare of its still-molten form is agony to witches, for it conjures the all-consuming blaze of the pyre, and twists their powers against them.

The bearer has the following ability:

Rune of Brass (Aura): While an enemy **PSYKER** unit is within 12" of the bearer:

- Each time a Psychic test is taken for that unit, it suffers Perils of the Warp on any dice roll that includes a double, instead of only a double 1 or double 6.
- Each time that unit suffers Perils of the Warp, it suffers D6 mortal wounds instead of D3.

BLOOD-DRINKER TALISMAN

Seized from the blasted surface of a crone world, this sentient gemstone resides within the warp-wrought body of its daemonic master. There it pulses with malign murderlust, drinking in the blood that sprays its host's flesh during battle and channelling the stolen life force to reknit the corporeal form of the daemon within which it resides.

Each time the bearer fights, after resolving its attacks, roll one D6 for each enemy model that was destroyed by those attacks. On a 5+, the bearer regains 1 lost wound. The bearer cannot regain more than 6 lost wounds in each Fight phase.

A'RGATH, THE KING OF BLADES

When a daemon is bound within a weapon by its infernal master, it rarely submits willingly to this terrible incarceration. The same cannot be said for A'rgath. A lifetime of slaughter and zealous dedication saw this butcher granted daemonhood. Such was his devotion to Khorne that instead of accepting immortality as a Daemon Prince, he instead chose to take the form of a deadly blade so that he could spill the lifeblood of Khorne's greatest enemies. Their hand guided by A'rgath's spirit, this weapon's wielder becomes nigh on unstoppable. Countless are the rival champions and mortal heroes that have fallen to his power.

Select one melee weapon the bearer is equipped with.

- Add 1 to the Damage characteristic of that weapon.
- Each time the bearer makes a melee attack with that weapon, you can ignore any or all modifiers to that attack's hit roll and any or all modifiers to that attack's wound roll.
- That weapon is now considered to be a Relic for all rules purposes.

SKULLREAVER

This monstrous axe forms the prison for a Bloodthirster defeated in a duel against a rival champion of Khorne. The rage of the trammelled daemon causes the blade's infernal runes to blaze with the heat of a captive star, and keeps its edge so supernaturally sharp that a single blow from Skullreaver can lop the head from the mightiest foe or decapitate an entire rank of lesser victims.

Model equipped with axe of Khorne only. This Relic replaces an axe of Khorne and has the following profile:

WEAPON	RANGE	TYPE	S	AP	D
Skullreaver	Each time an attack is made with this weapon, select one of the profiles below to make that attack with.				
- Mighty strike	Melee	Melee	+4	-4	D6
- Sweeping blow	Melee	Melee	User	-3	1

Abilities: Each time an attack is made against a **VEHICLE** or **MONSTER** unit with this weapon's mighty strike profile, that attack has a Strength characteristic of x2 and a Damage characteristic of D3+3. Each time an attack is made with this weapon's sweeping blow profile, make 2 hit rolls instead of 1.

SKARBRAND

17 POWER

Some of this model's characteristics change as it suffers damage, as shown below:

No.	Name	M	WS	BS	S	T	W	A	Ld	DSv
1	Skarbrand (12+ wounds remaining)	8"	2+	2+	8	8	22	8	9	4+/4+
	Skarbrand (6-11 wounds remaining)	7"	3+	2+	8	8	N/A	9	9	4+/4+
	Skarbrand (1-5 wounds remaining)	6"	4+	2+	8	8	N/A	10	9	4+/4+

Skarbrand is equipped with: bellow of endless fury; Slaughter and Carnage. Your army can only include one **SKARBRAND** model.

WEAPON	RANGE	TYPE	S	AP	D	ABILITIES
Bellow of endless fury	12"	Assault 2D6	5	-1	1	Each time an attack is made with this weapon, that attack automatically hits the target.
Slaughter and Carnage		Each time an attack is made with this weapon, select one of the profiles below to make that attack with.				
- Mighty strike	Melee	Melee	x2	-4	D3+3	Each time an attack is made with this weapon profile, invulnerable saving throws cannot be made against that attack.
- Sweeping blow	Melee	Melee	User	-2	2	Each time an attack is made with this weapon profile, make 2 hit rolls instead of 1.

ABILITIES

Daemonic (pg 56)

Witchbane: This unit cannot be targeted or affected by psychic powers.

Rage Embodied (Aura): While a unit is within 6" of this model:
- Add 1 to the Attacks characteristic of models in that unit.
- Each time a Morale test is taken for that unit, it is automatically passed.
- Each time that unit is selected to Fall Back, the controlling player rolls 3D6. If the total is greater than that unit's Leadership characteristic, that unit cannot Fall Back.

FACTION KEYWORDS: CHAOS, LEGIONES DAEMONICA, KHORNE
KEYWORDS: MONSTER, CHARACTER, DAEMON, GREATER DAEMON, WARP LOCUS, BLOODTHIRSTER, SKARBRAND

Never pausing, never relenting, Skarbrand storms across realspace hacking apart every luckless foe that stands in its path. Worse, all who find themselves in the daemon's presence are seized by its feral murderlust, a madness that sees elegant strategies collapse into orgies of primal savagery.

KHORNE'S FALLEN FAVOURED

Mortals say of Skarbrand that no daemon ever served Khorne more faithfully, nor shed blood more enthusiastically. Yet legend has it that though the Greater Daemon rose high in the Blood God's favour, it became wild and prideful of its conquests and left itself open to manipulation. The Changer of the Ways, they say, was the one to note this weakness and to exploit it with subtle whispers until one day Skarbrand's fury overflowed. Taking up its axes, the mighty daemon struck a blow at Khorne himself.

The legends speak of Khorne's rage at this betrayal as a thing fit to burn out the stars in the heavens. Some even claim this as literal truth, preaching that every star ever to burst in furious supernova since that day has done so as an echo of the Blood God's wrath. Khorne is said to have

gripped his wayward servant about the throat, choking until nothing remained within Skarbrand but mindless rage, then to have hurled the Bloodthirster across the heavens as a blazing meteor.

What arose from the impact crater of Skarbrand's final fall was a ruined and wrathful thing whose wings were reduced to gristle-gore tatters, and whose monstrous visage was as much flayed skull as daemonic flesh. Yet the rage that had driven the exile to strike at its master remained and burned hotter than ever. This, the storytellers claim, accounts for the madness said to fall upon friend and foe alike at Skarbrand's coming. Even the meekest coward becomes a murderous berserker in the exile's presence, and the bloodshed that ripples out from the daemon in waves has caused gory apocalypses that have consumed countless worlds.

BLOODTHIRSTER

16 POWER

Some of this model's characteristics change as it suffers damage, as shown below:

No.	Name	M	WS	BS	S	T	W	A	Ld	DSv
1	Bloodthirster (11+ wounds remaining)	12"	2+	2+	8	8	20	8	10	4+/4+
	Bloodthirster (6-10 wounds remaining)	10"	3+	2+	8	8	N/A	7	10	4+/4+
	Bloodthirster (1-5 wounds remaining)	8"	4+	2+	8	8	N/A	6	10	4+/4+

A Bloodthirster is equipped with: hellfire breath; great axe of Khorne.

WEAPON	RANGE	TYPE	S	AP	D	ABILITIES
Bloodflail	12"	Assault 1	x2	-4	3D3	Each time an attack is made with this weapon, excess damage it inflicts is not lost. Instead, keep allocating excess damage to another model in the target unit until either all the excess damage has been allocated or the target unit is destroyed.
Hellfire breath	12"	Assault D6	5	-2	1	Each time an attack is made with this weapon, that attack automatically hits the target.
Lash of Khorne	12"	Assault 6	User	-1	2	-
Axe of Khorne	Each time an attack is made with this weapon, select one of the profiles below to make that attack with.					
- Mighty strike	Melee	Melee	+4	-4	D6	-
- Sweeping blow	Melee	Melee	User	-3	1	Each time an attack is made with this weapon profile, make 2 hit rolls instead of 1.
Great axe of Khorne	Each time an attack is made with this weapon, select one of the profiles below to make that attack with.					
- Mighty strike	Melee	Melee	x2	-4	D3+3	-
- Sweeping blow	Melee	Melee	User	-3	2	Each time an attack is made with this weapon profile, make 2 hit rolls instead of 1.

WARGEAR OPTIONS

• This model's great axe of Khorne can be replaced with 1 axe of Khorne and one of the following: 1 bloodflail; 1 lash of Khorne.

ABILITIES

Daemonic (pg 56)

Daemon Lord of Khorne (Aura): While a friendly LEGIONES DAEMONICA KHORNE CORE unit is within 6" of this model, each time a model in that unit makes an attack, re-roll a hit roll of 1.

Relentless Carnage: At the end of the Fight phase, select one enemy unit within Engagement Range of this model and roll one D6 (subtracting 2 from the result if that unit is an INFANTRY CHARACTER unit): on a 2+, that unit suffers D3 mortal wounds.

FACTION KEYWORDS: CHAOS, LEGIONES DAEMONICA, KHORNE
KEYWORDS: MONSTER, CHARACTER, FLY, DAEMON, GREATER DAEMON, BLOODTHIRSTER

Bloodthirsters are supreme warriors, ferocious embodiments of the Blood God's rage and murderlust. Commanders and champions of the Khornate daemon legions, Bloodthirsters are possessed of supreme martial skill. They wield baroque weapons of appalling power, and slaughter all in their paths.

SKULLTAKER

6 POWER

No.	Name	M	WS	BS	S	T	W	A	Ld	DSv
1	Skulltaker	6"	2+	3+	6	6	5	6	8	4+/4+

Skulltaker is equipped with: the Slayer Sword. Your army can only include one **SKULLTAKER** model.

WEAPON	RANGE	TYPE	S	AP	D	ABILITIES
The Slayer Sword	Melee	Melee	User	-3	3	Each time an attack is made with this weapon, invulnerable saving throws cannot be made against that attack.

ABILITIES

Daemonic (pg 56)

Skulls for Khorne:

• Each time this model makes a melee attack against an enemy **CHARACTER** unit, you can re-roll the hit roll and you can re-roll the wound roll.

• Each time an enemy **CHARACTER** unit is destroyed by an attack made by this model, increase the range of this model's Herald of Khorne and Lord of Decapitations abilities (see right) by 3" (to a maximum of 12").

Herald of Khorne (Aura): While a friendly **LEGIONES DAEMONICA KHORNE CORE** unit is within 6" of this model, each time a model in that unit makes an attack, you can re-roll a wound roll of 1.

Lord of Decapitations: In your Command phase, select one friendly **BLOODLETTERS CORE** unit within 6" of this model. Until the start of your next Command phase, each time a model in that unit makes a melee attack, add 1 to that attack's hit roll.

FACTION KEYWORDS: CHAOS, LEGIONES DAEMONICA, KHORNE
KEYWORDS: INFANTRY, CHARACTER, DAEMON, BLOODLETTERS, HERALD, SKULLTAKER

Skulltaker is Khorne's executioner. Wielding the terrifying Slayer Sword, Skulltaker's every blow lops another head from an enemy's shoulders. Fighting at the head of the Cohort of Blood – a dread assemblage of the mightiest Bloodletters – Skulltaker reaps an ever-greater tally of worthy skulls for Khorne.

BLOODMASTER

5 POWER

No.	Name	M	WS	BS	S	T	W	A	Ld	DSv
1	Bloodmaster	6"	2+	3+	6	5	4	5	8	4+/4+

A Bloodmaster is equipped with: blade of blood.

WEAPON	RANGE	TYPE	S	AP	D	ABILITIES
Blade of blood	Melee	Melee	User	-3	3	-

ABILITIES

Daemonic (pg 56)

Herald of Khorne (Aura): While a friendly **LEGIONES DAEMONICA KHORNE CORE** unit is within 6" of this model, each time a model in that unit makes an attack, you can re-roll a wound roll of 1.

Bloodmaster: In your Command phase, select one friendly **BLOODLETTERS CORE** unit within 6" of this model. Until the start of your next Command phase, each time a model in that unit makes a melee attack, an unmodified hit roll of 6 automatically wounds the target.

FACTION KEYWORDS: CHAOS, LEGIONES DAEMONICA, KHORNE
KEYWORDS: INFANTRY, CHARACTER, DAEMON, BLOODLETTERS, HERALD, BLOODMASTER

Risen victorious from the horrors of the Skullpit, Bloodmasters lead Khorne's Bloodletters hosts in battle. The presence of these hulking daemonic slaughterers imbues their infernal followers with even greater fury and might, even as the Bloodmasters themselves carve a gory path through their luckless foes.

SKULLMASTER

7 POWER

No.	Name	M	WS	BS	S	T	W	A	Ld	DSv
1	Skullmaster	10"	2+	3+	6	6	7	5	8	4+/4+

A Skullmaster is equipped with: blade of blood; bladed horn.

WEAPON	RANGE	TYPE	S	AP	D	ABILITIES
Blade of blood	Melee	Melee	User	-3	3	-
Bladed horn	Melee	Melee	User	-2	1	Malefic 4. Each time the bearer fights, if it made a charge move this turn, then until that fight is resolved, change the Strength characteristic of this weapon to +2.

ABILITIES

Daemonic (pg 56)

Herald of Khorne (Aura): While a friendly LEGIONES DAEMONICA KHORNE CORE unit is within 6" of this model, each time a model in that unit makes an attack, you can re-roll a wound roll of 1.

Skullmaster: In your Command phase, select one friendly BLOODLETTERS CORE unit within 6" of this model. Until the start of your next Command phase, each time a model in that unit makes a melee attack, an unmodified hit roll of 6 automatically wounds the target.

FACTION KEYWORDS: CHAOS, LEGIONES DAEMONICA, KHORNE
KEYWORDS: CAVALRY, CHARACTER, DAEMON, BLOODLETTERS, HERALD, SKULLMASTER

Skullmasters ride daemon steeds known as Juggernauts. Mounted upon these beasts of living brass and molten fury, Skullmasters lead the Khornate cavalry charge into the heart of the enemy lines, hacking, beheading, impaling and crushing. Few are the foes that can stand against this devastating stampede.

RENDMASTER ON BLOOD THRONE

7 POWER

No.	Name	M	WS	BS	S	T	W	A	Ld	DSv
1	Rendmaster on Blood Throne	8"	2+	3+	6	7	9	5	8	4+/4+

A Rendmaster on Blood Throne is equipped with: attendants' hellblades; blade of blood.

WEAPON	RANGE	TYPE	S	AP	D	ABILITIES
Attendants' hellblades	Melee	Melee	User	-3	2	Malefic 4
Blade of blood	Melee	Melee	User	-3	3	-

ABILITIES

Daemonic (pg 56)

Champion Slayer: Each time this model makes a melee attack against an enemy CHARACTER or MONSTER unit, you can re-roll the wound roll.

Herald of Khorne (Aura): While a friendly LEGIONES DAEMONICA KHORNE CORE unit is within 6" of this model, each time a model in that unit makes an attack, you can re-roll a wound roll of 1.

Blood Throne: In your Command phase, select one friendly BLOODLETTERS CORE unit within 9" of this model. Until the start of your next Command phase, each time a model in that unit makes a melee attack, an unmodified hit roll of 6 automatically wounds the target.

FACTION KEYWORDS: CHAOS, LEGIONES DAEMONICA, KHORNE
KEYWORDS: VEHICLE, CHARACTER, DAEMON, BLOODLETTERS, HERALD, BLOOD THRONE, RENDMASTER

The greatest of Khorne's heralds are Rendmasters, who ride to battle atop monstrous Daemon Engines known as Blood Thrones. Infernal lore suggests these engines are fashioned from slivers of the Blood God's own throne, and that wherever they plough into the foe, Khorne's legions fight beneath his lowering gaze.

KARANAK

5 POWER

No.	Name	M	WS	BS	S	T	W	A	Ld	DSv
1	Karanak	12"	2+	-	6	5	5	6	8	5+/4+

Karanak is equipped with: soul-rending fangs. Your army can only include one **KARANAK** model.

WEAPON	RANGE	TYPE	S	AP	D	ABILITIES
Soul-rending fangs	Melee	Melee	User	-2	2	-

ABILITIES

Daemonic (pg 56)

Brass Collar of Bloody Vengeance: In your opponent's Psychic phase, this model can attempt to deny two psychic powers as if it were a **PSYKER**.

Pack Leader (Aura): While a friendly **FLESH HOUNDS CORE** unit is within 6" of this model, each time a model in that unit makes an attack, re-roll a wound roll of 1. If the target is a **PSYKER** unit, you can re-roll the wound roll instead.

Prey of the Blood God: In your first Command phase, select one enemy **CHARACTER** unit. Each time this model makes an attack against that **CHARACTER** unit, a successful wound roll inflicts 2 mortal wounds on the target and the attack sequence ends.

FACTION KEYWORDS: Chaos, Legiones Daemonica, Khorne
KEYWORDS: Beast, Daemon, Character, Flesh Hounds, Karanak

Karanak hunts those who give insult to Khorne. Scenting its prey across time and space, it is an inescapable predator. Karanak's incorporeal howls summon the Blood Hunt of Khorne to join it in the chase, a cavalcade of ferocious daemons set on mayhem and slaughter.

BLOODLETTERS

6 POWER

No.	Name	M	WS	BS	S	T	W	A	Ld	DSv
9	Bloodletter	6"	3+	3+	5	4	1	2	6	5+/4+
1	Bloodreaper	6"	3+	3+	5	4	1	3	7	5+/4+

Every model is equipped with: hellblade.

WEAPON	RANGE	TYPE	S	AP	D	ABILITIES
Hellblade	Melee	Melee	User	-3	2	-

OTHER WARGEAR	ABILITIES
Daemonic icon	While this unit contains any models equipped with a daemonic icon: • It has the **ICON** keyword. • Each time a Combat Attrition test is taken for this unit, you can ignore any or all modifiers.
Instrument of Chaos	While this unit contains any models equipped with an instrument of Chaos: • It has the **INSTRUMENT** keyword. • Add 1 to the Leadership characteristic of models in this unit.

WARGEAR OPTIONS

• One Bloodletter that is not equipped with a daemonic icon can be equipped with 1 instrument of Chaos.
• One Bloodletter that is not equipped with an instrument of Chaos can be equipped with 1 daemonic icon.

ABILITIES

Daemonic (pg 56)

FACTION KEYWORDS: Chaos, Legiones Daemonica, Khorne
KEYWORDS: Infantry, Daemon, Core, Bloodletters

Bloodletters are hate and violence made manifest. Attacking in berserk packs or in martial, marching ranks, they hack apart their victims with monstrous hellblades. These weapons glow red-hot with the fury of their wielders, and even the slightest wound they inflict can see the victim bled dry in seconds.

BLOODCRUSHERS

6 POWER

No.	Name	M	WS	BS	S	T	W	A	Ld	DSv
2-5	Bloodcrusher	10"	3+	3+	5	5	4	3	7	4+/4+
1	Bloodhunter	10"	3+	3+	5	5	4	4	8	4+/4+

If this unit contains 4 or more models it has **Power Rating 12**. Every model is equipped with: bladed horn; hellblade.

WEAPON	RANGE	TYPE	S	AP	D	ABILITIES
Bladed horn	Melee	Melee	User	-2	1	Malefic 4. Each time the bearer fights, if it made a charge move this turn, then until that fight is resolved, change the Strength characteristic of this weapon to +2.
Hellblade	Melee	Melee	User	-3	2	-

OTHER WARGEAR	ABILITIES
Daemonic icon	While this unit contains any models equipped with a daemonic icon: • It has the **Icon** keyword. • Each time a Combat Attrition test is taken for this unit, you can ignore any or all modifiers.
Instrument of Chaos	While this unit contains any models equipped with an instrument of Chaos: • It has the **Instrument** keyword. • Add 1 to the Leadership characteristic of models in this unit.

WARGEAR OPTIONS

• One Bloodcrusher that is not equipped with a daemonic icon can be equipped with 1 instrument of Chaos.
• One Bloodcrusher that is not equipped with an instrument of Chaos can be equipped with 1 daemonic icon.

ABILITIES

Daemonic (pg 56)

FACTION KEYWORDS: Chaos, Legiones Daemonica, Khorne
KEYWORDS: Cavalry, Daemon, Bloodletters, Core, Bloodcrushers

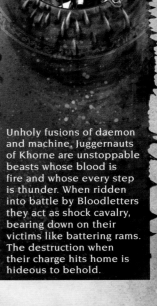

Unholy fusions of daemon and machine, Juggernauts of Khorne are unstoppable beasts whose blood is fire and whose every step is thunder. When ridden into battle by Bloodletters they act as shock cavalry, bearing down on their victims like battering rams. The destruction when their charge hits home is hideous to behold.

FLESH HOUNDS

5 POWER

No.	Name	M	WS	BS	S	T	W	A	Ld	DSv
4-9	Flesh Hound	12"	3+	-	5	4	2	3	7	5+/4+
1	Gore Hound	12"	3+	-	5	4	2	4	8	5+/4+

If this unit contains 6 or more models it has **Power Rating 10**. Every Flesh Hound is equipped with: gore-drenched fangs. The Gore Hound is equipped with: burning roar; gore-drenched fangs.

WEAPON	RANGE	TYPE	S	AP	D	ABILITIES
Burning roar	12"	Assault D6	4	-1	1	Each time an attack is made with this weapon, that attack automatically hits the target.
Gore-drenched fangs	Melee	Melee	User	-2	1	-

ABILITIES

Daemonic (pg 56)

Collar of Khorne: In your opponent's Psychic phase, this unit can attempt to deny one psychic power as if it were a **PSYKER**.

Savage Pounce: Each time a model in this unit makes an attack with its gore-drenched fangs, if that model's unit made a charge move or performed a Heroic Intervention this turn, add 1 to that attack's Damage characteristic.

FACTION KEYWORDS: CHAOS, LEGIONES DAEMONICA, KHORNE
KEYWORDS: BEAST, DAEMON, CORE, FLESH HOUNDS

These hunting hounds of Khorne track the terror spoor of their prey across interstellar gulfs. The brass collars about their necks ward away even the most potent sorceries of their desperate prey, before the slavering Flesh Hounds launch themselves onto their victims swinging vicious talons and sinking foot-long fangs deep.

SKULL CANNON

5 POWER

No.	Name	M	WS	BS	S	T	W	A	Ld	DSv
1	Skull Cannon	8"	3+	3+	6	7	9	2	7	4+/4+

A Skull Cannon is equipped with: skull cannon; attendants' hellblades; biting maw.

WEAPON	RANGE	TYPE	S	AP	D	ABILITIES
Skull cannon	48"	Heavy D3+3	8	-2	2	Blast. Each time an attack is made with this weapon, the target does not receive the benefits of cover against that attack.
Attendants' hellblades	Melee	Melee	User	-3	2	Malefic 4
Biting maw	Melee	Melee	User	-1	2	-

ABILITIES

Daemonic (pg 56)

FACTION KEYWORDS: CHAOS, LEGIONES DAEMONICA, KHORNE
KEYWORDS: VEHICLE, DAEMON, BLOODLETTERS, SKULL CANNON

Grotesque brazen war engines that rumble into battle with obscene eagerness, Skull Cannons are fed the corpses of the fallen to fuel their charnel fury. When they fire, these infernal weapons spit blazing skulls that arc through the air like meteors before exploding with thunderous violence upon impact.

SKULL ALTAR

3 POWER

No.	Name	M	WS	BS	S	T	W	A	Ld	DSv
1	Skull Altar	-	-	-	6	8	9	-	7	4+/4+

A Skull Altar has no equipment.

ABILITIES

Daemonic (pg 56)

Witchbane (Aura): While a **Psyker** unit is within 18" of this model, subtract 2 from Psychic tests taken for that unit.

War Altar: While a model is embarked within this **Transport** model, this **Transport** model has the same aura abilities as the embarked model.

Ritual Slaughter: While there is a model embarked within this **Transport** model, this **Transport** model can attempt the following action:

Ritual Slaughter (Action): At the end of your Movement phase, this model can start to perform this action. The action is completed at the end of your next Charge phase. Once completed, roll one D6 for each **Legiones Daemonica Khorne** unit from your army within 12" of this model and within Engagement Range of any enemy units: for each 4+, gain 1 Warp Storm point.

TRANSPORT

This model has a transport capacity of 1 **Khorne Infantry Herald** model.

FACTION KEYWORDS: Chaos, Legiones Daemonica, Khorne
KEYWORDS: Building, Vehicle, Transport, Warp Locus, Skull Altar

Rumbling up from the tortured ground amidst geysers of gore and skulls, these grotesque altars mar the land wherever the daemons of Khorne advance. They are sites of sacrifice, the blood shed atop them causing waves of wrathful unreality to roll out across the battlefield spreading hate and destruction.

THE BOOK OF CHANGE

Ever shifting changing flowing one into another sorcery becomes flame becomes diamond talons and always they gibber and shriek and whisper and tell their truthful lies while again the shifting flow of fiery change becomes warp becomes reality and in madness in flux in pandemonium they rule…

In this section you will find the following rules:

EXALTED LORDS OF CHANGE (PG 76)

Lords of Change can be upgraded with potent new abilities. The rules for how you can upgrade these models and the abilities they bestow are described in this section.

TZEENTCH STRATAGEMS (PG 77)

Tzeentch armies have access to unique battlefield strategies and tactics that they can utilise to best their foes in any theatre of war; these are represented by the Stratagems in this section, and you can spend Command points to use them in your games. You can find out more about Stratagems and Command points in the Warhammer 40,000 Core Book.

PANDAEMONIAC DISCIPLINE (PG 78)

If your army includes any Tzeentch PSYKER units, they can be given additional psychic powers from the Pandaemoniac discipline. This represents the different arcane lore and particular talents of each individual psyker. You can find out more about psychic powers in the Warhammer 40,000 Core Book.

TZEENTCH WARLORD TRAITS (PG 79)

Tzeentch WARLORD models can have one of the traits presented in this section. These help to better reflect their individual combat and command style on the battlefield.

RELICS OF TZEENTCH (PG 80)

Tzeentch's greatest champions can be equipped with powerful artefacts called Relics of Tzeentch; these Relics and the rules they bestow are described in this section.

TZEENTCH DATASHEETS (PG 81-87)

This section is essential to all Chaos Daemons players who wish to include TZEENTCH units in their army, regardless of preferred play style, containing as it does the datasheets for LEGIONES DAEMONICA TZEENTCH units. Each datasheet describes, among other things, the profiles of its models, the wargear they can be equipped with and the abilities they have. You can find out more about datasheets in the Warhammer 40,000 Core Book.

EXALTED LORDS OF CHANGE

Highest amongst the Lords of Change are those entities whose plotting, foresight and esoteric lore please Tzeentch most greatly. Such malevolent manipulators weave webs of fate and deception that span soaring gulfs of time and space. They oversee the sanity-blasting campaigns of Tzeentch's daemon legions, manipulate his cult followers in realspace, and apply themselves to twisting both the warp and reality to most greatly empower the Dark God they serve. For such efforts, Tzeentch rewards his favoured daemons with mind-bending blessings of empyric power.

If your army includes any **Legiones Daemonica** Detachments (excluding Auxiliary Support, Super-heavy Auxiliary or Fortification Network Detachments), then when you muster your army, you can upgrade any **Lord of Change** models from your army to be exalted. When a model is upgraded to be exalted it gains Exalted abilities.

You can select one of the Exalted abilities (see right) for that model. That model's Power Rating is increased accordingly, as shown in the table below. If you are playing a matched play game, or a game that uses a points limit, then the points value of that unit is also increased by the amount shown in the same table. Make a note on your army roster each time you upgrade a unit using these rules, specifying the ability it has gained.

Named characters (e.g. **Kairos Fateweaver**, page 81) cannot be given Exalted abilities. Each model can only be upgraded to have Exalted abilities once. An army (or a Crusade force) cannot include the same Exalted ability more than once.

A Crusade force cannot start with any models having Exalted abilities – to include one in a Crusade force, you must use the Exalted Daemon Requisition (pg 132).

EXALTED ABILITY	POWER	POINTS
Architect of Deception	+2	+35
Master Mutator	+2	+30
Nexus of Fate	+1	+20

EXALTED ABILITIES

ARCHITECT OF DECEPTION
No foe, be they mortal or daemonic, can trust their perceptions around this most cunning of daemons. A veil of sorcerous illusion wreathes it so densely that its enemies may not discern the daemon's true location even should they stand in its very shadow.

Each time a ranged attack is made against this model, subtract 1 from that attack's hit roll.

MASTER MUTATOR
The merest touch of this daemon's magicks causes the fabric of realspace to twist and distort. Screaming victims find their bodies and wargear erupting into grotesque mutant growth that soon reduces even the most stoic or magnificent warrior to a mewling heap of fleshy ruination.

At the end of your Psychic phase, roll one D6 for each enemy unit that suffered any mortal wounds as a result of a psychic power manifested by this model this turn: on a 2+, that unit suffers 1 mortal wound.

NEXUS OF FATE
Orbited by glowing runes that dance through the air like will-o'-the-wisps, the fates of all its allies and foes play out before the bottomless wells of this daemon's unblinking eyes.

In your Command phase, if this model is on the battlefield, roll one D6: on a 4+, you gain one Command point.

TZEENTCH STRATAGEMS

If your army includes any **LEGIONES DAEMONICA TZEENTCH** units (excluding units in Auxiliary Support, Super-heavy Auxiliary or Fortification Network Detachments), you have access to these Stratagems, and can spend CPs to use them.

MINIONS OF MAGIC   1CP

Legions of Tzeentch – Battle Tactic Stratagem

The mutating change-fires unleashed by the freakish daemons of Tzeentch pour through or melt away even the most formidable armour.

Use this Stratagem in your Shooting phase, when a **HORRORS CORE** unit is selected to shoot. Until the end of the phase, each time a ranged attack is made by a model in that unit, on an unmodified wound roll of 6, change the Armour Penetration characteristic of that attack to -3.

BURNING WARPFIRE   1CP/2CP

Legions of Tzeentch – Battle Tactic Stratagem

Employing their rubbery flesh as a conduit for the raw energies of the warp, these daemons spew the resultant torrent of warp-stuff as wave upon wave of mutating flame.

Use this Stratagem in your Shooting phase, when a **FLAMERS** unit is selected to shoot. Until the end of the phase, each time a model in that unit makes an attack with flickering flames or the pink fire profile of fire of Tzeentch that targets an enemy unit that contains 11 or more models, when determining how many attacks that model makes with that weapon, count results of less than 9 as 9. If that **FLAMERS** unit contains 4 or more models, this Stratagem costs 2CP; otherwise, it costs 1CP.

WARP JAWS   1CP

Legions of Tzeentch – Battle Tactic Stratagem

Many Tzeentchian daemons possess slavering maws that drool corrosive warp-stuff quite capable of eating through or transmogrifying the toughest corporeal armour.

Use this Stratagem in the Fight phase, when a **SCREAMERS**, **FATESKIMMER** or **BURNING CHARIOT** unit from your army is selected to fight. Until the end of the phase, each time an attack is made with a lamprey bite or Screamer bites by a model in that unit, add 1 to that attack's wound roll.

MAGICAL BOON   1CP

Legions of Tzeentch – Epic Deed Stratagem

Arcane knowledge and mystical power have ever been the domain of Tzeentch and his minions.

Use this Stratagem at the start of your Psychic phase. Select one **LEGIONES DAEMONICA TZEENTCH PSYKER** unit from your army. That unit can attempt to manifest one additional psychic power this turn.

RELICS OF THE IMPOSSIBLE FORTRESS   1CP

Legions of Tzeentch – Requisition Stratagem

Many are the arcane devices wielded by the servants of Tzeentch.

Use this Stratagem before the battle, when you are mustering your army. Select one **LEGIONES DAEMONICA TZEENTCH CHARACTER** model from your army and give them one Relic of Tzeentch (this must be a Relic they can have). Each Relic in your army must be unique, and you cannot use this Stratagem to give a model two Relics. You can only use this Stratagem once, unless you are playing a Strike Force battle (in which case, you can use this Stratagem twice) or an Onslaught battle (in which case, you can use this Stratagem three times).

WARP PORTAL   1CP/2CP

Legions of Tzeentch – Strategic Ploy Stratagem

This daemon prises open an unnatural shortcut through the warp.

Use this Stratagem in your Movement phase, when you select a **LEGIONES DAEMONICA TZEENTCH CHARACTER** model from your army to make a Normal Move. Instead of moving it as normal, remove that unit from the battlefield and set it up anywhere on the battlefield that is more than 9" from any enemy models. If that **CHARACTER** model has the **HERALD** keyword, this Stratagem costs 1CP, otherwise, it costs 2CP.

FLAMES OF MUTATION   1CP

Legions of Tzeentch – Strategic Ploy Stratagem

Tzeentchian daemons advance wreathed in kaleidoscopic flame.

Use this Stratagem at the end of the Fight phase. Select one **HORRORS** unit from your army that had any models destroyed during this phase. Select one enemy unit within Engagement Range of that unit, and roll one D6 for each model in that **HORRORS** unit that was destroyed during this phase. For each 6, that enemy unit suffers 1 mortal wound. A unit can only suffer a maximum of 6 mortal wounds per phase as a result of this Stratagem.

BLASTED STANDARD   1CP

Legions of Tzeentch – Wargear Stratagem

The daemons unleash transmutational energies from their icon.

Use this Stratagem at the start of your Psychic phase. Select one **LEGIONES DAEMONICA TZEENTCH ICON** unit from your army. Until the end of the phase, each time you make an unmodified Psychic test of 9 or more for a friendly **LEGIONES DAEMONICA TZEENTCH PSYKER** unit within 12" of that unit, the closest enemy unit within 24" of and visible to that selected unit suffers 1 mortal wound.

PANDAEMONIAC DISCIPLINE

Before the battle, generate the psychic powers for **PSYKER** models in your army that know powers from the Pandaemoniac discipline using the table below. You can either roll one D6 to generate each power randomly (re-rolling duplicate results), or you can select which powers the **PSYKER** model knows.

1. BOON OF CHANGE

As the daemon chants, its minions begin to twist and new forms take shape as the will of Tzeentch demands.

Blessing: *Boon of Change* has a warp charge value of 6. If manifested, select one friendly **LEGIONES DAEMONICA TZEENTCH** unit within 18" of this **PSYKER** and roll one D3. Until the start of your next Psychic phase, that unit gains the relevant bonus from the table below:

D3	EFFECT
1	**Extra Limbs:** Add 2" to the Move characteristic of models in that unit.
2	**Mystical Strength:** Add 1 to the Strength characteristic of models in that unit.
3	**Resilient Hide:** Add 1 to the Toughness characteristic of models in that unit.

If the result of the Psychic test was 9 or more, you can select which result applies instead of rolling a D3.

2. BOLT OF CHANGE

The daemon unleashes a bolt of warp energy that afflicts the foe with sickening and uncontrollable mutations.

Witchfire: *Bolt of Change* has a warp charge value of 7. If manifested, select one enemy unit within 18" of and visible to this **PSYKER**, and roll nine D6:

- For each 5+, that enemy unit suffers 1 mortal wound.
- For each model destroyed as a result of these mortal wounds, that unit suffers 1 additional mortal wound (to a maximum of 3). These additional mortal wounds cannot generate any additional mortal wounds.

3. GAZE OF FATE

Using its powers of precognition to unravel the strands of destiny, this daemon extracts secrets from the sea of souls and channels them through its own potent form.

Blessing: *Gaze of Fate* has a warp charge value of 7. If manifested, at the end of the battle round, if this **PSYKER** is on the battlefield, you can retain up to 2 unspent Warp Storm points (pg 58).

4. TREASON OF TZEENTCH

The psyker reaches into the mind of its victim, subverting their will and turning them upon their own allies.

Malediction: *Treason of Tzeentch* has a warp charge value of 7. If manifested, select one enemy unit within 18" of and visible to this **PSYKER**. Until the start of your next Psychic phase, that enemy unit is not affected by the aura abilities of other enemy units.

5. INFERNAL FLAMES

Cackling madly, the psyker's minions are wreathed in pink and blue flames that leap forth to consume their foes.

Blessing: *Infernal Flames* has a warp charge value of 7. If manifested, select one friendly **LEGIONES DAEMONICA TZEENTCH CORE** unit within 18" of and visible to this **PSYKER**. Until the start of your next Psychic phase, each time a model in that unit makes a ranged attack, add 1 to that attack's wound roll.

6. INFERNAL GATEWAY

Opening a portal to the warp, this daemon creates a tear in the fabric of the mortal plane that sucks foes into certain oblivion.

Witchfire: *Infernal Gateway* has a warp charge value of 8. If manifested, the closest enemy unit within 18" of and visible to this **PSYKER** and each other enemy unit within 3" of that enemy unit suffers D3 mortal wounds. If the result of the Psychic test was 12 or more, each affected unit suffers 3 mortal wounds instead.

'The Gibberling Prince speaks truth in every lie. The God of Puppets offers freedom with every tug of his strings. The Nine Blinded Eyes see all in the nothing. That Which Knows All covets knowledge in the void. The Weaver of Fates spins a twisted skein of ever-fraying ends. The Changer of the Ways entraps all souls upon the paths they believe they have chosen. All that ever you know of Almighty Tzeentch is that of which you are most ignorant.'

- The Chant of Untruths, Ninety-ninth verse

TZEENTCH WARLORD TRAITS

If a **Legiones Daemonica Tzeentch Character** model from your army gains a Warlord Trait, you can use the Tzeentch Warlord Traits table below to determine which Warlord Trait they have. You can either roll one D6 to randomly generate one, or you can select one.

If a **Tzeentch Herald** model is your **Warlord**, they can only have the Born of Sorcery, Incorporeal Form or Fractal Mind Warlord Traits. You can either roll one D3 to randomly generate one, or you can select one.

1. BORN OF SORCERY
Tapping into the infinite power of the warp comes as easily to this daemon as breathing air does to a mortal.

Add 1 to Psychic tests taken for this **Warlord**.

2. INCORPOREAL FORM
This daemon's body flickers constantly in and out of reality, making it difficult for adversaries to land a telling blow against it.

Each time an attack is made against this **Warlord**, subtract 1 from that attack's wound roll.

3. FRACTAL MIND
This daemon's consciousness is a many-faceted tangle of infinite complexity that allows it to divide its perceptions and attention in a way that would drive mortal minds to madness.

If this **Warlord** attempts to perform a psychic action in your Psychic phase, it can still attempt to manifest one psychic power during that phase without that psychic action failing.

4. WARP TETHER
This daemon embeds its essence into realspace like a thorn, then exudes tendrils of energy that anchor its minions within corporeal reality.

- This **Warlord** has the **Warp Locus** keyword.
- This **Warlord** has the following ability:

Warp Tether (Aura): While a friendly **Legiones Daemonica Tzeentch** unit is within 12" of this model, each time a Morale test is taken for that unit, you can re-roll the result.

5. LOREKEEPER OF TZEENTCH
Like some malevolent arachnid, this daemon extends its web ever further, ensnaring mortal wisdom and arcane lore and devouring it.

Each time this **Warlord** successfully manifests a psychic power from the Pandaemoniac discipline (pg 78), add 6" to the range of that psychic power. If that psychic power specifies more than one range, only add 6" to the first range specified.

6. TYRANT OF THE WARP
The sheer ensorcelled might of this daemon's presence in the warp is enough to dissuade rival entities and predatory sentiences from attempting to assail it on the metaphysical battleground.

- This **Warlord** never suffers Perils of the Warp.
- Each time this **Warlord** would lose a wound as the result of a mortal wound, roll one D6: on a 5+, that wound is not lost.

NAMED CHARACTERS AND WARLORD TRAITS
If one of the following characters gains a Warlord Trait, they must have the relevant one shown below:

Named Character	Warlord Trait
Kairos Fateweaver	Tyrant of the Warp
The Blue Scribes	Incorporeal Form
The Changeling	Warp Tether

RELICS OF TZEENTCH

If a **LEGIONES DAEMONICA TZEENTCH CHARACTER** model gains a Relic, you can give them one of the following Relics of Tzeentch. Named characters and **VEHICLE** models cannot be given any of the following Relics.

Note that some Relics replace one of the model's existing items of wargear. Where this is the case, you must, if you are using points values, still pay the cost of the wargear that is being replaced. Write down any Relics of Tzeentch your models have on your army roster.

THE ENDLESS GRIMOIRE

Within the pages of this magical tome lie the secrets of every cantrip, incantation and spell ever conceived. Though the bearer of this grimoire has access to the infinite knowledge bound within, they must battle the temptation simply to fall into the flickering pages of the tome and drink in endless reams of knowledge until they lose all grasp or influence upon the events transpiring around them.

PSYKER model only. The bearer can attempt the following action:

Study Grimoire (Action): At the start of your Shooting phase, the bearer can start to perform this action. This action is completed at the start of your next Command phase. If completed, select one psychic power from the Pandaemoniac discipline (pg 78). Until the end of the battle, the bearer knows that psychic power in addition to any others it knows.

THE IMPOSSIBLE ROBE

The wearer of this robe exists between several realities at once. Thus can a daemonic commander potentially control Tzeentch's interests in multiple times and places simultaneously to further multiple aspects of the Great Plan. This effect makes it hard for foes to truly harm the wearer, who flickers between planes of reality in an unpredictable fashion. However, the robe is capricious, and has been known to rip its wearer out of reality altogether should they lose control of its powers.

Once per phase, when a saving throw is failed for the bearer, you can use this ability. If you do so, the Damage characteristic of that attack is changed to 0.

THE EVERSTAVE

This staff blazes with vibrant warpflame. As soon as its master takes up the eldritch weapon, they too are wreathed in the same daemonic fire. From within this magenta inferno, the Everstave's daemonic bearer hurls searing gouts of Tzeentch's pink fire, turning armour to ash and immolating or irrevocably mutating the flesh beneath.

PSYKER model only. Each time the bearer attempts to manifest a Witchfire psychic power or *Smite*, on an unmodified Psychic test of 9 or more, that psychic power cannot be denied.

WARPFIRE BLADE

Existing in nine times nine dimensions, the Warpfire Blade flickers with its bearer's sorcerous power. Every iteration of the blade strikes in differing forms and at varying angles – a plane of sharpened will, an outstretched hand of friendship, a wave of stellar fire – seeking a route through every sub-existence to sever the soul of those it strikes.

Select one melee weapon the bearer is equipped with.

- Add 1 to the Damage characteristic of that weapon.
- Each time an attack is made with that weapon, an unmodified wound roll of 6 inflicts 1 mortal wound on the target in addition to any normal damage.
- That weapon is now considered to be a Relic for all rules purposes.

SOULBANE

This incorporeal blade inflicts no harm upon its victim's physical body, instead carving its way through the stuff of their very soul. So ephemeral and unreal is this strange weapon that it is impossible to cross blades with Soulbane, for its ghostly edge will pass straight through any guard. Those struck by Soulbane collapse in agony, writhing and screaming as their lacerated essences slowly bleed away into the immaterium.

Model equipped with rod of sorcery only. This Relic replaces a rod of sorcery and has the following profile:

WEAPON	RANGE	TYPE	S	AP	D
Soulbane	12"	Assault 3D3	6	–2	3

SOUL-EATER STAVE

Invisible to those without witch-sight, ethereal pseudopods, grasping talons and maws of non-matter surround this twisted staff, ever alert to the cry of a soul newly torn from its body. Riding the power channelled by the staff's bearer, they hungrily devour every scrap of life essence they can catch before it is lost to the maelstrom of the warp's myriad predators. This unholy feast serves to infuse the stave's daemon wielder with stolen vigour, which flows from the weapon into its master through its nightmarish web of tendrils and parasitic tethers.

PSYKER model only. Each time an enemy model is destroyed by a mortal wound inflicted as a result of a psychic power manifested by the bearer, roll one D6: on a 4+, the bearer regains 1 lost wound. The bearer cannot regain more than 6 lost wounds in each Psychic phase as a result of this ability.

KAIROS FATEWEAVER
16 POWER

Some of this model's characteristics change as it suffers damage, as shown below:

No.	Name	M	WS	BS	S	T	W	A	Ld	DSv
1	Kairos Fateweaver (12+ wounds remaining)	12"	3+	3+	6	7	22	5	10	5+/3+
	Kairos Fateweaver (6-11 wounds remaining)	10"	4+	3+	6	7	N/A	4	10	5+/3+
	Kairos Fateweaver (1-5 wounds remaining)	8"	5+	3+	6	7	N/A	3	10	5+/3+

Kairos Fateweaver is equipped with: Staff of Tomorrow. Your army can only include one **KAIROS FATEWEAVER** model.

WEAPON	RANGE	TYPE	S	AP	D	ABILITIES
Staff of Tomorrow	Melee	Melee	+2	-3	2D3	-

ABILITIES

Daemonic (pg 56)

Daemon Lord of Tzeentch (Aura): While a friendly **LEGIONES DAEMONICA TZEENTCH CORE** unit is within 6" of this model, each time a model in that unit makes an attack, re-roll a hit roll of 1.

One Head Looks Forward: Each time a Psychic test is taken for this model, add the current battle round number to the result.

One Head Looks Back: Once per battle, when your opponent uses a Stratagem (excluding the Command Re-roll Stratagem, see the Warhammer 40,000 Core Book) you can use this ability. If you do so, until the end of the battle, the CP cost your opponent must pay to use that Stratagem again is increased by 1.

PSYKER

This model can attempt to manifest three psychic powers in your Psychic phase, and attempt to deny three psychic powers in your opponent's Psychic phase. It knows *Smite* and all of the psychic powers from the Pandaemoniac discipline (pg 78).

FACTION KEYWORDS: CHAOS, LEGIONES DAEMONICA, TZEENTCH
KEYWORDS: MONSTER, CHARACTER, DAEMON, FLY, PSYKER, GREATER DAEMON, WARP LOCUS, LORD OF CHANGE, KAIROS FATEWEAVER

Wielding the warp-forged Staff of Tomorrow, and with the ability to predict all that may come to pass while knowing all that has already transpired, Kairos Fateweaver is amongst the galaxy's most canny strategists. What the daemon lacks in physical and martial prowess, it more than makes up for in pure Tzeentchian cunning.

LORD OF CHANGE
15 POWER

Some of this model's characteristics change as it suffers damage, as shown below:

No.	Name	M	WS	BS	S	T	W	A	Ld	DSv
1	Lord of Change (11+ wounds remaining)	12"	3+	3+	6	7	20	5	10	5+/3+
	Lord of Change (6-10 wounds remaining)	10"	4+	3+	6	7	N/A	4	10	5+/3+
	Lord of Change (1-5 wounds remaining)	8"	5+	3+	6	7	N/A	3	10	5+/3+

A Lord of Change is equipped with: staff of Tzeentch.

WEAPON	RANGE	TYPE	S	AP	D	ABILITIES
Rod of sorcery	12"	Assault D6	6	-1	2	-
Baleful sword	Melee	Melee	+1	-3	3	Malefic 3
Staff of Tzeentch	Melee	Melee	User	-2	3	-

WARGEAR OPTIONS

• This model can be equipped with one of the following: 1 baleful sword; 1 rod of sorcery.

ABILITIES

Daemonic (pg 56)

Daemon Lord of Tzeentch (Aura): While a friendly **LEGIONES DAEMONICA TZEENTCH CORE** unit is within 6" of this model, each time a model in that unit makes an attack, re-roll a hit roll of 1.

Master of Magicks: Each time a Psychic test is taken for this model, add 1 the result. If this model has 10 or more wounds remaining, add 2 to the result instead.

PSYKER

This model can attempt to manifest three psychic powers in your Psychic phase, and attempt to deny two psychic powers in your opponent's Psychic phase. It knows *Smite* and three psychic powers from the Pandaemoniac discipline (pg 78).

FACTION KEYWORDS: CHAOS, LEGIONES DAEMONICA, TZEENTCH
KEYWORDS: MONSTER, CHARACTER, DAEMON, FLY, PSYKER, GREATER DAEMON, LORD OF CHANGE

These Greater Daemons of Tzeentch are infinitely cunning sorcerers and manipulators. Their malevolent gaze lays bare the souls of their victims and blasts the sanity of even the staunchest mortal, while their ensorcelled weapons and unholy magicks violently reshape reality itself into ever-mutating forms.

THE CHANGELING

5 POWER

No.	Name	M	WS	BS	S	T	W	A	Ld	DSv
1	The Changeling	6"	4+	3+	3	5	5	2	8	5+/3+

The Changeling is equipped with: Trickster's staff. Your army can only include one **The Changeling** model.

WEAPON	RANGE	TYPE	S	AP	D	ABILITIES
Trickster's staff	Melee	Melee	User	0	1	Each time the bearer is selected to fight, you can select one melee weapon an enemy **INFANTRY** model within Engagement Range of the bearer is equipped with. Until that fight is resolved, this weapon has the same profile as the selected weapon.

ABILITIES

Daemonic (pg 56)

Formless Horror: Each time this model is selected to fight, you can select one enemy **INFANTRY** model within Engagement Range of this model. Until that fight is resolved, this model has the same Weapon Skill, Strength and Attacks characteristics as the selected model.

Herald of Tzeentch (Aura): While a friendly **LEGIONES DAEMONICA TZEENTCH CORE** unit is within 6" of this model, each time a model in that unit makes an attack, you can re-roll a wound roll of 1.

PSYKER

This model can attempt to manifest one psychic power in your Psychic phase, and attempt to deny one psychic power in your opponent's Psychic phase. It knows *Smite* and one psychic power from the Pandaemoniac discipline (pg 78).

FACTION KEYWORDS: CHAOS, LEGIONES DAEMONICA, TZEENTCH
KEYWORDS: INFANTRY, CHARACTER, DAEMON, PSYKER, HERALD, HORRORS, THE CHANGELING

Known also as the Trickster of Tzeentch, the Changeling can alter its form at will to mimic mortal beings from the smallest insect to the most titanic monster. The daemon's favourite game is to impersonate pivotal mortal leaders or heroes, and then to wreak untold mischief by abusing their power and position.

FATESKIMMER

7 POWER

No.	Name	M	WS	BS	S	T	W	A	Ld	DSv
1	Fateskimmer	14"	4+	3+	3	6	9	2	8	5+/3+

A Fateskimmer is equipped with: ritual dagger; Screamer bites.

WEAPON	RANGE	TYPE	S	AP	D	ABILITIES
Staff of change	18"	Assault 3	+4	-4	2	-
Ritual dagger	Melee	Melee	User	-1	1	-
Screamer bites	Melee	Melee	6	-3	2	Malefic 6

OTHER WARGEAR	ABILITIES
Retinue of Horrors	Add 1 to Psychic tests taken for the bearer.

WARGEAR OPTIONS

- This model's ritual dagger can be replaced with 1 staff of change.
- This model can be equipped with 1 retinue of Horrors.

ABILITIES

Daemonic (pg 56)

Herald of Tzeentch (Aura): While a friendly **LEGIONES DAEMONICA TZEENTCH CORE** unit is within 6" of this model, each time a model in that unit makes an attack, you can re-roll a wound roll of 1.

Fateskimmer: In your Command phase, select one friendly **SCREAMERS** unit within 6" of this model. Until the start of your next Command phase, each time a model in that unit makes a melee attack, an unmodified hit roll of 6 automatically wounds the target.

PSYKER

This model can attempt to manifest two psychic powers in your Psychic phase, and attempt to deny one psychic power in your opponent's Psychic phase. It knows *Smite* and two psychic powers from the Pandaemoniac discipline (pg 78).

FACTION KEYWORDS: CHAOS, LEGIONES DAEMONICA, TZEENTCH
KEYWORDS: VEHICLE, CHARACTER, DAEMON, FLY, PSYKER, HERALD, HORRORS, FATESKIMMER

These daemons ride upon Burning Chariots, arcane constructs fashioned from the energies of dread omens and foretelling. They hurtle along anarchic and illogical trajectories that defy all physical laws, often surrounded by shoals of predatory daemonic entities empowered and emboldened by the herald's presence.

FLUXMASTER

6 POWER

No.	Name	M	WS	BS	S	T	W	A	Ld	DSv
1	Fluxmaster	12"	4+	3+	3	4	6	2	8	6+/3+

A Fluxmaster is equipped with: Disc blades; ritual dagger.

WEAPON	RANGE	TYPE	S	AP	D	ABILITIES
Staff of change	18"	Assault 3	+4	-4	2	-
Disc blades	Melee	Melee	4	0	1	Malefic 1
Ritual dagger	Melee	Melee	User	-1	1	-

WARGEAR OPTIONS

• This model can be equipped with 1 staff of change.

ABILITIES

Daemonic (pg 56)

Herald of Tzeentch (Aura): While a friendly **Legiones Daemonica Tzeentch Core** unit is within 6" of this model, each time a model in that unit makes an attack, you can re-roll a wound roll of 1.

Fluxmaster: In your Command phase, select one friendly **Horrors Core** unit within 6" of this model. Until the start of your next Command phase, each time a model in that unit makes a ranged attack, an unmodified hit roll of 6 automatically wounds the target.

PSYKER

This model can attempt to manifest two psychic powers in your Psychic phase, and attempt to deny one psychic power in your opponent's Psychic phase. It knows *Smite* and two psychic powers from the Pandaemoniac discipline (pg 78).

FACTION KEYWORDS: Chaos, Legiones Daemonica, Tzeentch
KEYWORDS: Infantry, Character, Daemon, Fly, Psyker, Herald, Horrors, Fluxmaster

Fluxmasters are Heralds of Tzeentch gifted with daemonic Discs as steeds. They streak through the air like scintillating comets, trailing a wake of altered reality behind them in which fate turns in the favour of Tzeentch's servants and all their endeavours are rendered especially successful and potent.

THE BLUE SCRIBES

5 POWER

No.	Name	M	WS	BS	S	T	W	A	Ld	DSv
1	The Blue Scribes	12"	4+	4+	3	4	5	2	8	5+/3+

The Blue Scribes are equipped with: disc blades; sharp quills. Your army can only include one **The Blue Scribes** model.

WEAPON	RANGE	TYPE	S	AP	D	ABILITIES
Disc blades	Melee	Melee	4	0	1	Malefic 1
Sharp quills	Melee	Melee	User	0	1	-

ABILITIES

Daemonic (pg 56)

P'tarix's Sorcerous Syphon (Aura): While an enemy **Psyker** unit is within 12" of this model:

• Subtract 1 from Psychic tests taken for that unit.

• Each time a Psychic test is failed for that unit, that psychic power is syphoned, and until the end of the battle, that unit cannot attempt to manifest that psychic power. Psychic actions are unaffected.

Xirat'p's Sorcerous Barrage: At the start of your Psychic phase, you can resolve each of the following effects once, in any order:

• Roll two D6 and select one result. This model can automatically manifest the psychic power from the Pandaemoniac discipline (pg 78) that corresponds with that number.

• If this model successfully syphoned any psychic powers in the previous enemy Psychic phase (see left), it can automatically manifest the *Smite* psychic power.

These powers are considered to have been manifested with a roll equal to their warp charge value (do not make a Psychic test), and they cannot be denied.

FACTION KEYWORDS: Chaos, Legiones Daemonica, Tzeentch
KEYWORDS: Cavalry, Character, Daemon, Fly, Horrors, The Blue Scribes

These quarrelsome daemons flit through time and space upon their skimming Disc, seeking scattered shards of the sorcerous wisdom of Tzeentch. P'tarix leeches away the secrets and power of enemy sorcerers, even as Xirat'p unleashes storms of sorcerous destruction drawn from their arcane stash of lore.

CHANGECASTER

4 POWER

No.	Name	M	WS	BS	S	T	W	A	Ld	DSv
1	Changecaster	6"	4+	3+	3	4	5	2	8	6+/3+

A Changecaster is equipped with: ritual dagger.

WEAPON	RANGE	TYPE	S	AP	D	ABILITIES
Staff of change	18"	Assault 3	+4	-4	2	-
Ritual dagger	Melee	Melee	User	-1	1	-

WARGEAR OPTIONS

• This model's ritual dagger can be replaced with 1 staff of change.

ABILITIES

Daemonic (pg 56)

Herald of Tzeentch (Aura): While a friendly **LEGIONES DAEMONICA TZEENTCH CORE** unit is within 6" of this model, each time a model in that unit makes an attack, you can re-roll a wound roll of 1.

Changecaster: In your Command phase, select one friendly **HORRORS CORE** unit within 6" of this model. Until the start of your next Command phase, each time a model in that unit makes a melee attack, an unmodified hit roll of 6 automatically wounds the target.

PSYKER

This model can attempt to manifest two psychic powers in your Psychic phase, and attempt to deny one psychic power in your opponent's Psychic phase. It knows *Smite* and two psychic powers from the Pandaemoniac discipline (pg 78).

FACTION KEYWORDS: **CHAOS, LEGIONES DAEMONICA, TZEENTCH**
KEYWORDS: **INFANTRY, CHARACTER, DAEMON, PSYKER, HERALD, HORRORS, CHANGECASTER**

Whirling amidst capering masses of daemonic Horrors, these Heralds are potent sorcerers whose presence causes the fires of their fellow daemons to burn hotter. Changecasters unleash storms of mutating sorcery against their enemies, jabbering and cackling as they wreak gruesome havoc through the enemy lines.

BLUE HORRORS

3 POWER

No.	Name	M	WS	BS	S	T	W	A	Ld	DSv
10	Blue Horror	6"	5+	4+	2	3	1	1	5	6+/4+
-	Brimstone Horror	6"	5+	4+	1	3	1	1	4	6+/5+

Every model is equipped with: coruscating flames.

WEAPON	RANGE	TYPE	S	AP	D	ABILITIES
Coruscating flames	18"	Assault 2	+1	-1	1	-

ABILITIES

Daemonic (pg 56)

Capering Horrors:

• This unit cannot perform actions (see the Warhammer 40,000 Core Book).

• This unit can never gain the Objective Secured ability (see the Warhammer 40,000 Core Book).

Split: Each time an enemy unit shoots or fights, after resolving those attacks, if any Blue Horrors models in this unit were destroyed as a result of those attacks but this unit was not destroyed, make a Split roll for each destroyed model. To make a Split roll, roll one D6: on a 4+, that model splits and you can add 1 Brimstone Horror model to this unit. When doing so, that Brimstone Horror model cannot be set up within Engagement Range of any enemy units unless those enemy units are already within Engagement Range of its unit.

FACTION KEYWORDS: **CHAOS, LEGIONES DAEMONICA, TZEENTCH**
KEYWORDS: **INFANTRY, DAEMON, CORE, HORRORS, BLUE HORRORS**

Blue Horrors are sullen, malevolent entities, as likely to throttle victims with their rubbery fingers out of sheer spite as to melt them like tallow with conjured gouts of mutating warpflame. Should one of these wretched beings be slain it bursts into a roiling cloud of fume from which a pair of crackling Brimstone Horrors emerge.

PINK HORRORS

7 POWER

No.	Name	M	WS	BS	S	T	W	A	Ld	DSv
9	Pink Horror	6"	4+	3+	3	3	1	1	6	6+/3+
1	Iridescent Horror	6"	4+	3+	3	3	1	2	7	6+/3+
-	Blue Horror	6"	5+	4+	2	3	1	1	5	6+/4+
-	Brimstone Horror	6"	5+	4+	1	3	1	1	4	6+/5+

Every model is equipped with: coruscating flames.

WEAPON	RANGE	TYPE	S	AP	D	ABILITIES
Coruscating flames	18"	Assault 2	+1	-1	1	-

OTHER WARGEAR	ABILITIES
Daemonic icon	While this unit contains any models equipped with a daemonic icon: • It has the **ICON** keyword. • Each time a Combat Attrition test is taken for this unit, you can ignore any or all modifiers.
Instrument of Chaos	While this unit contains any models equipped with an instrument of Chaos: • It has the **INSTRUMENT** keyword. • Add 1 to the Leadership characteristic of models in this unit.

WARGEAR OPTIONS

- One Pink Horror that is not equipped with a daemonic icon can be equipped with 1 instrument of Chaos.
- One Pink Horror that is not equipped with an instrument of Chaos can be equipped with 1 daemonic icon.

ABILITIES

Daemonic (pg 56)

Exploding Horrors: While this unit only contains Blue Horror or Brimstone Horror models:
- This unit cannot perform actions (see the Warhammer 40,000 Core Book).
- This unit loses the Objective Secured ability (see the Warhammer 40,000 Core Book).

Split: Each time an enemy unit shoots or fights, after resolving those attacks, if any Pink Horror, Iridescent Horror or Blue Horror models in this unit were destroyed as a result of those attacks but this unit was not destroyed, make a Split roll for each destroyed model. To make a Split roll, roll one D6: on a 4+, that model splits:
- If a Pink Horror or Iridescent Horror model splits, you can add up to 2 Blue Horror models to this unit (this can increase the size of this unit above its Starting Strength and does not change this unit's Power Rating).
- If a Blue Horror model splits, you can add 1 Brimstone Horror model to this unit.
- Each time a model is added to this unit, that model cannot be set up within Engagement Range of any enemy units unless those enemy units are already within Engagement Range of its unit.

FACTION KEYWORDS: CHAOS, LEGIONES DAEMONICA, TZEENTCH
KEYWORDS: INFANTRY, DAEMON, CORE, HORRORS, PINK HORRORS

Magic made manifest, these cavorting grotesques hurl balls of warpfire into the enemy ranks where they transmogrify and immolate their victims. Pink Horrors cackle, riddle and caper endlessly, their unsettling glee ending only in the moment when their mortal form is destroyed and forced to split messily into two Blue Horrors.

FLAMERS

3 POWER

No.	Name	M	WS	BS	S	T	W	A	Ld	DSv
2-5	Flamer	12"	4+	3+	5	4	3	3	7	6+/3+
1	Pyrocaster	12"	4+	3+	5	4	3	4	8	6+/3+

If this unit contains 4 or more models it has **Power Rating 6**. Every model is equipped with: flickering flames.

WEAPON	RANGE	TYPE	S	AP	D	ABILITIES
Flickering flames	12"	Assault D6+3	User	-2	1	Each time an attack is made with this weapon, that attack automatically hits the target.

ABILITIES

Daemonic (pg 56)

FACTION KEYWORDS: CHAOS, LEGIONES DAEMONICA, TZEENTCH
KEYWORDS: INFANTRY, DAEMON, CORE, FLY, FLAMERS

These bizarre daemons bound through the air in convulsive leaps. The warpflame that drools from their many maws seethes with the raw power of change. When spat forth in roaring sheets, it sends its victims into agonies of mutation, their forms altering again and again before collapsing into distorted ruin.

EXALTED FLAMER

4 POWER

No.	Name	M	WS	BS	S	T	W	A	Ld	DSv
1	Exalted Flamer	10"	3+	3+	6	5	5	4	8	6+/3+

An Exalted Flamer is equipped with: fire of Tzeentch.

WEAPON	RANGE	TYPE	S	AP	D	ABILITIES
Fire of Tzeentch	Before selecting targets, select one of the profiles below to make attacks with.					
- Blue fire	18"	Assault 3	+3	-4	3	-
- Pink fire	12"	Assault 2D6	User	-2	1	Each time an attack is made with this weapon profile, that attack automatically hits the target.

ABILITIES

Daemonic (pg 56)

Manifestation of Destruction: This model can never have a Relic or a Warlord Trait.

Blazing Warpfire (Aura): While a friendly FLAMERS unit is within 6" of this model, each time a model in that unit makes an attack with flickering flames, that attack has a Strength characteristic of +1.

FACTION KEYWORDS: CHAOS, LEGIONES DAEMONICA, TZEENTCH
KEYWORDS: INFANTRY, CHARACTER, DAEMON, FLAMERS, FLY, EXALTED FLAMER

Champions of their kind, Exalted Flamers lead packs of lesser entities to battle. Some swoop upon the backs of Burning Chariots, unleashing focused jets of devastating blue fire, or indiscriminate rains of searing pink fire that clings and spreads like panic given animus until nothing remains in its wake but glowing ashes.

SCREAMERS

4 POWER

No.	Name	M	WS	BS	S	T	W	A	Ld	DSv
3-6	Screamer	16"	4+	-	4	4	3	3	8	6+/3+

If this unit contains 4 or more models it has **Power Rating 8**. Every model is equipped with: lamprey bite.

WEAPON	RANGE	TYPE	S	AP	D	ABILITIES
Lamprey bite	Melee	Melee	+2	-3	2	-

ABILITIES

Daemonic (pg 56)

Riders of the Immaterial Winds: Each time this unit Advances, you can instead remove this unit from the battlefield and set it up again anywhere on the battlefield that is more than 9" away from any enemy models.

Slashing Dive: In your Movement phase, after this unit makes a Normal Move or Advances, if you did not set this unit up again using the Riders of the Immaterial Winds ability (see left), you can select one enemy unit this unit moved across as part of that move. Roll one D6 for each model in this unit that moved across that enemy unit: on a 4+, that enemy unit suffers 1 mortal wound.

FACTION KEYWORDS: Chaos, Legiones Daemonica, Tzeentch
KEYWORDS: Beast, Daemon, Core, Fly, Screamers

These predatory daemons strike like sudden and inescapable change. They emit unearthly shrieks as they swoop down upon their prey upon scintillating tides of sorcery, slicing victims to ribbons with razor-keen fins and latching on with fanged jaws from which corrosive empyric energies flow.

BURNING CHARIOT

6 POWER

No.	Name	M	WS	BS	S	T	W	A	Ld	DSv
1	Burning Chariot	14"	4+	3+	6	6	9	4	8	4+/4+

A Burning Chariot is equipped with: fire of Tzeentch; Screamer bites.

WEAPON	RANGE	TYPE	S	AP	D	ABILITIES
Fire of Tzeentch	Before selecting targets, select one of the profiles below to make attacks with.					
- Blue fire	18"	Assault 3	+3	-4	3	-
- Pink fire	12"	Assault 2D6	User	-2	1	Each time an attack is made with this weapon profile, that attack automatically hits the target.
Screamer bites	Melee	Melee	6	-3	2	Malefic 6

OTHER WARGEAR	ABILITIES
	This model has the following ability:
Horror infestation	**Horror Infestation (Aura):** While an enemy unit is within 12" of this model, subtract 1 from Psychic tests taken for that unit.

WARGEAR OPTIONS

• This model can be equipped with 1 Horror infestation.

ABILITIES

Daemonic (pg 56)

Blazing Warpfire (Aura): While a friendly **FLAMERS** unit is within 6" of this model, each time a model in that unit makes an attack with flickering flames, that attack has a Strength characteristic of +1.

FACTION KEYWORDS: Chaos, Legiones Daemonica, Tzeentch
KEYWORDS: Vehicle, Daemon, Fly, Exalted Flamer, Flamers, Burning Chariot

Burning Chariots of Tzeentch are often seen in the visions and nightmares of mortals as blazing omens of ill fortune. Upon the battlefield such warnings become self-fulfilling prophecies, the eldritch war engines serving as the agents of the very devastation and misery their coming is said to warn of.

THE BOOK OF CONTAGION

Bountiful the gruesome gifts they offer in their ghastly glee. Droning the count and droning the pestilential swarms that bring despair to all. Thrice toll the bells, seven times thrice, for the Plague Legions are come to sow the rotting of all things…

In this section you will find the following rules:

EXALTED GREAT UNCLEAN ONES (PG 90)
Great Unclean Ones can be upgraded with potent new abilities. The rules for how you can upgrade these models and the abilities they bestow are described in this section.

NURGLE STRATAGEMS (PG 91)
Nurgle armies have access to unique battlefield strategies and tactics that they can utilise to best their foes in any theatre of war; these are represented by the Stratagems in this section, and you can spend Command points to use them in your games. You can find out more about Stratagems and Command points in the Warhammer 40,000 Core Book.

WARPROT DISCIPLINE (PG 92)
If your army includes any Nurgle **Psyker** units, they can be given additional psychic powers from the Warprot discipline. This represents the different arcane lore and particular talents of each individual psyker. You can find out more about psychic powers in the Warhammer 40,000 Core Book.

NURGLE WARLORD TRAITS (PG 93)
Nurgle **Warlord** models can have one of the traits presented in this section. These help to better reflect their individual combat and command style on the battlefield.

RELICS OF NURGLE (PG 94)
Nurgle's greatest champions can be equipped with powerful artefacts called Relics of Nurgle; these Relics and the rules they bestow are described in this section.

NURGLE DATASHEETS (PG 95-103)
This section is essential to all Chaos Daemons players who wish to include **Nurgle** units in their army, regardless of preferred play style, containing as it does the datasheets for **Legiones Daemonica Nurgle** units. Each datasheet describes, among other things, the profiles of its models, the wargear they can be equipped with and the abilities they have. You can find out more about datasheets in the Warhammer 40,000 Core Book.

EXALTED GREAT UNCLEAN ONES

Just as the power of disease waxes and wanes through outbreak and remission, so does Nurgle's favour see some of his Great Unclean Ones swell almost to bursting with power, even as the blessings of others seep away to naught. Those daemons highest in the Grandfather's regard boast a veritable cornucopia of malignant abilities and malodorous mutations.

If your army includes any **Legiones Daemonica** Detachments (excluding Auxiliary Support, Super-heavy Auxiliary or Fortification Network Detachments), then when you muster your army, you can upgrade any **Great Unclean One** models from your army to be exalted. When a model is upgraded to be exalted it gains Exalted abilities.

You can select one of the Exalted abilities (see right) for that model. That model's Power Rating is increased accordingly, as shown in the table below. If you are playing a matched play game, or a game that uses a points limit, then the points value of that unit is also increased by the amount shown in the same table. Make a note on your army roster each time you upgrade a unit using these rules, specifying the ability it has gained.

Named characters (e.g. **Rotigus**, page 95) cannot be given Exalted abilities. Each model can only be upgraded to have Exalted abilities once. An army (or a Crusade force) cannot include the same Exalted ability more than once.

A Crusade force cannot start with any models having Exalted abilities – to include one in a Crusade force, you must use the Exalted Daemon Requisition (pg 132).

EXALTED ABILITY	POWER	POINTS
Bountiful Gifts	+2	+25
Hideous Visage	+1	+20
Revoltingly Resilient	+2	+30

EXALTED ABILITIES

BOUNTIFUL GIFTS

Deep in this daemon's unnatural innards is a captive warp rent that leads to a near-infinite ocean of supernatural foulness. The Great Unclean One holds this tide of filth within itself, occasionally burping forth pure warp energy, invigorating its fellows with the noisome stench.

At the end of each battle round, if this model is on the battlefield, you can retain up to 2 unspent Warp Storm points (pg 58).

HIDEOUS VISAGE

To look upon this creature is to see the fate of all flesh, rotting and sloughing off the bone. Even the sternest warrior is shaken by the inevitability of decay.

This model has the following ability:

Hideous Visage (Aura): While an enemy unit is within 6" of this model, subtract 1 from the Leadership characteristic of models in that unit and subtract 1 from Combat Attrition tests taken for that unit.

REVOLTINGLY RESILIENT

Between the foul gases that belch from every rent in this daemon's diseased form, the swarms of biting plague-mites that engulf its victims, and the slick of fever-sweat and curdled pus that coats its hide, it is nigh on impossible for its enemies to land a clean blow.

Each time a melee attack is made against this model, subtract 1 from that attack's Damage characteristic (to a minimum of 1).

NURGLE STRATAGEMS

If your army includes any **LEGIONES DAEMONICA NURGLE** units (excluding units in Auxiliary Support, Super-heavy Auxiliary or Fortification Network Detachments), you have access to these Stratagems, and can spend CPs to use them.

REVOLTING CONSTITUTION — 1CP/2CP

Legions of Nurgle – Battle Tactic Stratagem

The supernatural corruption of Plaguebearers' physical forms is such that even the most grievous wounds do not trouble them.

Use this Stratagem when a **PLAGUEBEARERS** unit from your army is selected as the target of an attack. Until the end of the phase, each time an attack is made against that unit, an unmodified wound roll of 1-3 for that attack fails, irrespective of any abilities that the weapon or the model making the attack may have. If that unit has a Power Rating of 12 or more, this Stratagem costs 2CP, otherwise, it costs 1CP.

CHORTLING MURRAIN — 1CP

Legions of Nurgle – Epic Deed Stratagem

Sloppity Bilepipers are carriers of the deadly chortling murrain, a disease that causes those who contract it to laugh themselves to death.

Use this Stratagem in your Shooting phase. Select one enemy unit within 6" of a **SLOPPITY BILEPIPER** model from your army and roll one D6 for each model in that enemy unit. For each roll that exceeds that model's Toughness characteristic, that model's unit suffers 1 mortal wound. A unit can only suffer a maximum of 6 mortal wounds per phase as a result of this Stratagem. You can only use this Stratagem once.

PESTILENT INSPIRATION — 1CP

Legions of Nurgle – Epic Deed Stratagem

From the germ of an idea may grow the most perfect plagues.

Use this Stratagem at the start of your Psychic phase. Select one **LEGIONES DAEMONICA NURGLE PSYKER** model from your army. Until the end of the phase, that model knows all of the psychic powers from the Warprot discipline (pg 92).

RELICS OF THE GREAT GARDEN — 1CP

Legions of Nurgle – Requisition Stratagem

Nurgle is said to be all-too-generous with his glopsome gifts.

Use this Stratagem before the battle, when you are mustering your army. Select one **LEGIONES DAEMONICA NURGLE CHARACTER** model from your army and give them one Relic of Nurgle (this must be a Relic they can have). Each Relic in your army must be unique, and you cannot use this Stratagem to give a model two Relics. You can only use this Stratagem once, unless you are playing a Strike Force battle (in which case, you can use this Stratagem twice) or an Onslaught battle (in which case, you can use this Stratagem three times).

SLIME TRAIL — 1CP

Legions of Nurgle – Strategic Ploy Stratagem

The more slug-like of Nurgle's daemons exude a paralysing slime that leaves victims numbed and despairing.

Use this Stratagem at the start of your opponent's Movement phase. Select one **BEASTS OF NURGLE** or **HORTICULOUS SLIMUX** unit from your army. Each time an enemy unit (excluding **AIRCRAFT** or **TITANIC** units) within Engagement Range of that unit is selected to move, roll one D6: on a 4+, that enemy unit cannot Fall Back this turn.

SWARMING FLIES — 2CP

Legions of Nurgle – Strategic Ploy Stratagem

A tsunami of thrumming plague flies roars around the daemons of Nurgle at all times. They carpet the enemy, providing a horrible distraction as they swarm, bite and choke their victims.

Use this Stratagem in your opponent's Shooting phase or the Fight phase. Select one **LEGIONES DAEMONICA NURGLE** unit from your army. Until the end of the phase, each time an enemy model makes an attack against that unit, subtract 1 from that attack's hit roll.

CRUSHING BULK — 1CP

Legions of Nurgle – Strategic Ploy Stratagem

Many daemons of Nurgle manifest lumpen and ponderous physical forms whose sheer bulk is a weapon in its own right.

Use this Stratagem after a **PLAGUE DRONES**, **BEASTS OF NURGLE** or **GREAT UNCLEAN ONE** unit from your army finishes a charge move. Select one enemy unit within Engagement Range of that unit and roll one D6 for each model in the charging unit, adding 3 to the result if that unit is a **GREAT UNCLEAN ONE** unit:

- On a 6+, that unit suffers D3 mortal wounds.
- On a 9, that unit suffers D3+3 mortal wounds instead.

PLAGUE BANNER — 1CP

Legions of Nurgle – Wargear Stratagem

A pervasive aura of pestilence surrounds this icon, causing rusted blades to weep with even fouler and more toxic diseases.

Use this Stratagem in the Fight phase, when a **LEGIONES DAEMONICA NURGLE ICON** unit from your army is selected to fight. Until the end of the phase, each time a model in that unit makes a melee attack, on an unmodified wound roll of 6, that attack inflicts 1 mortal wound on the target and the attack sequence ends. Each unit can only suffer a maximum of 6 mortal wounds as a result of this Stratagem in each phase.

WARPROT DISCIPLINE

Before the battle, generate the psychic powers for **PSYKER** models in your army that know powers from the Warprot discipline using the table below. You can either roll one D6 to generate each power randomly (re-rolling duplicate results), or you can select which powers the **PSYKER** model knows.

1. STREAM OF CORRUPTION

The daemon's jaws stretch impossibly wide. Its rotten body convulses, heaving out clouds of rancid gas and flies before at last it ejects a jetting river of diseased vomit. So contagious and corrosive is this tide of foulness that those not drowned by it are often dissolved into organic gruel or left stricken by supernatural sickness.

Witchfire: *Stream of Corruption* has a warp charge value of 6. If manifested, the closest enemy unit within 12" of and visible to this **PSYKER** suffers D3 mortal wounds. If that unit contains 11 or more models, that unit suffers D3+2 mortal wounds instead.

2. FLESHY ABUNDANCE

The daemon blesses their allies with Nurgle's bountiful energies, swelling them into even more grotesquely resilient and corpulent forms.

Blessing: *Fleshy Abundance* has a warp charge value of 7. If manifested, select one friendly **LEGIONES DAEMONICA NURGLE CORE** unit within 18" of and visible to this **PSYKER**. Until the start of your next Psychic phase, add 1 to the Toughness characteristic of models in that unit.

3. NURGLE'S ROT

Gurgling praise to its god, the daemon exudes a wave of soul-pox that eats away the spiritual essence of those who lack Nurgle's blessings. Victims' eyes become glassy, their flesh sinks upon their bones and their limbs fall slack before they collapse and begin to rot before their horrified comrades' eyes.

Witchfire: *Nurgle's Rot* has a warp charge value of 7. If manifested, roll 2D6 for each enemy unit within 6" of this **PSYKER**. If the result is higher than the highest Toughness characteristic of models in that unit, that unit suffers D3 mortal wounds. If the result is at least double the highest Toughness characteristic of models in that unit, that unit suffers D6 mortal wounds instead.

4. SHRIVELLING POX

Muttering an unholy chant in a blighted tongue, the daemon calls down a foul malignancy that races through the enemies' ranks like wildfire and chews away at their flesh and organs like a tide of ravenous maggots.

Malediction: *Shrivelling Pox* has a warp charge value of 6. If manifested, select one enemy unit within 18" of and visible to this **PSYKER**. Until the start of your next Psychic phase, subtract 1 from the Toughness characteristic of models in that unit.

5. VIRULENT BLESSING

Calling upon the myriad gifts of Nurgle, the daemon infuses its allies' weapons, fangs and talons with a seething mix of supernatural maladies that render their merest touch inimical to their luckless victims.

Blessing: *Virulent Blessing* has a warp charge value of 6. If manifested, select one friendly **LEGIONES DAEMONICA NURGLE CORE** unit within 18" of and visible to this **PSYKER**. Until the start of your next Psychic phase, add 1 to the Damage characteristic of melee weapons models in that unit are equipped with.

6. MALODOROUS PALL

Chanting in a phlegm-choked drone, the daemon conjures forth a dense cloud of occluding corpse-gas and biting, blinding flies to engulf the enemy and leave them nauseated and reeling.

Malediction: *Malodorous Pall* has a warp charge value of 8. If manifested, select one enemy unit within 18" of and visible to this **PSYKER**. Until the start of your next Psychic phase, that enemy unit:

- Cannot perform actions (if that enemy unit is currently performing an action, it immediately fails).
- Loses the Objective Secured ability (see the Warhammer 40,000 Core Book).

'Slitherslop the rotpus guts, spatterpop the strainsome boil, festerdrip the rancid heart, scratch and rip the reeking flesh. Heave and spew the bilewet worms, purple-blue the bloated corpse, scrabblesquirm the glutton-mite, daemongerm the bounty ripe. Then the bubbling cauldron. Then the sevenfold plagues. Then the tri-lobe sickness a-spreading swift as flames.'

- *Extract,* The Dirge of Gleeful Despair

NURGLE WARLORD TRAITS

If a **LEGIONES DAEMONICA NURGLE CHARACTER** model from your army gains a Warlord Trait, you can use the Nurgle Warlord Traits table below to determine what Warlord Trait they have. You can either roll one D6 to randomly generate one, or you can select one.

If a **NURGLE HERALD** model is your **WARLORD**, they can only have the Heaving Mass, Acidic Ichor or Virulent Touch Warlord Traits. You can either roll one D3 to randomly generate one, or you can select one.

1. HEAVING MASS
Saturated with corruption and fatted upon a diet of mortal souls, this daemon's swollen frame seethes with unclean vitality.

Add 2 to this **WARLORD**'s Wounds characteristic.

2. ACIDIC ICHOR
Those that pierce this daemon's straining flesh are sprayed with sizzling bile that melts through armour, flesh and bone.

Each time this **WARLORD** loses a wound as a result of a melee attack made by an enemy unit, after the attacking model's unit has finished making its attacks, roll one D6: on a 4+, that enemy unit suffers 1 mortal wound. Each unit can only suffer a maximum of 6 mortal wounds per phase as a result of this ability.

3. VIRULENT TOUCH
So saturated with noxious toxins and poisons is this daemon that its merest touch causes its victims to erupt into spreading masses of buboes and sores that burst and redouble until their bodies collapse under the repugnant strain.

Each time this **WARLORD** makes a melee attack (excluding attacks made against **TITANIC** units), if a hit is scored, that attack automatically wounds the target.

4. PLAGUE FLY HIVE (AURA)
This daemon's hole-riddled hide supports a colony of plague flies that crawl busily in and out of its flesh, and swarm forth to bedevil the foe.

While an enemy unit is within 6" of this **WARLORD**:

- Each time a model in that unit makes a melee attack, subtract 1 from that attack's hit roll.
- That unit cannot start to perform any actions (see the Warhammer 40,000 Core Book).

5. OVERFLOWING FECUNDITY
This daemon's hurts are swiftly unmade amidst swift-clotting filth and rotten regrowth.

Each time an attack is made against this **WARLORD**, an unmodified wound roll of 1-3 for that attack automatically fails, irrespective of any abilities that the weapon or the model making the attack may have.

6. PESTILENT MIASMA
Those who venture too close to this daemon find their injuries blackening in seconds and their infected flesh swiftly turning to rancid soup.

At the start of the Fight phase, roll one D6 for each enemy unit within Engagement Range of this **WARLORD**:

- On a 2-5, that enemy unit suffers 1 mortal wound.
- On a 6, that enemy unit suffers D3 mortal wounds.

NAMED CHARACTERS AND WARLORD TRAITS
If one of the following characters gains a Warlord Trait, they must have the relevant one shown below:

Named Character	Warlord Trait
Epidemius	Virulent Touch
Horticulous Slimux	Acidic Ichor
Rotigus	Pestilent Miasma

RELICS OF NURGLE

If a **Legiones Daemonica Nurgle Character** model gains a Relic, you can give them one of the following Relics of Nurgle. Named characters and **Vehicle** models cannot be given any of the following Relics.

Note that some Relics replace one of the model's existing items of wargear. Where this is the case, you must, if you are using points values, still pay the cost of the wargear that is being replaced. Write down any Relics of Nurgle your models have on your army roster.

ARMY RULES

HORN OF NURGLE'S ROT

A daemon crowned with this repulsive horn can, with but a single touch, infect mortal victims with Nurgle's Rot. Even as the afflicted lay dying, their bodies and souls decay and deform, despair curdling their last moments. What were once enemy soldiers rise anew as Plaguebearers of Nurgle, and shamble to take their place in the festering ranks of their fellows.

Each time the bearer is selected to fight, after its attacks have been resolved you can select one friendly **Plaguebearers Infantry Core** unit wholly within 18" of the bearer to be replenished. Roll one D6 for each enemy model that was destroyed by the bearer this phase. For each 4+, you can return 1 destroyed model to that **Plaguebearers** unit with its full wounds remaining, to a maximum of 3 models per turn. These models cannot be set up within Engagement Range of any enemy units unless those enemy units are already within Engagement Range of its unit. Each unit can only be replenished once per turn.

THE ENTROPIC KNELL

To hear the grim tolling of this great bell upon the winds is a death sentence, for its sound heralds the arrival of the Plague Legions. Such is its dread power that a single peal reverberates for long minutes, spreading despair even over the clangour of battle.

In your Command phase, select one enemy unit within 12" of this model. Until the start of your next Command phase:

- Enemy units cannot benefit from that enemy unit's aura abilities.
- For the purposes of determining which player controls an objective marker, treat the number of models in that unit as half its current number (rounding up).

TOME OF A THOUSAND POXES

How this rotten volume found its way out of the diseased libraries of the scholar Ku'gath may never be known, but within its foetid daemon-hide pages are the secrets of many of that daemon's most ruinous plagues. Even the simplest infection can bloom into new and vibrant potency by using the arcane incantations it contains, each inscribed in divine ichor.

Psyker model only.

- The bearer knows one additional psychic power from the Warprot discipline (pg 92).
- Each time the bearer attempts to manifest a psychic power from the Warprot discipline, if the result of the Psychic test is 7, that psychic power cannot be denied.

CORRUPTION

This fabled weapon is the physical manifestation of corruption. Constantly dripping with foul ooze, the merest scratch from its edge is enough to lay low the hardiest foe, and its toxins can effortlessly overcome even the resilience of a Space Marine.

Select one melee weapon the bearer is equipped with:

- Add 1 to the Damage characteristic of that weapon.
- Each time an attack made with that weapon is allocated to a model, that model cannot use any rules to ignore the wounds it loses.
- That weapon is now considered to be a Relic for all rules purposes.

EFFLUVIOR

Within the hanging skulls of this accursed flail, there is a rancid rot-hole burrowing through reality itself. Down these vile channels rush torrents of liquid warp-filth, the raw and seething slops of the Garden of Nurgle. With every ponderous swing and bludgeoning impact, Effluvior's skulls spray fans of this lethal slime, causing victims to contort as flesh, metal and bone putrefy. Those not pulverised by the daemon's attacks are instead reduced to a slick of slime that seeps back into Nurgle's metaphysical realm.

Model equipped with plague flail only. This Relic replaces a plague flail and has the following profile:

WEAPON	RANGE	TYPE	S	AP	D
Effluvior	7"	Assault 3D3	+1	-3	3

Abilities: Each time an attack is made with this weapon, excess damage it inflicts is not lost. Instead, keep allocating excess damage to another model in the target unit until either all the excess damage has been allocated or the target unit is destroyed.

THE ENDLESS GIFT

Only the most accomplished plague daemons are granted the Endless Gift. A disease of unutterable malignancy and repulsive beneficence, it changes form constantly from plague to infestation to malaise. The one constant is its ability to reknit its sufferer's corporeal form from even the most catastrophic of wounds. One moment, infernal bacteria may multiply like wildfire until their gelid mass fills a fleshy rent with fresh daemon-flesh. The next, pestilential vapours may billow from the daemon's yawning maw, veiling its ravaged bulk before tattering away to reveal a form healed of its recent hurts. However it happens, the longer the enemy must watch their efforts to fell the daemon falter, the more their despair feeds into the gift and increases its supernatural potency until its vessel is all but immune to banishment.

At the start of your Command phase, the bearer regains up to a number of lost wounds equal to the current battle round number.

ROTIGUS

Some of this model's characteristics change as it suffers damage, as shown below:

No.	Name	M	WS	BS	S	T	W	A	Ld	DSv
1	Rotigus (13+ wounds remaining)	7"	2+	3+	7	9	24	6	10	5+/4+
	Rotigus (7-12 wounds remaining)	6"	3+	3+	7	9	N/A	5	10	5+/4+
	Rotigus (1-6 wounds remaining)	5"	4+	3+	7	9	N/A	4	10	5+/4+

Rotigus is equipped with: streams of brackish filth; fanged maw; gnarlrod; Nurgling claws. Your army can only include one **ROTIGUS** model.

WEAPON	RANGE	TYPE	S	AP	D	ABILITIES
Streams of brackish filth	12"	Assault 2D6	6	-3	1	Each time an attack is made with this weapon, that attack automatically hits the target.
Fanged maw	Melee	Melee	User	-1	2	Malefic 1
Gnarlrod		Each time an attack is made with this weapon, select one of the profiles below to make that attack with.				
- Mighty strike	Melee	Melee	+1	-3	3	Each time an attack is made with this weapon profile, an unmodified hit roll of 6 automatically wounds the target.
- Sweeping blow	Melee	Melee	User	-2	1	Each time an attack is made with this weapon profile, make 2 hit rolls instead of 1.
Nurgling claws	Melee	Melee	2	0	1	Malefic 7

ABILITIES

Daemonic (pg 56)

Deluge of Nurgle: Each time this model successfully manifests a psychic power, if the result of the Psychic test was 7+, after resolving that psychic power, the closest enemy unit within 24" suffers D3 mortal wounds.

Daemon Lord of Nurgle (Aura): While a friendly **LEGIONES DAEMONICA NURGLE CORE** unit is within 6" of this model, each time a model in that unit makes an attack, re-roll a hit roll of 1.

PSYKER

This model can attempt to manifest two psychic powers in your Psychic phase, and attempt to deny two psychic powers in your opponent's Psychic phase. It knows *Smite* and two psychic powers from the Warprot discipline (pg 92).

FACTION KEYWORDS: CHAOS, LEGIONES DAEMONICA, NURGLE
KEYWORDS: MONSTER, CHARACTER, DAEMON, PSYKER, GREATER DAEMON, WARP LOCUS, GREAT UNCLEAN ONE, ROTIGUS

Rotigus Rainfather lumbers into battle vomiting jetting rivers of corrosive, plague-laden filth across all who stand in its path. In its bloated fist it clutches a gnarlrod, while an endless and infectious downpour accompanies the daemon, a fecund flood fit to drown, corrupt and mutate all it touches.

THE BOUNTIFUL ONE

Generosity. It is a word seldom heard in so dark and desperate an age, its allure all the stronger for that. Yet one should be mindful that overabundance can be just as much a curse as can scarcity. Drought; starvation; sterility – each a doom that brings slow extinction, that inflicts pain and misery enough to wear down the resolve of the unwary until, in their utmost need, they cry out for salvation from any that can offer it. The servants of Nurgle scent such despair upon the winds of the warp. They hear the threnody of sorrow's choir echoing across impossible gulfs and they follow it, full of malevolent mirth, for they know what lies at its source. And when at last the cry goes up from mortal throats, when the final bargain is struck, the get of Grandfather Nurgle are only too pleased to demonstrate their largesse. At such times, none is more giving than Rotigus Rainfather.

At his bidding did the sterile agri-beasts of Ullden begin birthing young once more, and the locals rejoiced until it became clear that this spawning would not stop, until they were buried beneath the crushing weight of mewling and mutant flesh. It was Rotigus, too, who offered freely his gifts to the T'au of Dh'artan in the form of a planetwide deluge that banished the hated drought, yet welled then into an endless flood of brackish and diseased swamp water that saw all they had made disappear beneath the waves. The overflowing corpse-starch vats that filled Hive Yuras to bursting and beyond; the omniphagic infestation that consumed the Necrons of Jula II, but then turned as well on the frightened locals who had prayed for it; the Last Banquet of Pordec's Reach and the Everwave of Amalicar – all these and more have been Rainfather's boons to reality.

GREAT UNCLEAN ONE

15 POWER

Some of this model's characteristics change as it suffers damage, as shown below:

No.	Name	M	WS	BS	S	T	W	A	Ld	DSv
1	Great Unclean One (12+ wounds remaining)	7"	2+	3+	7	9	22	6	10	5+/4+
	Great Unclean One (6-11 wounds remaining)	6"	3+	3+	7	9	N/A	5	10	5+/4+
	Great Unclean One (1-5 wounds remaining)	5"	4+	3+	7	9	N/A	4	10	5+/4+

A Great Unclean One is equipped with: plague flail; putrid vomit; bilesword; Nurgling claws.

WEAPON	RANGE	TYPE	S	AP	D	ABILITIES
Plague flail	7"	Assault D6+3	User	-3	2	-
Putrid vomit	12"	Assault D6	5	-2	1	Each time an attack is made with this weapon, that attack automatically hits the target.
Bileblade	Melee	Melee	User	-3	2	Each time an attack is made with this weapon, you can re-roll the wound roll.
Bilesword	Each time an attack is made with this weapon, select one of the profiles below to make that attack with.					
- Mighty strike	Melee	Melee	+1	-3	D6	Each time an attack is made with this weapon profile, an unmodified hit roll of 6 automatically wounds the target.
- Sweeping blow	Melee	Melee	User	-3	1	Each time an attack is made with this weapon profile, make 2 hit rolls instead of 1.
Doomsday bell	Melee	Melee	+1	-1	2	-
Nurgling claws	Melee	Melee	2	0	1	Malefic 7

OTHER WARGEAR	ABILITIES
Bileblade	Each time the bearer attempts to manifest a psychic power, before taking the Psychic test, you can select for this model to suffer 1 mortal wound. If you do so, add 1 to that Psychic test.
Doomsday bell	In your Command phase, you can select one friendly **Plaguebearers Core** unit within 12" of the bearer to be replenished. You can return one destroyed model from that unit to the battlefield with its full wounds remaining. If that unit is an **Infantry** unit, you return D3 destroyed models instead. These models cannot be set up within Engagement Range of any enemy units unless those enemy units are already within Engagement Range of its unit. Each unit can only be replenished once per turn.

WARGEAR OPTIONS

- This model's bilesword can be replaced with 1 doomsday bell.
- This model's plague flail can be replaced with 1 bileblade.

ABILITIES

Daemonic (pg 56)

Daemon Lord of Nurgle (Aura): While a friendly **Legiones Daemonica Nurgle Core** unit is within 6" of this model, each time a model in that unit makes an attack, re-roll a hit roll of 1.

PSYKER

This model can attempt to manifest two psychic powers in your Psychic phase, and attempt to deny one psychic power in your opponent's Psychic phase. It knows *Smite* and two psychic powers from the Warprot discipline (pg 92).

FACTION KEYWORDS: Chaos, Legiones Daemonica, Nurgle
KEYWORDS: Monster, Character, Daemon, Psyker, Greater Daemon, Great Unclean One

These Greater Daemons possess the same boundless energy and drive to corrupt as a swift-spreading virus. Their booming voices roll across the battlefield, their cruel jollity and the perverse pride they take in their underlings' achievements horribly at odds with the misery and disease they spread.

POXBRINGER

5 POWER

No.	Name	M	WS	BS	S	T	W	A	Ld	DSv
1	Poxbringer	5"	2+	3+	5	6	6	3	8	5+/4+

A Poxbringer is equipped with: foul balesword.

WEAPON	RANGE	TYPE	S	AP	D	ABILITIES
Foul balesword	Melee	Melee	User	-3	2	Each time an attack is made with this weapon, an unmodified hit roll of 6 automatically wounds the target.

ABILITIES

Daemonic (pg 56)

Herald of Nurgle (Aura): While a friendly **LEGIONES DAEMONICA NURGLE CORE** unit is within 6" of this model, each time a model in that unit makes an attack, you can re-roll a wound roll of 1.

Poxbringer: In your Command phase, select one friendly **PLAGUEBEARERS CORE** unit within 6" of this model. Until the start of your next Command phase, each time a model in that unit makes a melee attack, on an unmodified wound roll of 6, add 1 to the Damage characteristic of that attack.

PSYKER

This model can attempt to manifest one psychic power in your Psychic phase, and attempt to deny one psychic power in your opponent's Psychic phase. It knows *Smite* and one psychic power from the Warprot discipline (pg 92).

FACTION KEYWORDS: CHAOS, LEGIONES DAEMONICA, NURGLE
KEYWORDS: INFANTRY, CHARACTER, DAEMON, PLAGUEBEARERS, PSYKER, HERALD, POXBRINGER

Poxbringers are the largest and foulest of Plaguebearers, their corporeal forms brimming with unclean vitality even as they exude an air of feculent despair. A miasmal haze of disease hangs about them, clotting upon the plagueswords of their fellow daemons and rendering their touch all the more infectious.

SPOILPOX SCRIVENER

5 POWER

No.	Name	M	WS	BS	S	T	W	A	Ld	DSv
1	Spoilpox Scrivener	5"	2+	3+	5	6	6	3	8	5+/4+

A Spoilpox Scrivener is equipped with: disgusting sneezes; distended maw; plaguesword.

WEAPON	RANGE	TYPE	S	AP	D	ABILITIES
Disgusting sneezes	6"	Assault D6	4	0	1	Each time an attack is made with this weapon, that attack automatically hits the target.
Distended maw	Melee	Melee	+1	-1	3	Malefic 1
Plaguesword	Melee	Melee	User	-2	1	Each time an attack is made with this weapon, an unmodified hit roll of 6 automatically wounds the target.

ABILITIES

Daemonic (pg 56)

Herald of Nurgle (Aura): While a friendly **LEGIONES DAEMONICA NURGLE CORE** unit is within 6" of this model, each time a model in that unit makes an attack, you can re-roll a wound roll of 1.

Keep Counting! Meet Your Quota!: In your Command phase, select one friendly **PLAGUEBEARERS CORE** unit within 6" of this model. Until the start of your next Command phase:
- Each time a model in that unit makes a melee attack, add 1 to that attack's hit roll.
- That unit has the Objective Secured ability (see the Warhammer 40,000 Core Book). If that unit already has the Objective Secured ability, then for the purposes of determining which player controls an objective marker, each model in that unit counts as two models.

FACTION KEYWORDS: CHAOS, LEGIONES DAEMONICA, NURGLE
KEYWORDS: INFANTRY, CHARACTER, DAEMON, PLAGUEBEARERS, HERALD, SPOILPOX SCRIVENER

Spiteful and pedantic, these daemons are tasked with auditing the endless disease-tally of the Plaguebearers. The presence of the Scriveners is cruelly motivational to their fellows. Moreover, they can easily bite enemy warriors in half, or drown them in the foul mucus that issues from their distended maws.

EPIDEMIUS

5 POWER

No.	Name	M	WS	BS	S	T	W	A	Ld	DSv
1	Epidemius	5"	2+	3+	5	6	9	4	8	5+/4+

Epidemius is equipped with: foul balesword; Nurgling claws. Your army can only include one EPIDEMIUS model.

WEAPON	RANGE	TYPE	S	AP	D	ABILITIES
Foul balesword	Melee	Melee	User	-3	2	Each time an attack is made with this weapon, an unmodified hit roll of 6 automatically wounds the target.
Nurgling claws	Melee	Melee	2	0	1	Malefic 7

ABILITIES

Daemonic (pg 56)

Herald of Nurgle (Aura): While a friendly LEGIONES DAEMONICA NURGLE CORE unit is within 6" of this model, each time a model in that unit makes an attack, you can re-roll a wound roll of 1.

Tally of Pestilence: While this model is on the battlefield, keep a tally of how many enemy models are destroyed by attacks made by LEGIONES DAEMONICA NURGLE units from your army. At the start of each battle round, if there are 7 or more marks on that tally, after making a Warp Storm roll (pg 58), gain 1 additional Warp Storm point, and reset that tally to 0. If this model is destroyed, any marks on that tally are lost.

FACTION KEYWORDS: CHAOS, LEGIONES DAEMONICA, NURGLE
KEYWORDS: INFANTRY, CHARACTER, DAEMON, PLAGUEBEARERS, HERALD, EPIDEMIUS

Borne upon his throne by a scrabbling mound of Nurglings, Epidemius endlessly catalogues the infinite plagues and maladies released upon realspace by the followers of Nurgle. The higher Epidemius' tally rises upon any given battlefield, the more favourably the Plague God smiles upon his servants in the vicinity.

SLOPPITY BILEPIPER

5 POWER

No.	Name	M	WS	BS	S	T	W	A	Ld	DSv
1	Sloppity Bilepiper	5"	2+	3+	5	6	6	3	8	5+/4+

A Sloppity Bilepiper is equipped with: marotter.

WEAPON	RANGE	TYPE	S	AP	D	ABILITIES
Marotter	Melee	Melee	User	0	1	Each time an attack is made with this weapon, an unmodified hit roll of 6 automatically wounds the target.

ABILITIES

Daemonic (pg 56)

Herald of Nurgle (Aura): While a friendly LEGIONES DAEMONICA NURGLE CORE unit is within 6" of this model, each time a model in that unit makes an attack, you can re-roll a wound roll of 1.

Jolly Gutpipes: In your Command phase, select one friendly GREAT UNCLEAN ONE, NURGLINGS or PLAGUEBEARERS CORE unit within 6" of this model. Until the start of your next Command phase:
• Add 1 to the Move characteristic of models in that unit.
• Add 1 to Advance and charge rolls made for this unit.

Disease of Mirth: In the Morale phase, you can select one enemy unit within 12" of this model and roll 3D6: if the result is greater than that enemy unit's Leadership characteristic, select one of the results below to take effect until the start of the next Morale phase. Each unit can only be selected for this ability once per phase.
• The selected unit cannot perform actions (see the Warhammer 40,000 Core Book), and if that unit is currently performing an action, it immediately fails.
• The selected unit loses the Objective Secured ability (see the Warhammer 40,000 Core Book).

FACTION KEYWORDS: CHAOS, LEGIONES DAEMONICA, NURGLE
KEYWORDS: INFANTRY, CHARACTER, DAEMON, PLAGUEBEARERS, HERALD, SLOPPITY BILEPIPER

Infected with the Chortling Murrain, these desperately grinning daemons caper and quip as they play discordant dirges on their foul gutpipes. Their antics either amuse or irritate their fellow daemons so much that they hasten into the press of battle, while mortals infected with the murrain may literally laugh themselves to death.

HORTICULOUS SLIMUX

7 POWER

No.	Name	M	WS	BS	S	T	W	A	Ld	DSv
1	Horticulous Slimux	5"	2+	2+	5	7	9	4	8	4+/4+

Horticulous Slimux is equipped with: acidic maw; lopping shears. Your army can only include one **HORTICULOUS SLIMUX** model.

WEAPON	RANGE	TYPE	S	AP	D	ABILITIES
Acidic maw	Melee	Melee	7	-4	3	Malefic 2
Lopping shears	Melee	Melee	+1	-3	2	Each time an attack is made with this weapon, an unmodified hit roll of 6 automatically wounds the target.

Horticulous Slimux is the Grand Cultivator, roaming realspace to sow the seeds of corruption in all unspoilt lands. Sat atop the heaving bulk of the snail-like daemon Mulch, Slimux goads packs of thrashing plague beasts into battle even as it lops mortal heads with thwicker-snick flashes of its wickedly sharp lopping shears.

ABILITIES

Daemonic (pg 56)

Herald of Nurgle (Aura): While a friendly **LEGIONES DAEMONICA NURGLE CORE** unit is within 6" of this model, each time a model in that unit makes an attack, you can re-roll a wound roll of 1.

Beast Handler: In your Command phase, you can select one friendly **BEASTS OF NURGLE** or **PLAGUE DRONES** unit within 9" of this model. Until the start of your next Command phase:
• You can re-roll charge rolls made for that unit.
• Each time a model in that unit makes a melee attack, add 1 to that attack's hit roll.

Seed the Garden of Nurgle: At the end of your Movement phase, if this model is wholly within an Area Terrain feature, you can select for that Area Terrain feature to be seeded. If you do so, until the end of the battle:
• Enemy units treat that Area Terrain feature as if it had the Difficult Ground terrain trait.
• Each time an enemy unit ends any type of move (excluding pile-in or consolidation moves) within that Area Terrain feature, roll one D6: on a 2+, that enemy unit suffers D3 mortal wounds.

FACTION KEYWORDS: **CHAOS, LEGIONES DAEMONICA, NURGLE**
KEYWORDS: **CAVALRY, CHARACTER, DAEMON, PLAGUEBEARERS, HERALD, HORTICULOUS SLIMUX**

PLAGUEBEARERS

7 POWER

No.	Name	M	WS	BS	S	T	W	A	Ld	DSv
9	Plaguebearer	5"	4+	4+	4	5	2	2	6	5+/4+
1	Plagueridden	5"	4+	4+	4	5	2	3	7	5+/4+

Every model is equipped with: plaguesword.

WEAPON	RANGE	TYPE	S	AP	D	ABILITIES
Plaguesword	Melee	Melee	User	-2	1	Each time an attack is made with this weapon, an unmodified hit roll of 6 automatically wounds the target.

OTHER WARGEAR	ABILITIES
Daemonic icon	While this unit contains any models equipped with a daemonic icon: • It has the **ICON** keyword. • Each time a Combat Attrition test is taken for this unit, you can ignore any or all modifiers.
Instrument of Chaos	While this unit contains any models equipped with an instrument of Chaos: • It has the **INSTRUMENT** keyword. • Add 1 to the Leadership characteristic of models in this unit.

WARGEAR OPTIONS

• One Plaguebearer that is not equipped with a daemonic icon can be equipped with 1 instrument of Chaos.
• One Plaguebearer that is not equipped with an instrument of Chaos can be equipped with 1 daemonic icon.

ABILITIES

Daemonic (pg 56)

FACTION KEYWORDS: **CHAOS, LEGIONES DAEMONICA, NURGLE**
KEYWORDS: **INFANTRY, DAEMON, CORE, PLAGUEBEARERS**

Born from the souls of those who die of Nurgle's Rot, Plaguebearers are the foot soldiers of Nurgle. They wield plagueswords that drip with infectious slime, and are surrounded by the endless drone of counting as they pursue their hopeless and eternal task of tallying each new outbreak of the Plague God's many diseases.

NURGLINGS

3 POWER

No.	Name	M	WS	BS	S	T	W	A	Ld	DSv
3-9	Nurgling Swarm	5"	4+	4+	2	3	4	4	6	6+/5+

If this unit contains 4-6 models, it has **Power Rating 6**. If this unit contains 7 or more models, it has **Power Rating 9**. Every model is equipped with: diseased claws and teeth.

WEAPON	RANGE	TYPE	S	AP	D	ABILITIES
Diseased claws and teeth	Melee	Melee	User	0	1	Each time an attack is made with this weapon, an unmodified hit roll of 6 automatically wounds the target.

ABILITIES

Daemonic (pg 56)

Bothersome Scamps: Each time an attack is made against this unit, subtract 1 from that attack's hit roll.

Mischief Makers: During deployment, when you set up this unit, it can be set up anywhere on the battlefield that is more than 9" away from your opponent's deployment zone and any enemy models.

Tide of Tiny Bodies: If your army is Battle-forged, this unit cannot be selected to fill a compulsory Battlefield Role slot in a Detachment.

FACTION KEYWORDS: **CHAOS, LEGIONES DAEMONICA, NURGLE**
KEYWORDS: **SWARM, DAEMON, NURGLINGS**

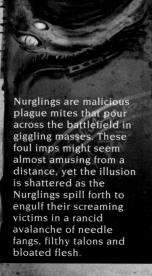

Nurglings are malicious plague mites that pour across the battlefield in giggling masses. These foul imps might seem almost amusing from a distance, yet the illusion is shattered as the Nurglings spill forth to engulf their screaming victims in a rancid avalanche of needle fangs, filthy talons and bloated flesh.

BEASTS OF NURGLE

4 POWER

No.	Name	M	WS	BS	S	T	W	A	Ld	DSv
1-3	Beast of Nurgle	6"	4+	-	6	6	7	6	7	5+/4+

If this unit contains 2 models it has **Power Rating 8**. If this unit contains 3 models it has **Power Rating 12**. Every model is equipped with: putrid appendages.

WEAPON	RANGE	TYPE	S	AP	D	ABILITIES
Putrid appendages	Melee	Melee	User	-2	2	Each time an attack is made with this weapon, an unmodified hit roll of 6 inflicts 2 mortal wounds on the target and the attack sequence ends.

ABILITIES

Daemonic (pg 56)

Attention Seeker: This unit is eligible to perform Heroic Interventions as if it were a **CHARACTER** unit. This unit is eligible to perform a Heroic Intervention if it is within 6" horizontally and 5" vertically of any enemy unit, instead of 3" horizontally and 5" vertically. Each time this unit makes a Heroic Intervention move, it can move up to 6". All other rules for Heroic Interventions still apply.

Grotesque Regeneration: At the end of each phase, if a model in this unit has lost any wounds but was not destroyed, that model regains all of its lost wounds.

Gooey Demise: Each time a model in this unit is destroyed, roll one D6 before removing it from play. On a 6 it explodes, and each enemy unit within 3" suffers 1 mortal wound.

FACTION KEYWORDS: CHAOS, LEGIONES DAEMONICA, NURGLE
KEYWORDS: BEAST, DAEMON, BEASTS OF NURGLE

Filled with dim-witted ebullience at odds with their plague-ridden and nightmarish forms, Beasts of Nurgle flollop into battle like eager hounds. They are drawn instinctively to mortal playthings, whose desperate cries and frantic flight they mistake for participation, at least until their luckless new friends have twitched their last.

PLAGUE DRONES

6 POWER

No.	Name	M	WS	BS	S	T	W	A	Ld	DSv
2-5	Plague Drone	10"	4+	4+	5	6	5	2	7	5+/4+
1	Plaguebringer	10"	4+	4+	5	6	5	3	8	5+/4+

If this unit contains 4 or more models, it has **Power Rating 12**. Every model is equipped with: death's heads; foul mouthparts; plaguesword.

WEAPON	RANGE	TYPE	S	AP	D	ABILITIES
Death's heads	12"	Assault D3	4	-1	1	Blast
Foul mouthparts	Melee	Melee	5	-2	2	Malefic 2
Plaguesword	Melee	Melee	User	-2	1	Each time an attack is made with this weapon, an unmodified hit roll of 6 automatically wounds the target.
Prehensile proboscis	Melee	Melee	4	-2	1	Malefic 4

OTHER WARGEAR	ABILITIES
Daemonic Icon	While this unit contains any models equipped with a daemonic icon: • It has the **ICON** keyword. • Each time a Combat Attrition test is taken for this unit, you can ignore any or all modifiers.
Instrument of Chaos	While this unit contains any models equipped with an instrument of Chaos: • It has the **INSTRUMENT** keyword. • Add 1 to the Leadership characteristic of models in this unit.

WARGEAR OPTIONS

- One Plague Drone that is not equipped with a daemonic icon can be equipped with 1 instrument of Chaos.
- One Plague Drone that is not equipped with an instrument of Chaos can be equipped with 1 daemonic icon.
- Any model's foul mouthparts can be replaced with 1 prehensile proboscis.

ABILITIES

Daemonic (pg 56)

FACTION KEYWORDS: **CHAOS, LEGIONES DAEMONICA, NURGLE**
KEYWORDS: **CAVALRY, DAEMON, CORE, FLY, PLAGUEBEARERS, PLAGUE DRONES**

Plague Drones ride monstrous Rot Flies to war. These vile steeds scrabble and bite at their prey, impaling them on dripping probosces or biting off and gulping down the heads of their victims. The finest stolen craniums are recovered and fashioned into filth-swollen projectiles –death's heads – for the daemonic riders to hurl at their foes.

FECULENT GNARLMAW

4 POWER

No.	Name	M	WS	BS	S	T	W	A	Ld	DSv
1	Feculent Gnarlmaw	-	-	-	6	7	9	-	7	4+/3+

A Feculent Gnarlmaw has no equipment.

ABILITIES

Daemonic (pg 56)

The Garden Grows: During deployment, when you set up this unit, it can be set up anywhere on the battlefield that is more than 9" away from your opponent's deployment zone and any enemy models.

Sickness Blossoms: At the start of each turn, roll one D6 for each enemy unit within Engagement Range of this model:

- On a 2-5, that enemy unit suffers 1 mortal wound.
- On a 6, that enemy unit suffers D3 mortal wounds.

If any enemy models are destroyed as a result of these mortal wounds, gain 1 Warp Storm point (pg 58).

Shroud of Flies (Aura): While a friendly LEGIONES DAEMONICA NURGLE unit (excluding VEHICLE and MONSTER units) is within 6" of this model, each time a ranged attack is made against that unit, subtract 1 from that attack's hit roll.

The Plague Bells Chime: In your Command phase, you can select one friendly PLAGUEBEARERS INFANTRY CORE unit within 6" of this model to be replenished. If you do so, roll seven D6. For each 6, return 1 destroyed model to that unit with its full wounds remaining. These models cannot be set up within Engagement Range of any enemy units unless those enemy units are already within Engagement Range of its unit. Each unit can only be replenished once per turn.

FACTION KEYWORDS: CHAOS, LEGIONES DAEMONICA, NURGLE
KEYWORDS: WARP LOCUS, FECULENT GNARLMAW

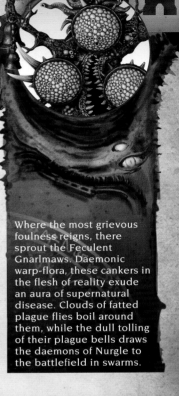

Where the most grievous foulness reigns, there sprout the Feculent Gnarlmaws. Daemonic warp-flora, these cankers in the flesh of reality exude an aura of supernatural disease. Clouds of fatted plague flies boil around them, while the dull tolling of their plague bells draws the daemons of Nurgle to the battlefield in swarms.

THE BOOK OF EXCESS

They are joy turned to horror, want become need become obsession. Surging sinuous across the field of war, their every caress is a knife thrust, their every sighing exhalation a howl that bursts hearts and shatters bones. Hideously beautiful, savagely delicate, they promise only delightful misery garbed in the desperate finery of unattainable fulfilment.

In this section you will find the following rules:

EXALTED KEEPERS OF SECRETS (PG 106)

Keepers of Secrets can be upgraded with potent new abilities. The rules for how you can upgrade these models and the abilities they bestow are described in this section.

SLAANESH STRATAGEMS (PG 107)

Slaanesh armies have access to unique battlefield strategies and tactics that they can utilise to best their foes in any theatre of war; these are represented by the Stratagems in this section, and you can spend Command points to use them in your games. You can find out more about Stratagems and Command points in the Warhammer 40,000 Core Book.

SOULSTAIN DISCIPLINE (PG 108)

If your army includes any Slaanesh **Psyker** units, they can be given additional psychic powers from the Soulstain discipline. This represents the different arcane lore and particular talents of each individual psyker. You can find out more about psychic powers in the Warhammer 40,000 Core Book.

SLAANESH WARLORD TRAITS (PG 109)

Slaanesh **Warlord** models can have one of the traits presented in this section. These help to better reflect their individual combat and command style on the battlefield.

RELICS OF SLAANESH (PG 110)

Slaanesh's greatest champions can be equipped with powerful artefacts called Relics of Slaanesh; these Relics and the rules they bestow are described in this section.

SLAANESH DATASHEETS (PG 111-121)

This section is essential to all Chaos Daemons players who wish to include **Slaanesh** units in their army, regardless of preferred play style, containing as it does the datasheets for **Legiones Daemonica Slaanesh** units. Each datasheet describes, among other things, the profiles of its models, the wargear they can be equipped with and the abilities they have. You can find out more about datasheets in the Warhammer 40,000 Core Book.

EXALTED KEEPERS OF SECRETS

The most gifted amongst the Greater Daemons of Slaanesh are living embodiments of unfettered excess and sensory overload. At once sublimely graceful and menacingly bestial, they terrify and repulse mortals even as they beguile them and bewitch their every sense. To stand against such a sublime nightmare given corporeal form is to endure a test of will and resolve that few mortals stand any chance of passing.

If your army includes any **LEGIONES DAEMONICA** Detachments (excluding Auxiliary Support, Super-heavy Auxiliary or Fortification Network Detachments), then when you muster your army, you can upgrade any **KEEPER OF SECRETS** models from your army to be exalted. When a model is upgraded to be exalted it gains Exalted abilities.

You can select one of the Exalted abilities (see right) for that model. That model's Power Rating is increased accordingly, as shown in the table below. If you are playing a matched play game, or a game that uses a points limit, then the points value of that unit is also increased by the amount shown in the same table. Make a note on your army roster each time you upgrade a unit using these rules, specifying the ability it has gained.

Named characters (e.g. **SHALAXI HELBANE**, page 111) cannot be given Exalted abilities. Each model can only be upgraded to have Exalted abilities once. An army (or a Crusade force) cannot include the same Exalted ability more than once.

A Crusade force cannot start with any models having Exalted abilities – to include one in a Crusade force, you must use the Exalted Daemon Requisition (pg 132).

EXALTED ABILITY	POWER	POINTS
Diaphanous Panoply	+2	+35
Epicurean of Agonies	+2	+25
Insatiable Onslaught	+1	+20

EXALTED ABILITIES

DIAPHANOUS PANOPLY
Though the smooth flesh and flowing silken finery of this daemon appear almost delicate, they are as impenetrable as a mind lost to the deepest throes of addiction. Even the largest calibre shots rebound from them as though the blows were no more than the kiss of a perfumed breeze.

Each time a ranged attack is made against this model, subtract 1 from that attack's wound roll.

EPICUREAN OF AGONIES
It is in this daemon's gift to know the innermost secrets, the most desperate desires and deeply harboured fears of all those it looks upon. It delights in exploiting such stolen insights to maximise the torments of its victims, dissecting their bodies with precise, nerve-shredding blows even as it drowns their minds in sadistic illusions that leave them all but unable to resist.

Each time this model makes a melee attack, an unmodified hit roll of 6 scores 1 additional hit.

INSATIABLE ONSLAUGHT
The unfulfilled desires of myriad desperate souls surge through this daemon, filling it with a ravenous appetite for cruelty and slaughter that drives it on with ever-greater urgency.

Add 2 to Advance rolls and charge rolls made for this model.

SLAANESH STRATAGEMS

If your army includes any LEGIONES DAEMONICA SLAANESH units (excluding units in Auxiliary Support, Super-heavy Auxiliary or Fortification Network Detachments), you have access to these Stratagems, and can spend CPs to use them.

THIRST FOR SOULS   1CP

Legions of Slaanesh – Battle Tactic Stratagem

As extensions of their patron deity, the daemons of Slaanesh salivate with undisguised desire at the thought of devouring Aeldari souls.

Use this Stratagem in the Fight phase, when a LEGIONES DAEMONICA SLAANESH unit from your army is selected to fight. Until the end of the phase, each time a model in that unit makes a melee attack against an AELDARI unit, you can re-roll the hit roll and you can re-roll the wound roll.

RAZOR-SHARP CARESS   1CP

Legions of Slaanesh – Battle Tactic Stratagem

The keenness of the Daemonettes' desire to torment their foes manifests in the razored kiss of their vicious talons.

Use this Stratagem in the Fight phase, when a DAEMONETTES unit from your army is selected to fight. Until the end of the phase, each time a model in that unit makes a melee attack, on an unmodified wound roll of 6, improve the Armour Penetration characteristic of that attack by 1.

THE ENDLESS DANCE   1CP

Legions of Slaanesh – Battle Tactic Stratagem

These daemons flow ever-onward through the steps of an immortal ballet, a hideously graceful and wholly unnatural performance that speeds them across the battlefields of realspace.

Use this Stratagem in the Fight phase, when a DAEMONETTES unit from your army is selected to fight. Until the end of the phase, each time a model in that unit makes a pile-in or consolidation move, it can move up to an additional 3". This is not cumulative with any other rule that increases the distance models can pile in or consolidate.

IMPOSSIBLE ELEGANCE   1CP

Legions of Slaanesh – Epic Deed Stratagem

The greatest of Slaanesh's daemons move with an idealised grace and agility rendered hideous by its sheer precision and impossibility.

Use this Stratagem at the start of the Fight phase. Select one LEGIONES DAEMONICA SLAANESH CHARACTER model from your army (excluding VEHICLE units). Until the end of the phase, each time a melee attack is made against that unit, an unmodified hit roll of 1-3 always fails, irrespective of any abilities that the weapon or the model making the attack may have.

EXQUISITE GIFTS   1CP

Legions of Slaanesh – Requisition Stratagem

The most exalted of Slaanesh's daemons wield mighty artefacts, powerful symbols of the favour of the Dark Prince.

Use this Stratagem before the battle. Select one LEGIONES DAEMONICA SLAANESH CHARACTER model from your army and give them one Relic of Slaanesh (this must be a Relic they can have). Each Relic in your army must be unique, and you cannot use this Stratagem to give a model two Relics. You can only use this Stratagem once, unless you are playing a Strike Force battle (in which case, you can use this Stratagem twice) or an Onslaught battle (in which case, you can use this Stratagem three times).

MELODIC DELIRIUM   1CP

Legions of Slaanesh – Strategic Ploy Stratagem

Fiends sing a strange dirge, its melodies catching in the minds of enemy psykers like hooks in flesh and flooding their thoughts with feverish bewilderment.

Use this Stratagem at the start of your opponent's Psychic phase. Select one FIENDS unit from your army. Until the end of the phase, that unit has the following ability:

Melodic Delirium (Aura): While an enemy PSYKER unit is within 12" of this unit, each time a Psychic test is taken for that unit, subtract 2 from the result.

RACE THROUGH THE WARP   1CP

Legions of Slaanesh – Strategic Ploy Stratagem

Slicing the skein of reality, Slaaneshi charioteers steer their charge into the warp before re-emerging to run the enemy down.

Use this Stratagem in your Command phase. Select one LEGIONES DAEMONICA SLAANESH VEHICLE unit (excluding SOUL GRINDER units) from your army. Remove that unit from the battlefield and place it into Strategic Reserves.

RAPTUROUS STANDARD   1CP

Legions of Slaanesh - Wargear Stratagem

This icon fills all who gaze upon it with such euphoria that they stand slack and glazed even as the daemons of Slaanesh descend upon them.

Use this Stratagem at the start of the Fight phase. Select one LEGIONES DAEMONICA SLAANESH ICON unit from your army. Until the end of the phase, each time a model in that unit makes a melee attack, you can re-roll the hit roll.

SOULSTAIN DISCIPLINE

Before the battle, generate the psychic powers for **PSYKER** models in your army that know powers from the Soulstain discipline using the table below. You can either roll one D6 to generate each power randomly (re-rolling duplicate results), or you can select which powers the **PSYKER** model knows.

1. CACOPHONIC CHOIR
The daemon emits an ear-piercing chorus of warp-infused screams that erupt from its distended maw and shatter the sanity of its foes.

Witchfire: *Cacophonic Choir* has a warp charge value of 7. If manifested, roll 3D6. The closest enemy unit within 18" of and visible to this **PSYKER** suffers 1 mortal wound for each point that the result exceeds that enemy unit's Leadership characteristic by (to a maximum of 6 mortal wounds).

2. SYMPHONY OF PAIN
Drawing in all the screams of pain and pleasure from across the battlefield, the daemon melds them into a disorienting and otherworldly music that beguiles even as it torments.

Malediction: *Symphony of Pain* has a warp charge value of 7. If manifested, select one enemy unit within 18" of and visible to this **PSYKER**. Until the start of your next Psychic phase, each time a melee attack is made by a model in that unit, subtract 1 from that attack's hit roll and wound roll.

3. HYSTERICAL FRENZY
The daemon sends a barbed lash of deranged fervour and furious bliss uncoiling across the battlefield to goad its allies to greater efforts.

Blessing: *Hysterical Frenzy* has a warp charge value of 7. If manifested, select one friendly **LEGIONES DAEMONICA SLAANESH CORE** unit within 18" of and visible to this **PSYKER**. Until the start of your next Psychic phase:

- Add 1 to the Attacks characteristic of models in that unit.
- Each time a model in that unit makes a melee attack, on an unmodified hit roll of 6, that attack scores 1 additional hit.

4. DELIGHTFUL AGONIES
Manipulating the very stuff of its allies' corporeal manifestations, the daemon turns their physical hurts to euphoric stimuli, allowing them to fight on even with their physical selves in tatters.

Blessing: *Delightful Agonies* has a warp charge value of 6. If manifested, select one friendly **LEGIONES DAEMONICA SLAANESH CORE** unit within 18" of and visible to this **PSYKER**. Until the start of your next Psychic phase, each time a model in that unit would lose a wound, roll one D6: on a 5+, that wound is not lost.

5. PAVANE OF SLAANESH
Compelled by this daemon's plaintive urging, its victims begin an ever-more-desperate dance, flailing and contorting with wild abandon until flesh tears and bones snap from the unnatural contortions.

Witchfire: *Pavane of Slaanesh* has a warp charge value of 6. If manifested, select one enemy unit within 18" of and visible to this **PSYKER**. Roll one D6 for each model in that unit. For each 5+, that unit suffers 1 mortal wound (to a maximum of 6 mortal wounds).

6. PHANTASMAGORIA
Fixing its malevolent gaze upon its chosen victims, the daemon floods their minds with rapturous visions of delight and horror. These escalate to such overwhelming heights that soon those foes not tearing themselves or one another to pieces instead simply drop dead from insupportable sensory overload.

Witchfire: *Phantasmagoria* has a warp charge value of 7. If manifested, select one enemy unit within 18" of and visible to this **PSYKER** and roll six D6. For each 5+, that unit suffers 1 mortal wound. Until the start of your next Psychic phase, each time that unit suffers a mortal wound as a result of this psychic power, subtract 1 from the Leadership characteristic of models in that unit.

'Every shudder of pain and moment of delight, every peak of agony or ecstasy, each moment of mortal bliss or langour or desire, all give succour and form to the daemons of Slaanesh. No intensity of sensation goes unsampled, no pit of hedonistic indulgence left to waste. Only through numb and absolute unfeeling could the sentient races of the galaxy defeat the excesses of the Dark Prince, and so, of course, it shall never be.'

- Rucharis, the *Grimoire of Infernal Entities*

SLAANESH WARLORD TRAITS

If a LEGIONES DAEMONICA SLAANESH CHARACTER model gains a Warlord Trait, you can use the Slaanesh Warlord Traits table below to determine what Warlord Trait they have. You can either roll one D6 to randomly generate one, or you can select one.

If a SLAANESH HERALD model is your WARLORD, they can only have the Warp Mists, Fatal Caress or The Murderdance Warlord Traits. You can either roll one D3 to randomly generate one, or you can select one.

1. WARP MISTS
The stuff of the warp clings to this daemon's form, swirling around it like iridescent silks.

At the end of each battle round, if this WARLORD is on the battlefield, you can retain up to 2 unspent Warp Storm points (pg 58).

2. FATAL CARESS
With a swift flick of a blade or razor-sharp claw, this daemon can inflict agonising pleasures that drive the victim instantly insane.

Each time this WARLORD makes a melee attack, on an unmodified successful wound roll of 5+, invulnerable saving throws cannot be made against that attack.

3. THE MURDERDANCE
A performer in the maniacal dance of death, this daemon hacks and cavorts its way through the enemy ranks without ever missing a step.

Each time this WARLORD fights, if it made a charge move this turn, then until that fight is resolved, add D3 to its Attacks characteristic.

4. QUICKSILVER DUELLIST
A corporeal embodiment of arrogance, this daemon redoubles its efforts when humbling an enemy champion.

Each time this WARLORD makes a melee attack:

- You can re-roll the hit roll.
- If that attack is made against an enemy CHARACTER model, you can re-roll the wound roll.

5. SAVAGE HEDONIST
This daemon is a glutton for violence, striking ever harder to maintain the thrill of combat.

At the start of each battle round, add 1 to this WARLORD's Strength characteristic (to a maximum of +3).

6. AURA OF BEWITCHMENT (AURA)
Even the most disciplined warriors succumb to this daemon's beguilements, all thoughts lost in a haze of hallucinatory desire.

While an enemy unit is within 6" of this WARLORD, that unit cannot perform actions (see the Warhammer 40,000 Core Book). If that unit is performing an action when it comes into range of this ability, it immediately fails.

NAMED CHARACTERS AND WARLORD TRAITS
If one of the following characters gains a Warlord Trait, they must have the relevant one shown below:

Named Character	Warlord Trait
Shalaxi Helbane	Quicksilver Duellist
Syll'Esske	Aura of Bewitchment
The Masque of Slaanesh	The Murderdance

At the end of your need, should all other containment measures and wardings fail you, the entity and grimoire both maybe be destroyed but only by means of eglghaa lly uulgha'tuk r'yelth aaslanaash, s'ir'yk kharankar, ul'yt'isk ghumrglyth, ph'tak'yr t'zaadytch octu anmih'lk immat'yr ent'khul alayma'k'gh'eh glaghaa lly uulgha'tuk r'yelth aaslanaash, s'ir'yk kharankar, ph'tak'yr t'zaadytch octu anmih'lk immat'yr ent'khul alayma'k'gh'eh glaghaa lly uulgha'tuk r'yelth aaslanaash, s'ir'yk kharankar, ul'yt'isk ghumrglyth, ph'tak'yr t'zaadytch OC'TU EG'KLASH T'SKAH URUSHAK K'TZAR KH'ARTH TZ'ENETH NURG'LATH TSLAANA'TSH

RELICS OF SLAANESH

If a **Legiones Daemonica Slaanesh Character** model gains a Relic, you can give them one of the following Relics of Slaanesh. Named characters cannot be given any of the following Relics.

Note that some Relics replace one of the model's existing items of wargear. Where this is the case, you must, if you are using points values, still pay the cost of the wargear that is being replaced. Write down any Relics of Slaanesh your models have on your army roster.

THE FORBIDDEN GEM

This gem was the purest diamond in the Aeldari empire in the time before the Fall. It was a source of jealous pride to its keeper, a noble by the name of Ydrisyll, who spent increasing amounts of time transfixed by its beauty. One of Slaanesh's first deeds after his apocalyptic birth was to capture Ydrisyll's soul and cage it within the very gem he once so coveted. Gazing upon this corrupted diamond now inspires uncontrollable jealousy, leaving mortal senses hopelessly addled.

In your Command phase, select one enemy unit within 12" of the bearer. Until the start of your next Command phase, any aura abilities that unit has have no effect.

THE MARK OF EXCESS

A daemon favoured with Slaanesh's own mark of excess faces an existence of constant, desperate addiction. Whenever the cursed recipient sheds the lifeblood of a worthy foe it is rewarded by a sensory explosion of bliss so all-consuming that the daemon will fight harder than ever to feel such sensations again.

- Add 1 to the bearer's Attacks characteristic.
- Each time the bearer makes a melee attack that destroys a **Character**, **Monster** or **Vehicle** unit, add 1 to the bearer's Attacks characteristic.

SOULSTEALER

This gluttonous blade gulps down the souls of its victims before invigorating the corporeal form of its wielder. Its greed stems from the starving Keeper of Secrets bound within – an arrogant entity that sought to devour enough Aeldari souls to challenge Slaanesh itself. As punishment for the daemon's monstrous hubris, Slaanesh trapped it within Soulstealer, condemning the Keeper of Secrets to sustain other daemons with its frenzied appetite while retaining nothing for itself.

Model equipped with witstealer sword or hellforged sword only. This Relic replaces a witstealer sword or hellforged sword and has the following profile:

WEAPON	RANGE	TYPE	S	AP	D
Soulstealer	Melee	Melee	+2	-3	3

Abilities: Each time a model is destroyed by an attack made with this weapon, the bearer regains 1 lost wound (to a maximum of 6 regained wounds per phase). Each time the bearer makes an attack with this weapon against an **Aeldari** unit, if a hit is scored, that attack automatically wounds the target.

SLOTHFUL CLAWS

Formed from the essence of a Keeper of Secrets, these claws have taken many guises and been bound to the corporeal forms of countless daemons. The slightest scratch from them imparts a smothering lethargy that weighs heavy on limbs, mind and soul alike, leaving victims mired in blissful lassitude.

Model equipped with ravaging claws or snapping claws only. Select 1 ravaging claws or snapping claws the bearer is equipped with.

- Add 1 to the Damage characteristic of that weapon.
- Each time an enemy model loses any wounds as a result of an attack made with that weapon, until the end of the phase, that enemy unit is not affected by the aura abilities of other enemy units.
- That weapon is now considered to be a Relic for all rules purposes.

SILVERSTRIKE

The blinding speed with which this blade flicks out makes it appear as if it does not even occupy the space between thrust and strike. This swiftness makes the weird languor the blade inflicts on its victims seem all the more grotesque by comparison, those struck responding with slow and witless smiles even as their flesh peels apart or their limbs thump heavily to the ground.

Model equipped with witstealer sword only. This Relic replaces a witstealer sword and has the following profile:

WEAPON	RANGE	TYPE	S	AP	D
Silverstrike	Melee	Melee	+3	-3	3

Abilities: Each time an enemy model loses any wounds as a result of an attack made with this weapon, until the end of the battle, each time that model makes a melee attack, subtract 1 from that attack's hit roll and wound roll.

WHIP OF AGONY

This twitching lash coils lazily and deceptively around its master's limbs, lurking innocently like a hidden compulsion until willed into a serpentine strike. The Whip of Agony exudes a psychic poison, linking its sentience with the nerves of any it touches. With the connection made, the whip's febrile imagination pours pain and horror into the sensoria of its victims.

Model equipped with living whip or lashes of torment only.

- Change the Type characteristic of any living whip or lashes of torment the bearer is equipped with to Assault 8.
- Each time the bearer makes an attack with a living whip or lashes of torment (excluding attacks made against **Vehicle** units), on an unmodified successful hit roll of 4+, that attack automatically wounds the target.

SHALAXI HELBANE

15 POWER

Some of this model's characteristics change as it suffers damage, as shown below:

No.	Name	M	WS	BS	S	T	W	A	Ld	DSv
1	Shalaxi Helbane (12+ wounds remaining)	16"	2+	2+	6	7	22	6	10	5+/4+
	Shalaxi Helbane (6-11 wounds remaining)	14"	3+	2+	6	7	N/A	5	10	5+/4+
	Shalaxi Helbane (1-5 wounds remaining)	12"	4+	2+	6	7	N/A	4	10	5+/4+

Shalaxi Helbane is equipped with: living whip; snapping claws; Soulpiercer. Your army can only include one **SHALAXI HELBANE** model.

WEAPON	RANGE	TYPE	S	AP	D	ABILITIES
Living whip	12"	Assault 6	6	-2	2	-
Snapping claws	Melee	Melee	User	-4	3	Malefic 4
Soulpiercer	Melee	Melee	x2	-4	3	Each time an attack is made with this weapon against a **CHARACTER** model, this weapon has a Damage characteristic of D3+3.

OTHER WARGEAR	ABILITIES
Shining aegis	The bearer has a Daemonic Save characteristic of 4+/4+.

WARGEAR OPTIONS

• This model's living whip can be replaced with 1 shining aegis.

ABILITIES

Daemonic (pg 56)

Daemon Lord of Slaanesh (Aura): While a friendly **LEGIONES DAEMONICA SLAANESH CORE** unit is within 6" of this model, each time a model in that unit makes an attack, re-roll a hit roll of 1.

Mesmerising Form: Each time an attack is made against this model, subtract 1 from that attack's hit roll.

Cloak of Constriction: Each time a melee attack is made against this model, subtract 1 from that attack's wound roll.

Monarch of the Hunt: This model is eligible to perform a Heroic Intervention if it is within 6" horizontally and 5" vertically of any enemy **CHARACTER** units, instead of 3" horizontally and 5" vertically. Each time this model makes a Heroic Intervention move, it can move up to 6" if it finishes that move within Engagement Range of an enemy **CHARACTER** unit. All other rules for Heroic Interventions still apply.

PSYKER

This model can attempt to manifest two psychic powers in your Psychic phase, and attempt to deny one psychic power in your opponent's Psychic phase. It knows *Smite* and two psychic powers from the Soulstain discipline (pg 108).

FACTION KEYWORDS: CHAOS, LEGIONES DAEMONICA, SLAANESH
KEYWORDS: MONSTER, CHARACTER, DAEMON, PSYKER, GREATER DAEMON, WARP LOCUS, KEEPER OF SECRETS, SHALAXI HELBANE

Cloven hooves pounding against broken earth, Shalaxi Helbane bears down upon its doomed quarry with the Soulpiercer gleaming in its grip. No prey can evade the Monarch of the Hunt, for the daemon's obsession with its victim is so singular and so powerful that no mortal means of flight could ever escape it.

PREDATOR AND PREY

How does one humble a god? What symbolic victory combines the metaphysical and the real in such a fashion as to make mock of the eternal and the divine? If whispered tales are to be believed, the daemon known as Shalaxi Helbane is tool and architect both of just such a feat. Unstinting huntress; obsessive duellist; inescapable bane of champions, regents, even daemons whose pride in their own martial achievements makes them prey for Helbane's spear; the Monarch of the Hunt manifests all these aspects and, in doing so, plants the flags of its victories firmly in territory that should belong to the Blood God, Khorne.

Yet Shalaxi Helbane's mockery extends not only to a single deity's realm. Myths tell how this entity quested deep into the Garden of Nurgle on the trail of the fecund Prince

of Corpseblooms, and how it returned to the Palace of Slaanesh to plant its quarry's final flower in soil saturated with deviance.

Then there are the stories told amongst the Asuryani, of a stolen blade that might otherwise have wakened their own slumbering god, and of the tireless pursuit of Yvraine who should be the end of death. Cruellest of all, tales of a battle unimaginable between this daemon predator and many great Aeldari heroes, wherein banishment and corporeal extinction appeared to be Helbane's end. Yet it seems that Shalaxi Helbane bested even the champions of the god-of-a-death-cheated, by sending nought but an illusion of self to battle them before revealing its own survival and cheating death itself.

KEEPER OF SECRETS

14 POWER

Some of this model's characteristics change as it suffers damage, as shown below:

No.	Name	M	WS	BS	S	T	W	A	Ld	DSv
1	Keeper of Secrets (11+ wounds remaining)	16"	2+	2+	6	7	20	6	10	5+/4+
	Keeper of Secrets (6-10 wounds remaining)	14"	3+	2+	6	7	N/A	5	10	5+/4+
	Keeper of Secrets (1-5 wounds remaining)	12"	4+	2+	6	7	N/A	4	10	5+/4+

A Keeper of Secrets is equipped with: ritual knife; snapping claws; witstealer sword.

WEAPON	RANGE	TYPE	S	AP	D	ABILITIES
Living whip	12"	Assault 6	6	-2	2	-
Snapping claws	Melee	Melee	User	-4	3	Malefic 4
Witstealer sword	Melee	Melee	+2	-3	3	Each time an enemy model loses any wounds as a result of an attack made with this weapon, until the end of the battle, each time that model makes a melee attack, subtract 1 from that attack's wound roll.

OTHER WARGEAR	ABILITIES
Ritual knife	At the end of the Fight phase, you can select one enemy model within 3" of the bearer that lost any wounds during that phase as a result of an attack made by the bearer. Roll one D6: on a 2+, that model suffers D3 mortal wounds.
Shining aegis	The bearer has a Daemonic Save characteristic of 4+/4+.
Sinistrous hand	At the end of the Fight phase, if any enemy models (excluding **VEHICLE** models) were destroyed by an attack made by the bearer that phase, the bearer regains up to D3 lost wounds.

WARGEAR OPTIONS

• This model's ritual knife can be replaced with one of the following: 1 living whip; 1 shining aegis; 1 sinistrous hand.

ABILITIES

Daemonic (pg 56)

Daemon Lord of Slaanesh (Aura): While a friendly **LEGIONES DAEMONICA SLAANESH CORE** unit is within 6" of this model, each time a model in that unit makes an attack, re-roll a hit roll of 1.

Mesmerising Form: Each time an attack is made against this model, subtract 1 from that attack's hit roll.

PSYKER

This model can attempt to manifest two psychic powers in your Psychic phase, and attempt to deny one psychic power in your opponent's Psychic phase. It knows *Smite* and two psychic powers from the Soulstain discipline (pg 108).

FACTION KEYWORDS: CHAOS, LEGIONES DAEMONICA, SLAANESH
KEYWORDS: MONSTER, CHARACTER, DAEMON, PSYKER, GREATER DAEMON, KEEPER OF SECRETS

Darkly intelligent, horribly beguiling and deadly in battle, the Keepers of Secrets are the greatest champions of Slaaneshi daemon legions. Wielding unclean yet beautiful weapons and unleashing the sorcerous powers of obsession and torment, these daemons cut an elegantly hideous swathe across the battlefield.

INFERNAL ENRAPTURESS

4 POWER

No.	Name	M	WS	BS	S	T	W	A	Ld	DSv
1	Infernal Enrapturess	9"	2+	3+	4	4	4	4	8	5+/4+

An Infernal Enrapturess is equipped with: heartstring lyre; ravaging claws.

WEAPON	RANGE	TYPE	S	AP	D	ABILITIES
Heartstring lyre	Before selecting targets, select one of the profiles below to make attacks with.					
- Cacophonous melody	18"	Assault 6	5	-1	1	-
- Euphonic blast	24"	Assault 1	9	-3	D3+3	-
Ravaging claws	Melee	Melee	User	-2	2	-

ABILITIES

Daemonic (pg 56)

Herald of Slaanesh (Aura): While a friendly LEGIONES DAEMONICA SLAANESH CORE unit is within 6" of this model, each time a model in that unit makes an attack, you can re-roll a wound roll of 1.

Discordant Disruption (Aura): While an enemy PSYKER unit is within 24" of this model, each time a Psychic test is taken for that unit, it suffers Perils of the Warp on any dice roll that includes a double, instead of only a double 1 or double 6.

Harmonic Alignment: In your Command phase, select one model with this ability from your army and one friendly LEGIONES DAEMONICA SLAANESH CORE unit from your army within 6" of that model. You can return one destroyed model from that unit to the battlefield with its full wounds remaining. If that unit is an INFANTRY unit, you can return up to D3 destroyed models instead. These models cannot be set up within Engagement Range of any enemy units unless those enemy units are already within Engagement Range of its unit.

FACTION KEYWORDS: **CHAOS, LEGIONES DAEMONICA, SLAANESH**
KEYWORDS: **INFANTRY, CHARACTER, DAEMON, WARP LOCUS, DAEMONETTES, HERALD, INFERNAL ENRAPTURESS**

The symphonies of torment and cacophonies of bliss unleashed by these daemons can tear their foes apart body and soul. Yet perhaps their greatest ability is to draw the disembodied energies of fellow Slaaneshi daemons to the battlefield, constantly bolstering their comrades' ranks with fresh and soul-hungry entities.

THE MASQUE OF SLAANESH

5 POWER

No.	Name	M	WS	BS	S	T	W	A	Ld	DSv
1	The Masque of Slaanesh	10"	2+	3+	4	4	4	6	8	4+/4+

The Masque of Slaanesh is equipped with: serrated claws. Your army can only include one THE MASQUE OF SLAANESH model.

WEAPON	RANGE	TYPE	S	AP	D	ABILITIES
Serrated claws	Melee	Melee	User	-3	2	-

ABILITIES

Daemonic (pg 56)

The Eternal Dance: At the start of the Fight phase, select one enemy unit within Engagement Range of this model. Then select one of the following effects:
- Until the end of the phase, each time a friendly LEGIONES DAEMONICA SLAANESH model makes a melee attack against that unit, add 1 to that attack's hit roll.
- Until the end of the phase, each time a model in that unit makes a melee attack, subtract 1 from that attack's hit roll.
- Until the end of the phase, each time a model in that unit makes a melee attack, subtract 1 from that attack's wound roll.

Herald of Slaanesh (Aura): While a friendly LEGIONES DAEMONICA SLAANESH CORE unit is within 6" of this model, each time a model in that unit makes an attack, you can re-roll a wound roll of 1.

Dazzling Acrobatics:
- Each time this model makes a Normal Move, Advances, Falls Back or makes a charge move, until that move is finished, this model can move horizontally through models and terrain features (it cannot finish a move on top of another model, or its base).
- This unit is eligible to charge in a turn in which it Fell Back.

FACTION KEYWORDS: **CHAOS, LEGIONES DAEMONICA, SLAANESH**
KEYWORDS: **INFANTRY, CHARACTER, DAEMON, DAEMONETTES, HERALD, THE MASQUE OF SLAANESH**

Once high in the favour of the Dark Prince, this daemon was cursed by its petulant deity to dance eternally across reality and beyond for an imagined slight. Its endless acrobatic performance beguiles and bewilders, drawing those who witness it into joining the revels even at the expense of their own survival.

SYLL'ESSKE

10 POWER

No.	Name	M	WS	BS	S	T	W	A	Ld	DSv
1	Syll'Esske	10"	2+	3+	4	6	8	6	9	5+/4+

Syll'Esske is equipped with: scourging whip; Axe of Dominion. Your army can only include one SYLL'ESSKE model.

WEAPON	RANGE	TYPE	S	AP	D	ABILITIES
Scourging whip (shooting)	9"	Assault 6	User	-2	1	-
Axe of Dominion	Melee	Melee	+3	-3	3	-
Scourging whip (melee)	Melee	Melee	User	-2	1	Malefic 6

ABILITIES

Daemonic (pg 56)

Prince of Chaos (Aura): While a friendly LEGIONES DAEMONICA SLAANESH CORE unit is within 6" of this model, each time a model in that unit makes an attack, re-roll a hit roll of 1.

Herald of Slaanesh (Aura): While a friendly LEGIONES DAEMONICA SLAANESH CORE unit is within 6" of this model, each time a model in that unit makes an attack, you can re-roll a wound roll of 1.

PSYKER

This model can attempt to manifest two psychic powers in your Psychic phase, and attempt to deny one psychic power in your opponent's Psychic phase. It knows *Smite* and two psychic powers from the Soulstain discipline (pg 108).

FACTION KEYWORDS: CHAOS, LEGIONES DAEMONICA, SLAANESH
KEYWORDS: MONSTER, CHARACTER, DAEMON, PSYKER, DAEMONETTES, HERALD, DAEMON PRINCE, SYLL'ESSKE

This strange alliance of the daemon herald Syll and the hulking Daemon Prince Esske has borne bloody fruit across countless battlefields. Not only do the pairing wreak red ruin amidst the foe themselves, but also their presence entices the daemons of Slaanesh to ever more excessive acts of cruelty and violence.

CONTORTED EPITOME

8 POWER

No.	Name	M	WS	BS	S	T	W	A	Ld	DSv
1	Contorted Epitome	12"	2+	3+	4	5	8	8	8	4+/4+

A Contorted Epitome is equipped with: coiled tentacles; ravaging claws.

WEAPON	RANGE	TYPE	S	AP	D	ABILITIES
Coiled tentacles	Melee	Melee	+1	-2	3	Malefic 3
Ravaging claws	Melee	Melee	User	-2	2	-

ABILITIES

Daemonic (pg 56)

Swallow Energy: Each time this model would lose a wound as a result of a mortal wound, roll one D6: on a 2+, that wound is not lost.

Herald of Slaanesh (Aura): While a friendly LEGIONES DAEMONICA SLAANESH CORE unit is within 6" of this model, each time a model in that unit makes an attack, you can re-roll a wound roll of 1.

Horrible Fascination (Aura): While an enemy unit is within 6" of this model, at the start of your opponent's Command phase, your opponent must roll 3D6 for that unit. If the result is higher than that unit's Leadership characteristic, until the start of your opponent's next Command phase:
• Halve the Move characteristic of models in that unit.
• Each time a model in that unit makes an attack, subtract 1 from that attack's hit roll.

PSYKER

This model can attempt to manifest two psychic powers in your Psychic phase, and attempt to deny two psychic powers in your opponent's Psychic phase. It knows *Smite* and two psychic powers from the Soulstain discipline (pg 108).

FACTION KEYWORDS: CHAOS, LEGIONES DAEMONICA, SLAANESH
KEYWORDS: CAVALRY, CHARACTER, DAEMON, PSYKER, DAEMONETTES, HERALD, CONTORTED EPITOME

These ghastly daemonic manifestations writhe into battle on nests of metallic tendrils, their leering attendants riding their twisted steeds to war. It reflects the darkest desires of those who look upon its surface, even as it swallows up the most potent energies and throws back overwhelming onslaughts of empyric devastation.

TORMENTBRINGER ON EXALTED SEEKER CHARIOT **6** POWER

Some of this model's characteristics change as it suffers damage, as shown below:

No.	Name	M	WS	BS	S	T	W	A	Ld	DSv
1	Tormentbringer on Exalted Seeker Chariot (7+ wounds remaining)	14"	2+	3+	4	5	12	8	8	4+/4+
	Tormentbringer on Exalted Seeker Chariot (4-6 wounds remaining)	12"	3+	3+	4	5	N/A	7	8	4+/4+
	Tormentbringer on Exalted Seeker Chariot (1-3 wounds remaining)	10"	4+	3+	4	5	N/A	6	8	4+/4+

A Tormentbringer on Exalted Seeker Chariot is equipped with: lashes of torment; exalted Seeker tongues; ravaging claws.

WEAPON	RANGE	TYPE	S	AP	D	ABILITIES
Lashes of torment	6"	Assault 6	4	-1	1	-
Exalted Seeker tongues	Melee	Melee	4	0	1	Malefic 8
Ravaging claws	Melee	Melee	User	-2	2	-

ABILITIES

Daemonic (pg 56)

Herald of Slaanesh (Aura): While a friendly LEGIONES DAEMONICA SLAANESH CORE unit is within 6" of this model, each time a model in that unit makes an attack, you can re-roll a wound roll of 1.

Tormentbringer: In your Command phase, select one friendly LEGIONES DAEMONICA SLAANESH CORE unit within 6" of this model. Until the start of your next Command phase, each time a model in that unit makes a melee attack, add 1 to that attack's hit roll.

Evasive Speed: Each time a ranged attack is made against this model, subtract 1 from that attack's hit roll.

Scything Impact: Each time this model finishes a charge move:
- Roll four D6 for each enemy unit within Engagement Range of this model. For each 5+, that enemy unit suffers 1 mortal wound.
- Until the end of the turn, add 2 to this model's Attacks characteristic.

PSYKER

This model can attempt to manifest one psychic power in your Psychic phase, and attempt to deny one psychic power in your opponent's Psychic phase. It knows *Smite* and one psychic power from the Soulstain discipline (pg 108).

FACTION KEYWORDS: CHAOS, LEGIONES DAEMONICA, SLAANESH
KEYWORDS: VEHICLE, CHARACTER, DAEMON, PSYKER, EXALTED SEEKER CHARIOT, HERALD, DAEMONETTES, TORMENTBRINGER

Riding to battle above the clatterslash blades of their Exalted Seeker Chariot, these wilfully vicious entities delight in ploughing screaming souls into the churned dirt of the battlefield. They strive to travel faster, strike harder, and leave even their lightning-fast fellow charioteers envious in their wakes.

TRANCEWEAVER

4 POWER

No.	Name	M	WS	BS	S	T	W	A	Ld	DSv
1	Tranceweaver	9"	2+	3+	4	4	4	5	8	5+/4+

A Tranceweaver is equipped with: ravaging claws.

WEAPON	RANGE	TYPE	S	AP	D	ABILITIES
Ravaging claws	Melee	Melee	User	-2	2	-

ABILITIES

Daemonic (pg 56)

Herald of Slaanesh (Aura): While a friendly **LEGIONES DAEMONICA SLAANESH CORE** unit is within 6" of this model, each time a model in that unit makes an attack, you can re-roll a wound roll of 1.

Tranceweaver: In your Command phase, select one friendly **DAEMONETTES CORE** unit within 6" of this model. Until the start of your next Command phase, each time a model in that unit makes a melee attack, improve the Armour Penetration characteristic of that attack by 1.

PSYKER

This model can attempt to manifest one psychic power in your Psychic phase, and attempt to deny one psychic power in your opponent's Psychic phase. It knows *Smite* and one psychic power from the Soulstain discipline (pg 108).

FACTION KEYWORDS: CHAOS, LEGIONES DAEMONICA, SLAANESH
KEYWORDS: INFANTRY, CHARACTER, DAEMON, PSYKER, DAEMONETTES, HERALD, TRANCEWEAVER

These favoured daemons of Slaanesh are raw manifestations of sensory excess and wilful cruelty. Heralds of the Dark Prince, they flow across the battlefield with inhuman grace, keening gleeful war cries as they exhort their fellows to greater acts of sadistic bliss-giving and lay enemies low with the razor caress of their talons.

TORMENTBRINGER ON SEEKER CHARIOT

5 POWER

No.	Name	M	WS	BS	S	T	W	A	Ld	DSv
1	Tormentbringer on Seeker Chariot	14"	2+	3+	4	5	7	8	8	4+/4+

A Tormentbringer on Seeker Chariot is equipped with: lashes of torment; ravaging claws; Seeker tongues.

WEAPON	RANGE	TYPE	S	AP	D	ABILITIES
Lashes of torment	6"	Assault 6	4	-1	1	-
Ravaging claws	Melee	Melee	User	-2	2	-
Seeker tongues	Melee	Melee	4	0	1	Malefic 4

ABILITIES

Daemonic (pg 56)

Herald of Slaanesh (Aura): While a friendly **LEGIONES DAEMONICA SLAANESH CORE** unit is within 6" of this model, each time a model in that unit makes an attack, you can re-roll a wound roll of 1.

Tormentbringer: In your Command phase, select one friendly **LEGIONES DAEMONICA SLAANESH CORE** unit within 6" of this model. Until the start of your next Command phase, each time a model in that unit makes a melee attack, add 1 to that attack's hit roll.

Evasive Speed: Each time a ranged attack is made against this model, subtract 1 from that attack's hit roll.

Scything Impact: Each time this model finishes a charge move:
- Roll four D6 for each enemy unit within Engagement Range of this model. For each 5+, that enemy unit suffers 1 mortal wound.
- Until the end of the turn, add 2 to this model's Attacks characteristic.

PSYKER

This model can attempt to manifest one psychic power in your Psychic phase, and attempt to deny one psychic power in your opponent's Psychic phase. It knows *Smite* and one psychic power from the Soulstain discipline (pg 108).

FACTION KEYWORDS: CHAOS, LEGIONES DAEMONICA, SLAANESH
KEYWORDS: VEHICLE, CHARACTER, DAEMON, PSYKER, SEEKER CHARIOT, HERALD, DAEMONETTES, TORMENTBRINGER

Even should the foe bring themselves to open fire upon entities of such ghastly beauty, they stand little chance of landing a hit upon the hurtling and swerving Tormentbringers aboard their Seeker Chariots. Whooping with wild exhilaration, the daemon Heralds slam into the enemy ranks in ecstatic eruptions of gore.

TORMENTBRINGER ON HELLFLAYER

No.	Name	M	WS	BS	S	T	W	A	Ld	DSv
1	Tormentbringer on Hellflayer	14"	2+	3+	4	5	7	8	8	4+/4+

A Tormentbringer on Hellflayer is equipped with: lashes of torment; bladed axle; ravaging claws; Seeker tongues.

WEAPON	RANGE	TYPE	S	AP	D	ABILITIES
Lashes of torment	6"	Assault 6	4	-1	1	-
Bladed axle	Melee	Melee	+2	-2	2	Malefic 4
Ravaging claws	Melee	Melee	User	-2	2	-
Seeker tongues	Melee	Melee	4	0	1	Malefic 4

ABILITIES

Daemonic (pg 56)

Herald of Slaanesh (Aura): While a friendly **Legiones Daemonica Slaanesh Core** unit is within 6" of this model, each time a model in that unit makes an attack, you can re-roll a wound roll of 1.

Tormentbringer: In your Command phase, select one friendly **Legiones Daemonica Slaanesh Core** unit within 6" of this model. Until the start of your next Command phase, each time a model in that unit makes a melee attack, add 1 to that attack's hit roll.

Evasive Speed: Each time a ranged attack is made against this model, subtract 1 from that attack's hit roll.

Cutting Down the Foe: Each time this model is selected to fight, if it made a charge move this turn, change this model's bladed axle's ability to Malefic 6.

PSYKER

This model can attempt to manifest one psychic power in your Psychic phase, and attempt to deny one psychic power in your opponent's Psychic phase. It knows *Smite* and one psychic power from the Soulstain discipline (pg 108).

FACTION KEYWORDS: Chaos, Legiones Daemonica, Slaanesh
KEYWORDS: Vehicle, Character, Daemon, Psyker, Hellflayer, Herald, Daemonettes, Tormentbringer

To these cruel and merciless Heralds falls the task of mowing down rank upon rank of screaming foes amidst spumes of blood and tattered flesh. Obsessive about ensuring the eradication of their victims, the Tormentbringers seed the ripped-up battlefield behind them with corpse-flesh and corruption.

DAEMONETTES

6 POWER

No.	Name	M	WS	BS	S	T	W	A	Ld	DSv
9	Daemonette	10"	3+	3+	4	3	1	4	6	5+/4+
1	Alluress	10"	3+	3+	4	3	1	5	7	5+/4+

Every model is equipped with: piercing claws.

WEAPON	RANGE	TYPE	S	AP	D	ABILITIES
Piercing claws	Melee	Melee	User	-2	1	-

OTHER WARGEAR	ABILITIES
Daemonic icon	While this unit contains any models equipped with a daemonic icon: • It has the **ICON** keyword. • Each time a Combat Attrition test is taken for this unit, you can ignore any or all modifiers.
Instrument of Chaos	While this unit contains any models equipped with an instrument of Chaos: • It has the **INSTRUMENT** keyword. • Add 1 to the Leadership characteristic of models in this unit.

WARGEAR OPTIONS

- One Daemonette that is not equipped with a daemonic icon can be equipped with 1 instrument of Chaos.
- One Daemonette that is not equipped with an instrument of Chaos can be equipped with 1 daemonic icon.

ABILITIES

Daemonic (pg 56)

FACTION KEYWORDS: **CHAOS, LEGIONES DAEMONICA, SLAANESH**
KEYWORDS: **INFANTRY, DAEMON, CORE, DAEMONETTES**

Known to mortals as the handmaidens of Slaanesh, these daemons are a mixture of the beautiful and the monstrous, made all the more disturbing by the visceral clash of both. They delight in the carnage of battle, weaving around enemies' clumsy blows as they shrill and sigh their delight amidst swift-taloned slaughter.

FIENDS

5 POWER

No.	Name	M	WS	BS	S	T	W	A	Ld	DSv
2-5	Fiend	14"	3+	-	5	4	4	4	7	5+/4+
1	Blissbringer	14"	3+	-	5	4	4	5	8	5+/4+

If this unit contains 4 or more models it has **Power Rating 10**. Every model is equipped with: barbed tail; dissecting claws.

WEAPON	RANGE	TYPE	S	AP	D	ABILITIES
Barbed tail	Melee	Melee	User	-3	3	Malefic 1
Dissecting claws	Melee	Melee	User	-2	2	-

ABILITIES

Daemonic (pg 56)

Soporific Musk (Aura): While an enemy unit (excluding **VEHICLE** and **TITANIC** units) is within Engagement Range of this unit, each time a model in that enemy unit makes an attack, subtract 1 from that attack's hit roll.

FACTION KEYWORDS: **CHAOS, LEGIONES DAEMONICA, SLAANESH**
KEYWORDS: **BEAST, DAEMON, CORE, FIENDS**

Few daemonic entities approach the sheer disturbing horror of the Fiends of Slaanesh. Malicious hunting beasts that croon their delight across the battlefield, these ghastly abominations are wreathed in a soporific musk that leaves their prey witless and helpless before their flashing talons and stabbing tails.

SEEKERS

5 POWER

No.	Name	M	WS	BS	S	T	W	A	Ld	DSv
4-9	Seeker	16"	3+	3+	4	4	2	4	7	5+/4+
1	Heartseeker	16"	3+	3+	4	4	2	5	8	5+/4+

If this unit contains 6 or more models it has **Power Rating 10**. Every model is equipped with: lashing tongue; piercing claws.

WEAPON	RANGE	TYPE	S	AP	D	ABILITIES
Lashing tongue	Melee	Melee	4	0	1	Malefic 2
Piercing claws	Melee	Melee	User	-2	1	-

OTHER WARGEAR	ABILITIES
Daemonic icon	While this unit contains any models equipped with a daemonic icon: • It has the **ICON** keyword. • Each time a Combat Attrition test is taken for this unit, you can ignore any or all modifiers.
Instrument of Chaos	While this unit contains any models equipped with an instrument of Chaos: • It has the **INSTRUMENT** keyword. • Add 1 to the Leadership characteristic of models in this unit.

WARGEAR OPTIONS

• One Seeker that is not equipped with a daemonic icon can be equipped with 1 instrument of Chaos.
• One Seeker that is not equipped with an instrument of Chaos can be equipped with 1 daemonic icon.

ABILITIES

Daemonic (pg 56)

Unholy Speed: Add 1 to charge rolls made for this unit.

FACTION KEYWORDS: CHAOS, LEGIONES DAEMONICA, SLAANESH
KEYWORDS: CAVALRY, DAEMON, CORE, DAEMONETTES, SEEKERS

Sat astride swift Steeds of Slaanesh, Seekers pursue their mortal prey with obsessive delight. Even the fastest of mortal vehicles cannot outpace these vicious entities, while those who stand and fight soon find their ranks smashed asunder by charging shock-cavalry drawn from the darkest depths of nightmare.

HELLFLAYER

4 POWER

No.	Name	M	WS	BS	S	T	W	A	Ld	DSv
1	Hellflayer	14"	3+	3+	4	5	7	8	8	4+/4+

A Hellflayer is equipped with: lashes of torment; bladed axle; piercing claws; Seeker tongues.

WEAPON	RANGE	TYPE	S	AP	D	ABILITIES
Lashes of torment	6"	Assault 6	4	-1	1	-
Bladed axle	Melee	Melee	+2	-2	2	Malefic 4
Piercing claws	Melee	Melee	User	-2	1	-
Seeker tongues	Melee	Melee	4	0	1	Malefic 4

ABILITIES

Daemonic (pg 56)

Evasive Speed: Each time a ranged attack is made against this model, subtract 1 from that attack's hit roll.

Cutting Down the Foe: Each time this model is selected to fight, if it made a charge move this turn, change this model's bladed axle's ability to Malefic 6.

FACTION KEYWORDS: Chaos, Legiones Daemonica, Slaanesh
KEYWORDS: Vehicle, Daemon, Daemonettes, Hellflayer

Mortal myth has it that the Hellflayers of Slaanesh began as devices for mowing the gruesome pleasure-gardens of the Dark Prince's realm, but that their efficacy in war was soon proven when their wild Daemonette crews unleashed the whirl-bladed murder engines upon the battlefields of realspace.

SEEKER CHARIOT

4 POWER

No.	Name	M	WS	BS	S	T	W	A	Ld	DSv
1	Seeker Chariot	14"	3+	3+	4	5	7	8	8	4+/4+

A Seeker Chariot is equipped with: lashes of torment; piercing claws; Seeker tongues.

WEAPON	RANGE	TYPE	S	AP	D	ABILITIES
Lashes of torment	6"	Assault 6	4	-1	1	-
Piercing claws	Melee	Melee	User	-2	1	-
Seeker tongues	Melee	Melee	4	0	1	Malefic 4

ABILITIES

Daemonic (pg 56)

Evasive Speed: Each time a ranged attack is made against this model, subtract 1 from that attack's hit roll.

Scything Impact: Each time this model finishes a charge move:
- Roll four D6 for each enemy unit within Engagement Range of this model. For each 5+, that enemy unit suffers 1 mortal wound.
- Until the end of the turn, add 2 to this model's Attacks characteristic.

FACTION KEYWORDS: Chaos, Legiones Daemonica, Slaanesh
KEYWORDS: Vehicle, Daemon, Daemonettes, Seeker Chariot

Lightweight, swift and completely deadly, entire cavalcades of Seeker Chariots tear through the veil of reality to bear down upon the enemies of Slaanesh. Their crews race wildly to be first into battle, their eagerness for speed turning to wild bloodlust the moment their clattering charge crashes home.

EXALTED SEEKER CHARIOT

5 POWER

Some of this model's characteristics change as it suffers damage, as shown below:

No.	Name	M	WS	BS	S	T	W	A	Ld	DSv
1	Exalted Seeker Chariot (7+ wounds remaining)	14"	2+	3+	4	5	12	8	8	4+/4+
	Exalted Seeker Chariot (4-6 wounds remaining)	12"	3+	3+	4	5	N/A	7	8	4+/4+
	Exalted Seeker Chariot (1-3 wounds remaining)	10"	4+	3+	4	5	N/A	6	8	4+/4+

An Exalted Seeker Chariot is equipped with: lashes of torment; exalted Seeker tongues; piercing claws.

WEAPON	RANGE	TYPE	S	AP	D	ABILITIES
Lashes of torment	6"	Assault 6	4	-1	1	-
Exalted Seeker tongues	Melee	Melee	4	0	1	Malefic 8
Piercing claws	Melee	Melee	User	-2	1	-

ABILITIES

Daemonic (pg 56)

Evasive Speed: Each time a ranged attack is made against this model, subtract 1 from that attack's hit roll.

Scything Impact: Each time this model finishes a charge move:
- Roll four D6 for each enemy unit within Engagement Range of this model. For each 5+, that enemy unit suffers 1 mortal wound.
- Until the end of the turn, add 2 to this model's Attacks characteristic.

FACTION KEYWORDS: Chaos, Legiones Daemonica, Slaanesh
KEYWORDS: Vehicle, Daemon, Daemonettes, Exalted Seeker Chariot

Larger and more deadly than Seeker Chariots, these infernal engines offer the legions of Slaanesh comparatively heavyweight weapons to break their victims' lines. Multi-hued wheels emitting blurred skeins of hypnotic light, axles screaming like damned souls, they tear through the enemy ranks again and again.

THE BOOK OF THE WARP

Warp space is an eternal and endless realm of roiling possibility and nightmarish dreamscapes, inhabited by every manner of supernatural entity mortal hearts and minds can conceive. It is a place of seething formless wastes haunted by carrion entities, of conjured realms and manifest deities. More than simply the animate will of the four true Dark Gods inhabits this infernal infinity.

In this section you will find the following rules:

NOCTIC DISCIPLINE (PG 124)

If your army includes Be'lakor, or you are using his Army of Renown, models in your army can be given additional psychic powers from the Noctic discipline. These represent the arcane lore and particular talents of each individual psyker. You can find out more about psychic powers in the Warhammer 40,000 Core Book.

DATASHEETS (PG 125-127)

This section is essential to all Chaos Daemons players regardless of preferred play style, containing as it does the datasheets for remaining **LEGIONES DAEMONICA** units which are not dedicated specifically to one of the Dark Gods. Each datasheet describes, among other things, the profiles of its models, the wargear they can be equipped with and the abilities they have. You can find out more about datasheets in the Warhammer 40,000 Core Book.

ARMY OF RENOWN: DISCIPLES OF BE'LAKOR (PG 128)

If your army includes Be'lakor, you can choose to use these Army of Renown rules for it. This army can also include units from *Codex: Chaos Space Marines*.

DISCIPLES OF BE'LAKOR STRATAGEMS (PG 129)

If you are using the Disciples of Be'lakor Army of Renown, you have access to these Stratagems and can spend Command points to use them during your battles.

ARMY OF RENOWN

An Army of Renown is a specialised force that has earned fame or infamy across the 41st Millennium, the experience of which has given its warriors unique skills to use on the battlefield.

An Army of Renown is a variant army list for a particular Faction in Warhammer 40,000 that is themed around a particular disposition of forces. Each imposes certain restrictions on what units can be included, but it also grants access to a wider range of rules such as Stratagems, Relics, etc. to reflect that Army of Renown's unique methods of waging war in the 41st Millennium.

If you wish for your army to become an Army of Renown, it must first adhere to all the restrictions laid out for that Army of Renown, it must be Battle-forged and it must not include any Specialist Detachments. You can then make a note in the Army Faction section of your army roster of which Army of Renown your army is. Some, or all the units in an Army of Renown then gain the benefits listed, such as new keywords, abilities, Stratagems, etc. Note that your army does not automatically become an Army of Renown just because it happens to abide by the restrictions – you must choose for it to be an Army of Renown.

CRUSADE ARMY OF RENOWN

You can use any of the rules listed in an Army of Renown to make a Crusade Army of Renown when you start a Crusade force. In this case, the Restrictions and Benefits apply to your entire Crusade force – replace all instances of 'army' listed in the Restrictions and Benefits sections to instead say 'Crusade force', and make a note in the Crusade Faction section of your Order of Battle of which Army of Renown your Crusade force is. Note that means that certain units can never be added to your Order of Battle; but it will result in a particularly focused and themed collection. Whenever you select a Crusade force from such an Order of Battle, it must be Battle-forged and cannot include any Specialist Detachments.

NOCTIC DISCIPLINE

Before the battle, generate the psychic powers for **Psyker** models in your army that know powers from the Noctic discipline using the table below. You can either roll one D6 to generate each power randomly (re-rolling duplicate results), or you can select which powers the **Psyker** model knows.

1. SHROUDED STEP

A black fume envelops the psyker's allies. It flows across the battlefield before coalescing into a roiling darkness from which they then emerge.

Blessing: *Shrouded Step* has a warp charge value of 6. If manifested, select one friendly **Legiones Daemonica Infantry** or **Disciples of Be'lakor Infantry** unit within 18" of this **Psyker**. Remove that unit from the battlefield and set it up anywhere on the battlefield that is more than 9" from any enemy models.

2. WREATHED IN SHADES

The psyker draws from the warp a churning mass of damned shades, abandoned worshippers of Be'lakor now doomed to conceal and protect his current servants.

Blessing: *Wreathed in Shades* has a warp charge value of 7. If manifested, select one friendly **Legiones Daemonica** or **Disciples of Be'lakor** unit (excluding **Monster** and **Vehicle** units) within 12" of this **Psyker**. Until the start of your next Psychic phase, enemy models cannot target that unit with ranged weapons unless that unit is the closest eligible target to the firing model or it is within 12" of the firing model.

3. PALL OF DESPAIR

The psyker draws forth every bleak imagining and hopeless terror their victims have ever felt, drowning their enemies' minds in misery until they barely have the will to keep breathing.

Malediction: *Pall of Despair* has a warp charge value of 7. If manifested, select one enemy unit within 18" of and visible to this **Psyker**. Roll 3D6: if the result is greater than that unit's Leadership characteristic, select one of the following to apply to that unit:

- Until the start of your next Psychic phase, if that unit has any aura abilities, select one of those abilities: that unit loses that ability.
- Until the start of your next Psychic phase, that unit cannot perform actions (see the Warhammer 40,000 Core Book). If that unit is currently performing an action, it immediately fails.
- Until the start of your next Psychic phase, in the Fight phase, that unit is not eligible to fight that phase until after all eligible units from your army have done so.

4. VOIDSLIVERS

Reaching with their mind into the darkest depths of the void, the psyker draws forth crystallised slivers of terror, misery and loss before hurling them in a storm at the foe. The darts rip through soul-matter, while leaving the enemy's corporeal forms lifeless but seemingly unharmed.

Witchfire: *Voidslivers* has a warp charge value of 5. If manifested, select one enemy model within 12" of and visible to this **Psyker**. Draw a line between any part of this **Psyker**'s base and any part of the selected model's base (or hull):

- The selected model's unit suffers 1 mortal wound (if that unit contains 11 or more models, it suffers D3 mortal wounds instead).
- Every other enemy unit that this line passes over or through suffers 1 mortal wound (if any of those units contains 11 or more models, it suffers D3 mortal wounds instead).

5. PENUMBRAL CURSE

The psyker curses the blades of the enemy, causing them to become as insubstantial as shadows, and to pass harmlessly through the very foes they should have hewn in two.

Malediction: *Penumbral Curse* has a warp charge value of 7. If manifested, select one enemy unit within 18" of this **Psyker**. Until the start of your next Psychic phase, each time a model in that unit makes a melee attack, subtract 1 from that attack's wound roll and worsen the Armour Penetration characteristic of that attack by 1.

6. BETRAYING SHADES

Falling to the psyker's whispered blandishments, the enemy's very shadows turn upon them, clawing and ripping at the mortal forms that cast them.

Witchfire: *Betraying Shades* has a warp charge value of 6. If manifested, select one enemy unit within 18" of and visible to this **Psyker**.

- Select up to 6 models in that unit, and add together the unmodified Attacks characteristics of those models.
- Roll a number of D6 equal to the total (for example, if five of the selected models had an Attacks characteristic of 2, and one had an Attacks characteristic of 3, you would roll thirteen D6).
- If the result of the Psychic test was 11 or more, add 1 to each dice result.
- For each roll of 6+, that unit suffers 1 mortal wound (to a maximum of 6 mortal wounds).

BE'LAKOR

21 POWER

Some of this model's characteristics change as it suffers damage, as shown below:

No.	NAME	M	WS	BS	S	T	W	A	Ld	DSv
1	Be'lakor (11+ wounds remaining)	12"	2+	2+	8	7	20	6	9	4+/4+
	Be'lakor (6-10 wounds remaining)	8"	2+	2+	7	7	N/A	5	9	4+/4+
	Be'lakor (1-5 wounds remaining)	6"	2+	2+	6	7	N/A	4	9	4+/4+

Be'lakor is equipped with: the Blade of Shadows. Your army can only include one **BE'LAKOR** model.

WEAPON	RANGE	TYPE	S	AP	D	ABILITIES
The Blade of Shadows						Each time an attack is made with this weapon, select one of the profiles below to make that attack with.
- Sweeping strike	Melee	Melee	User	-3	1	Each time an attack is made with this weapon profile, make 2 hit rolls instead of 1.
- Piercing strike	Melee	Melee	+4	-4	D3+3	Each time an attack is made with this weapon profile, invulnerable saving throws cannot be made against that attack.

ABILITIES

Daemonic (pg 56)

Shadow Form:
- Each time an attack is made against this model, your opponent cannot re-roll the hit roll.
- Each time an attack is made against this model, subtract 1 from that attack's hit roll and wound roll.
- Each time a ranged attack is made against this model, subtract 1 from that attack's Damage characteristic (to a minimum of 1).

Lord of Torment (Aura): While an enemy unit is within 6" of this model, subtract 1 from the Leadership characteristic of models in that unit, and each time a Combat Attrition test is taken for that unit, subtract 1 from that Combat Attrition test.

The Dark Master (Aura): While a friendly **LEGIONES DAEMONICA** or **DISCIPLES OF BE'LAKOR** unit (excluding **VEHICLE** units) is within 6" of this model, each time a model in that unit makes an attack, re-roll a hit roll of 1.

Spiteful Jealousy: If your army is Battle-forged, you cannot include this model in a Detachment that includes any other **DAEMON PRINCE** models. Each time this model makes an attack against a **DAEMON PRINCE** model, you can re-roll the hit roll and you can re-roll the wound roll.

PSYKER

This model can attempt to manifest two psychic powers in your Psychic phase and attempt to deny one psychic power in your opponent's Psychic phase. It knows *Smite* and two psychic powers from the Noctic discipline (pg 124).

FACTION KEYWORDS: **CHAOS, LEGIONES DAEMONICA, KHORNE, TZEENTCH, NURGLE, SLAANESH**
KEYWORDS: **MONSTER, CHARACTER, DAEMON, PSYKER, WARP LOCUS, SUPREME COMMANDER, FLY, DAEMON PRINCE, BE'LAKOR**

Few warp entities are as mighty or as insidious as Be'lakor. Wreathed in shadow and dancing witchlight, the Dark Master spreads terror and torment to all who behold him. Every blow of his Blade of Shadows leaves the hollow husks of slain enemies sprawled in its wake – just more victims lost to the encroaching darkness.

WARLORD TRAIT

If Be'lakor gains a Warlord Trait, he must have the one shown below:

SHADOW LORD

Be'lakor is a nexus for occluding shadow, veiling his enemies' sight and leaving them helpless to parry the vicious blows of his servants both mortal and daemonic.

In your Command phase, select one friendly **LEGIONES DAEMONICA CORE** or **DISCIPLES OF BE'LAKOR** unit (excluding **VEHICLE** units) within 9" of this **WARLORD**. Until the start of your next Command phase, each time a model in that unit makes an attack, you can re-roll the hit roll.

DAEMON PRINCE OF CHAOS

7 POWER

No.	Name	M	WS	BS	S	T	W	A	Ld	DSv
1	Daemon Prince of Chaos	8"	2+	2+	7	6	8	6	10	5+/4+

A Daemon Prince of Chaos is equipped with: hellforged sword; malefic talons.

WEAPON	RANGE	TYPE	S	AP	D	ABILITIES
Daemonic axe	Melee	Melee	+2	-2	3	-
Hellforged sword	Melee	Melee	+1	-3	3	-
Malefic talons	Melee	Melee	User	-1	2	Each time the bearer fights, it makes 1 additional attack with this weapon.

OTHER WARGEAR	ABILITIES
Wings	The bearer has a Move characteristic of 12" and the **FLY** keyword.

WARGEAR OPTIONS

- This model's hellforged sword can be replaced with one of the following: 1 daemonic axe; 1 malefic talons.
- This model can be equipped with 1 wings **(Power Rating +2)**.

ABILITIES

Daemonic (pg 56)

Prince of Chaos (Aura): While a friendly LEGIONES DAEMONICA <ALLEGIANCE> CORE unit is within 6" of this model, each time a model in that unit makes an attack, re-roll a hit roll of 1.

Daemonic Rewards:
- If this model has the KHORNE keyword, add 1 to this model's Strength characteristic and add 2 to this model's Attacks characteristic.
- If this model has the TZEENTCH keyword, it can attempt to manifest one additional psychic power in your Psychic phase and knows one additional psychic power from the Pandaemoniac discipline.
- If this model has the NURGLE keyword, add 1 to this model's Toughness characteristic.
- If this model has the SLAANESH keyword, add 2" to this model's Move characteristic.

PSYKER

If this model has the TZEENTCH, NURGLE or SLAANESH keyword, it has the PSYKER keyword. If this model is a PSYKER it can attempt to manifest one psychic power in your Psychic phase, and attempt to deny one psychic power in your opponent's Psychic phase. It knows *Smite* and:
- If this model has the TZEENTCH keyword, its knows one psychic power from the Pandaemoniac discipline (pg 78).
- If this model has the NURGLE keyword, its knows one psychic power from the Warprot discipline (pg 92).
- If this model has the SLAANESH keyword, its knows one psychic power from the Soulstain discipline (pg 108).

FACTION KEYWORDS: CHAOS, LEGIONES DAEMONICA, <ALLEGIANCE>
KEYWORDS: CHARACTER, MONSTER, DAEMON, DAEMON PRINCE

Blessed with apotheosis from mortal to daemonic form, a Daemon Prince is a monstrous entity well used to commanding cruel legions in battle. Their supernatural gifts are many and varied, from sorcerous powers to diseased fortitude, warp-forged weaponry, unholy swiftness or burning inner furnaces of unquenchable rage.

SOUL GRINDER

10 POWER

Some of this model's characteristics change as it suffers damage, as shown below:

No.	NAME	M	WS	BS	S	T	W	A	Ld	DSv
1	Soul Grinder (9+ wounds remaining)	8"	3+	3+	8	8	16	5	7	5+/4+
	Soul Grinder (5-8 wounds remaining)	6"	4+	4+	8	8	N/A	5	7	5+/4+
	Soul Grinder (1-4 wounds remaining)	4"	5+	5+	8	8	N/A	5	7	5+/4+

A Soul Grinder is equipped with: harvester cannon; phlegm bombardment; iron claw; warpsword.

WEAPON	RANGE	TYPE	S	AP	D	ABILITIES
Harvester cannon	36"	Heavy 6	7	-1	2	-
Phlegm bombardment	36"	Heavy D6	8	-2	3	Blast
Iron claw	Melee	Melee	x2	-3	D6	-
Warpclaw	Melee	Melee	User	-2	2	Malefic 4
Warpsword	Melee	Melee	User	-3	D3+3	Malefic 2

WARGEAR OPTIONS

• This model's warpsword can be replaced with 1 warpclaw.

ABILITIES

Daemonic (pg 56)

Explodes: When this model is destroyed, roll one D6 before removing it from play. On a 6 it explodes, and each unit within 6" suffers D3 mortal wounds.

Daemonic Rewards:
• If this model has the **KHORNE** keyword, add 2 to this model's Attacks characteristic.
• If this model has the **TZEENTCH** keyword, change this model's Daemonic Save characteristic to 4+/4+.
• If this model has the **NURGLE** keyword, add 1 to this model's Toughness characteristic.
• If this model has the **SLAANESH** keyword, add 4" to this model's Move characteristic.

FACTION KEYWORDS: CHAOS, LEGIONES DAEMONICA, <ALLEGIANCE>
KEYWORDS: VEHICLE, DAEMON, SOUL GRINDER

Daemons desperate to gain power above their station may strike an unwise bargain with the master of the Forge of Souls. Thus are they remade into the hulking war engines known as Soul Grinders, and given the might to crush and blast all in their path – for a steep, and ultimately never-ending price…

DISCIPLES OF BE'LAKOR

It pleases the Dark Master to be worshipped as a daemonic deity, and to have his devotees fight and die on his behalf. There is no shortage of heretics willing to do so. After all, Be'lakor promises great rewards to those who serve him, and he has had millennia to perfect his lies…

Heretic Astartes, mortal cultists and nightmarish daemons – all serve Be'lakor and fight amongst the ranks of his Disciples. These fanatical heretics have forsaken the Dark Gods in favour of worshipping their first and greatest champion, whom many of them view as at least a demigod in his own right. Be'lakor's servants manifest echoes of his own supernatural powers, exuding terrifying auras or flickering in and out of reality amidst cowls of animate shadow. Yet the price of power is eternal servitude, for Be'lakor will suffer no rival.

The Disciples of Be'lakor is an Army of Renown (pg 123).

RESTRICTIONS

- All units in your army (excluding **UNALIGNED** units) must have the **CHAOS** keyword.
- Your **WARLORD** must be **BE'LAKOR**. With the exception of **BE'LAKOR**, your army cannot include any named characters or **DAEMON PRINCE** models.
- Your army cannot include any **GREATER DAEMON**, **DAEMON ENGINE**, **WORLD EATERS**, **THOUSAND SONS**, **DEATH GUARD**, **EMPEROR'S CHILDREN**, **CHAOS KNIGHTS** (excluding one **HOUSE KORVAX** unit as described under Benefits), **TITANICUS TRAITORIS**, **KHORNE BERZERKERS**, **RUBRIC MARINES**, **PLAGUE MARINES** or **NOISE MARINES** units.
- You cannot include more **CULTISTS** units than other **TRAITORIS ASTARTES INFANTRY** units (excluding **CHARACTER** units) in each Detachment in your army.
- You cannot include **LEGIONES DAEMONICA** units and **TRAITORIS ASTARTES** units in the same Detachment.
- **TRAITORIS ASTARTES** units in your army cannot be given any Marks of Chaos (see *Codex: Chaos Space Marines*).
- If you upgrade a **HOUSE KORVAX DISCIPLES OF BE'LAKOR** unit to have a Favour of the Dark Gods, it must be Blessing of the Dark Master (see *Codex: Chaos Knights*).
- You cannot include a second **LEGIONES DAEMONICA** unit in your army with the same Allegiance keyword unless your army also includes at least one **LEGIONES DAEMONICA** unit with each of the other Allegiance keywords. You cannot include a third **LEGIONES DAEMONICA** unit in your army with the same Allegiance keyword until your army also includes at least two **LEGIONES DAEMONICA** units with each of the other Allegiance keywords, and so on. **BE'LAKOR** is excluded when considering this restriction.

*Example: If your army includes a **LEGIONES DAEMONICA KHORNE** unit, you cannot add a second **LEGIONES DAEMONICA KHORNE** unit to your army unless your army also includes one **LEGIONES DAEMONICA TZEENTCH** unit, one **LEGIONES DAEMONICA NURGLE** unit and one **LEGIONES DAEMONICA SLAANESH** unit.*

BENEFITS

- All units in your army (excluding **UNALIGNED** and **BUILDING** units) gain the **DISCIPLES OF BE'LAKOR** Faction keyword.
- All units in your army with the **TRAITORIS ASTARTES** Faction keyword (excluding **CULTISTS** units) gain the **LEGION DISCIPLES** keyword.
- All units in your army with the **LEGIONES DAEMONICA** Faction keyword gain the **DAEMONIC DISCIPLES** keyword.
- Your army can include up to one Super-heavy Auxiliary Detachment that contains one **CHAOS KNIGHTS HOUSE KORVAX** unit. That unit gains the **AGENT OF CHAOS** keyword. This Detachment still gains all the Detachment abilities available to **HOUSE KORVAX** units as listed in *Codex: Chaos Knights*, even though Super-heavy Auxiliary Detachments do not normally gain any Detachment abilities.
- All Troops units in your army gain the Objective Secured ability (see the Warhammer 40,000 Core Book).
- If a Detachment contains any units with the **TRAITORIS ASTARTES** Faction keyword, such a Detachment never counts as a Legion Detachment (see *Codex: Chaos Space Marines*), and you cannot use any Legion-specific Stratagems, Relics, Warlord Traits or psychic powers (e.g. even if such a Detachment only contained **TRAITORIS ASTARTES** units with the **BLACK LEGION** keyword, it would not count as a Legion Detachment, you cannot use Black Legion Stratagems, you cannot give a **BLACK LEGION CHARACTER** model a Black Legion Warlord Trait, etc.).
- You have access to the Disciples of Be'lakor Stratagems (pg 129).
- **DISCIPLES OF BE'LAKOR PSYKER** units from your army can generate their psychic powers from the Noctic discipline (pg 124).
- **LEGION DISCIPLES** units in your army cannot have a Legion Trait, but instead gain the Disciples of Shadows ability (see below).
- Your army can use the Warp Storm ability (pg 57) even if it includes any **TRAITORIS ASTARTES** units.

DISCIPLES OF SHADOWS

Fanatical worship of Be'lakor affords his disciples a fragment of his unnatural obfuscatory powers.

- Each time a Combat Attrition test is taken for this unit, add 1 to that Combat Attrition test.
- Each time a ranged attack is made against this unit, if the attacker is more than 12" away, subtract 1 from that attack's hit roll.

DISCIPLES OF BE'LAKOR STRATAGEMS

If your army is the Disciples of Be'lakor, you have access to these Stratagems, and can spend CPs to use them.

SHADOW PACT — 1CP

Disciples of Be'lakor – Battle Tactic Stratagem

Though they have forsaken the Chaos Gods in favour of Be'lakor, the Dark Master's mortal Disciples can still draw temporary power from offering soul-pacts to the daemons who fight in his service.

Use this Stratagem in your Command phase. Select one CHAOS UNDIVIDED LEGION DISCIPLES INFANTRY unit from your army (see *Codex: Chaos Space Marines*), then select one of the pacts below. Until the start of your next Command phase, that unit has that pact:

- **Pact of Blood:** Add 1 to the Attacks characteristic of models in that unit.
- **Pact of Fate:** Models in that unit have a 5+ invulnerable save.
- **Pact of Plague:** Add 1 to the Toughness characteristic of models in that unit.
- **Pact of Excess:** Add 1" to the Move characteristic of models in that unit. In addition, add 1 to Advance and charge rolls made for that unit.

DAEMONIC BOON — 1CP

Disciples of Be'lakor – Battle Tactic Stratagem

Mortal and daemon alike fight side by side in the service of the Dark Master, the energies of the immaterium flowing through and empowering both.

Use this Stratagem at the start of the Fight phase, when a LEGION DISCIPLES unit (excluding VEHICLE units) from your army that is within 6" of a friendly DAEMONIC DISCIPLES unit is selected to fight. Until the end of the phase:

- Add 1 to the Strength characteristic of models in that LEGION DISCIPLES unit.
- Each time a model in that LEGION DISCIPLES unit makes a melee attack, an unmodified hit roll of 6 automatically wounds the target.

LEGIONS OF SHADE — 1CP

Disciples of Be'lakor – Strategic Ploy Stratagem

The Disciples of Be'lakor flow around and through their enemies like wraiths from the depths of the warp.

Use this Stratagem at the start of your Movement phase or at the start of your Charge phase. Select one DISCIPLES OF BE'LAKOR unit from your army. Until the end of the phase, models in that unit can move horizontally through enemy models (they cannot finish a move on top of another model, or its base).

MORTAL BOON — 2CP

Disciples of Be'lakor – Strategic Ploy Stratagem

Be'lakor's daemonic hosts draw strength from the mortals fighting beside them, anchoring themselves in realspace by sinking ephemeral talons into the soul-stuff of their allies.

Use this Stratagem at the start of the Morale phase. Select one DAEMONIC DISCIPLES unit from your army that is within 6" of a friendly LEGION DISCIPLES unit (excluding VEHICLE units). Until the end of the phase, each time a Morale test is taken for that DAEMONIC DISCIPLES unit, it is automatically passed and counts as having been passed with an unmodified roll of a 1.

DRAUGHT OF TERROR — 1CP

Disciples of Be'lakor – Strategic Ploy Stratagem

The swelling fear of their mortal prey serves as an intoxicating elixir to Be'lakor's daemonic followers, each draught reknitting sundered warpflesh or drawing fresh and hungry entities through the veil to war.

Use this Stratagem at the start of the Morale phase. Select one DAEMONIC DISCIPLES unit from your army. Until the end of the phase, that unit gains the following ability:

Draught of Terror (Aura): While an enemy unit is within 6" of this unit, each time a model flees from that enemy unit:

- If any models in this unit have lost any wounds, one model in this unit regains 1 lost wound.
- If no models in this unit have lost any wounds, but it is not at its Starting Strength, one of this unit's destroyed models is returned with 1 wound remaining.
- Models returned to this unit in this way can only be set up within Engagement Range of enemy units that are already within Engagement Range of this unit.

BLESSING OF BE'LAKOR — 2CP

Disciples of Be'lakor – Epic Deed Stratagem

In the instant the enemy's blows fall, Be'lakor's blessings render his worshippers as insubstantial as shadow.

Use this Stratagem in any phase, when a saving throw made for a DISCIPLES OF BE'LAKOR model from your army against an attack is failed. If BE'LAKOR is on the battlefield, the Damage characteristic of that attack is changed to 0.

CRUSADE RULES

In this section you'll find additional rules for playing Crusade battles with Chaos Daemons, such as Agendas, Battle Traits and Crusade Relics that are bespoke to Chaos Daemons units. You can find out more about Crusade armies in the Warhammer 40,000 Core Book.

This section contains the following additional rules:

AGENDAS (PG 131)

LEGIONES DAEMONICA units can attempt to achieve unique Agendas in Crusade battles. These reflect the unique goals and methods of these armies. You can find out more about Agendas in Crusade mission packs, such as that presented in the Warhammer 40,000 Core Book.

REQUISITIONS (PG 132)

Chaos Daemons armies have access to a number of additional Requisitions, suited to their methods of waging war.

LOCI OF THE GODS (PG 133)

LEGIONES DAEMONICA CHARACTER units can gain these unique Battle Honours, giving them potent auras to empower their nearby allies.

THE GREAT GAME (PG 134-135)

On these pages you will find a series of rules allowing LEGIONES DAEMONICA units from your army to further the cause of their particular Dark Gods. Every success for these units will tip the balance of power in the warp, granting new abilities to whichever of the Dark Gods is in ascendancy.

FAVOURED REWARDS (PG 136)

GREATER DAEMON units can gain Lesser, Greater or Exalted Rewards based on their god's performance in the Great Game.

PSYCHIC FORTITUDES (PG 138)

When a LEGIONES DAEMONICA CHARACTER PSYKER unit gains a Battle Honour, they can be given a Psychic Fortitude chosen from this section.

BATTLE TRAITS (PG 139)

When a LEGIONES DAEMONICA CHARACTER model gains a Battle Trait, they can be given one of the ones found in this section instead of one from the Warhammer 40,000 Core Book.

CRUSADE RELICS (PG 140-141)

In addition to the Crusade Relics presented in the Warhammer 40,000 Core Book, LEGIONES DAEMONICA CHARACTER models can quest for one of the Crusade Relics described here.

SHOWCASE CRUSADE ARMY (PG 142-143)

Here you will find a beautifully painted Khorne Daemons Crusade army painted by Toby Liddiard, complete with a commentary on the composition, theme and characters of that force.

Ultramarines Hellblasters plant their feet and stand firm against the charge of the Blood Hunt. Yet no mere mortal warriors can hold back the fury of Skarbrand and Karanak and their baying hounds, not even the post-human warriors of the Adeptus Astartes.

AGENDAS

If your Crusade army includes any Legiones Daemonica units, you can select an Agenda from the Chaos Daemons Agendas listed below. This is a new category of Agendas, and follows all the normal rules for Agendas (for example, when you select Agendas, you cannot choose more than one Chaos Daemons Agenda).

 ## WORTHY TROPHIES
Chaos Daemons Agenda

Some mortal skulls are more worthy than others.

At the start of the battle, identify which 3 models in your opponent's army have the highest Wounds characteristics – these are trophy targets (if any units are tied, you can select which of those will be trophy targets). Each time a trophy target is destroyed by a melee attack made by a **Legiones Daemonica Khorne** model from your army, that **Legiones Daemonica Khorne** model's unit gains 2 experience points.

 ## FIRES OF TZEENTCH
Chaos Daemons Agenda

To the daemons of Tzeentch, unleashing the corrupting and mutating powers of sorcery is a victory in and of itself.

Keep a Fires of Tzeentch tally for each **Legiones Daemonica Tzeentch Psyker** unit from your army. Add 1 to a unit's Fires of Tzeentch tally each time it does any of the following:

- Manifests the *Smite* psychic power.
- Manifests a Witchfire psychic power.
- Destroys an enemy unit in your Psychic phase.

At the end of the battle, the unit in your army that has the highest Fires of Tzeentch tally gains 3 experience points, the unit with the second highest Fires of Tzeentch tally gains 2 experience points, and the unit with the third highest Fires of Tzeentch tally gains 1 experience point. If two or more units are tied, you can select which unit has the highest tally from those tied units.

 ## SEED THE GARDEN
Chaos Daemons Agenda

Where Nurgle's daemons wreak their butchery, the heaped slain swiftly fester and bloom with new life pleasing to the Plague God.

At the start of the battle, divide the battlefield into four even quarters. Keep a Seed the Garden tally for each **Legiones Daemonica Nurgle** unit from your army. The first time an enemy unit is destroyed in each battlefield quarter by a **Legiones Daemonica Nurgle** unit from your army, add 1 to that unit's Seed the Garden tally.

At the end of the battle, each unit gains 2 experience points for each mark on that unit's Seed the Garden tally.

 ## SAVAGE EXCESS
Chaos Daemons Agenda

Though despising the crude butchery of Khorne's daemons, those of Slaanesh delight in sudden explosions of elegant savagery.

Keep a Savage Excess tally for each **Legiones Daemonica Slaanesh** unit from your army. Add 1 to a unit's Savage Excess tally each time:

- A model in that unit makes a melee attack that destroys an enemy unit in the same turn that model made a charge move or performed a Heroic Intervention.
- A model in that unit makes a melee attack that destroys an enemy unit that made a charge move or performed a Heroic Intervention this turn.

At the end of the battle, the unit in your army that has the highest Savage Excess tally gains 3 experience points, the unit with the second highest Savage Excess tally gains 2 experience points, and the unit with the third highest Savage Excess tally gains 1 experience point. If two or more units are tied, you can select which unit has the highest tally from those tied units.

 ## CORRUPT ICONS
Chaos Daemons Agenda

The daemons of Chaos despoil that which their foes hold precious.

Keep a Corruption tally for each **Legiones Daemonica** unit in your army. Add 1 to a unit's Corruption tally each time it destroys an enemy unit that started the turn within 3" of an objective marker and each time it completes the Corrupt Icons action (see below).

If you selected this Agenda, **Legiones Daemonica Icon** units from your army can attempt the following action:

Corrupt Icons (Action): At the end of your Movement phase, one **Legiones Daemonica Icon** unit from your army within range of an objective marker that is not wholly within your deployment zone, can start to perform this action. A unit cannot start to perform this action while there are any enemy units (excluding **Aircraft** units) within range of the same objective marker. This action is completed at the start of your next Command phase.

At the end of the battle, each unit gains a number of experience points equal to their Corruption tally.

REQUISITIONS

A Crusade army that includes any LEGIONES DAEMONICA units can spend Requisition points (RPs) on any of the following Requisitions in addition to those presented in the Warhammer 40,000 Core Book.

EXALTED DAEMON   1RP

As the greatest daemons slaughter their way across reality, so they grow in power, earning rewards from their patron deity and learning how to shape realspace to augment their forms.

Purchase this Requisition when a GREATER DAEMON model from your Crusade force gains the Battle-hardened, Heroic or Legendary rank. That model is upgraded to be exalted.

- The rules for upgrading BLOODTHIRSTER models to be exalted can be found on page 62.
- The rules for upgrading LORD OF CHANGE models to be exalted can be found on page 76.
- The rules for upgrading GREAT UNCLEAN ONE models to be exalted can be found on page 90.
- The rules for upgrading KEEPER OF SECRETS models to be exalted can be found on page 106.

Increase this model's Power Rating accordingly and make a note on its Crusade card. You cannot purchase this Requisition if doing so would cause your total Power Level to exceed your Crusade force's Supply Limit.

DARK GAMBIT   1RP

The Great Game of the Dark Gods plays out across the battlefields of realspace, their servants taking great risks to claim the mightiest prizes. Should a daemonic general achieve some audacious victory, this reflects well upon the cause of their patron deity. Of course, the reverse is also true…

Purchase this Requisition before any battle, while you are influencing the Great Game (pg 134). If you win that battle, the god that shares an Allegiance keyword with your WARLORD gains D6 Ascendancy points (pg 134) instead of D3. If you lose the battle, the god that shares an Allegiance keyword with your WARLORD gains no Ascendancy points after that battle.

MONSTROUS DUEL   1-3RP

The Greater Daemons of the Dark Gods are eternal rivals, and their battles with one another transcend both bonds of loyalty and the bounds of reality. With each clash, the victor furthers the cause of their patron deity while diminishing the influence of their rival's master.

Purchase this Requisition at any time, while you are influencing the Great Game (pg 134). Select two GREATER DAEMON models from your Order of Battle that do not share an Allegiance keyword. Select one of these models to be the victor and one of them to be the defeated. The god that shares an Allegiance keyword with the victor gains 1 Ascendancy point for each RP spent on this Requisition, and the Dark God who shares an Allegiance keyword with the defeated loses 1 Ascendancy point for each RP spent on this Requisition.

IGNOBLE DEFEAT   1RP

Should a daemon's essence spill from its corporeal form, a rival may seize the opportunity to ritually bind it into a weapon. While imprisoned, the trammelled daemon lends supernatural power to its wielder's blows, all the time planning its eventual escape.

Purchase this Requisition when an Out of Action test is failed for a LEGIONES DAEMONICA CHARACTER model from your army. That model is now considered to be bound. Select one GREATER DAEMON model from your Order of Battle to be the binder, then select one melee weapon that model is equipped with (this cannot be a Relic or a malefic weapon) for the selected LEGIONES DAEMONICA CHARACTER model to be bound into. While that model is bound, the selected melee weapon gains the relevant ability below:

- If the bound model is a KHORNE model, add 1 to the Strength characteristic of that weapon.
- If the bound model is a TZEENTCH model, improve the Armour Penetration characteristic of that weapon by 1.
- If the bound model is a NURGLE model, add 1 to the Damage characteristic of that weapon.
- If the bound model is a SLAANESH model, each time an attack is made with that weapon, an unmodified wound roll of 6 inflicts 1 mortal wound on the target in addition to any normal damage.

While a model is bound:

- It cannot be included on your army roster.
- Keep a Bound tally for that model. After each battle in which the binder was included on your army roster, add 1 to this tally.

GLORIOUS RETURN   2RP

When daemons break out of captivity, they are able to put their new-found experience to great use while plotting their revenge.

Purchase this Requisition after any battle, while a LEGIONES DAEMONICA CHARACTER model from your army is bound (see Ignoble Defeat, above):

- That model is no longer bound.
- That model gains 1 experience point for each mark on their Bound tally. That tally is then removed.

LOCI OF THE GODS

Loci of the Gods are a new type of Battle Honour that can be given to **Greater Daemon** or **Herald** units. Each time such a model from your army would gain a Battle Honour, you can instead choose for it to gain a Locus of the Gods, from those found below. Each model on your Order of Battle can only have one Locus of the Gods.

Each Locus is an aura ability. If the model that has this ability is a **Greater Daemon** model, this ability has a range of 6"; otherwise, it has a range of 3".

As with any Battle Honour, make a note on the model's Crusade card when it gains a Locus of the Gods, and its Crusade points increase as described in the Warhammer 40,000 Core Book.

LOCUS OF UNSTOPPABLE FURY (AURA)
This daemon is a wellspring of supernatural rage, a bellowing berserker whose mere presence catalyses its underlings to new heights of apoplectic savagery and crunching violence.

Khorne model only. While a friendly **Legiones Daemonica Khorne Core** unit is within range of this ability, each time a model in that unit makes a melee attack, an unmodified hit roll of 6 automatically wounds the target.

LOCUS OF DIABOLICAL PURPOSE (AURA)
Khorne daemons rarely pause in their slaughter, their insatiable desire to reap the skulls of their foes driving them onwards.

Khorne model only. While a friendly **Legiones Daemonica Khorne Core** unit is within range of this ability, each time that unit makes a consolidation move, models in that unit can move an additional 3".

LOCUS OF CONJURATION (AURA)
This daemon is a walking rift, a prismatic lens through which the sorcerous energies of the warp flows in waves. Nearby daemons of Tzeentch harness the endless outpouring of power and weave it into fresh and potent magicks to hurl at their foes.

Tzeentch model only. While a friendly **Legiones Daemonica Tzeentch Psyker** unit is within range of this ability, each time a Psychic test is taken for that unit, you can re-roll any or all dice rolls of 1-2.

LOCUS OF TRANSMOGRIFICATION (AURA)
Change eternal is amongst the greatest powers of the daemons of Tzeentch, and one this entity turns to its advantage. Blows fated to banish its minions change to become fumbling failures. Wounded daemonic forms alter their nature to become hale and undamaged. With one rippling change after another, victory for the foe transforms into crushing and inexplicable defeat.

Tzeentch model only. While a friendly **Legiones Daemonica Tzeentch Core** unit is within range of this ability, each time a model in that unit would lose a wound, roll one D6: on a 6, that wound is not lost.

LOCUS OF POXES UNCOUNTED (AURA)
Like a swift-spreading plague rampaging through a frightened crowd, or a raging fever sweeping over its delirious host, the daemonic foot soldiers of Nurgle flicker across the battlefield to manifest suddenly amidst victims who believed themselves safely out of reach.

Nurgle model only. While a friendly **Plaguebearers Core** unit is within range of this ability, you can re-roll charge rolls made for that unit.

LOCUS OF FOETID REGENERATION (AURA)
The daemons of Nurgle are tremendously hard to destroy, all the more so in the presence of this walking font of unclean fecundity. Bountiful waves of diseased vigour roll off the daemon, its grotesque generosity an echo of Nurgle's own that mends ruptured corporeal forms, reknits burst innards and thickens leathery flesh with fresh layers of rancid blubber.

Nurgle model only. While a friendly **Legiones Daemonica Nurgle Core** unit is within range of this ability, each time an attack is allocated to a model in that unit, subtract 1 from the Damage characteristic of that attack (to a minimum of 1).

LOCUS OF DELICATE EVISCERATION (AURA)
The daemons of Slaanesh gift blissful agonies to their victims, each bladed caress causing organs to rupture and bones to shatter amidst convulsions of overwhelming pleasure.

Slaanesh model only. While a friendly **Legiones Daemonica Slaanesh Core** unit is within range of this ability, each time a model in that unit makes a melee attack, improve the Armour Penetration characteristic of that attack by 1.

LOCUS OF UNNATURAL SWIFTNESS (AURA)
Slaaneshi daemons dance across the battlefield with a grace and speed that defies belief. Their obsessive desire to close with their mortal playthings causes the stuff of reality to yield before them, allowing the daemons to cavort directly into battle with shrieks of wild delight.

Slaanesh model only. While a friendly **Legiones Daemonica Slaanesh Core** unit is within range of this ability, that unit is eligible to charge, even if it Advanced in the same turn.

THE GREAT GAME

If your Crusade army includes any **LEGIONES DAEMONICA** units, you can track what influence their actions have on the Great Game, the eternal battle between the Dark Gods for primacy.

When you are creating your Order of Battle, if it includes any **LEGIONES DAEMONICA** units, you can also start to influence the Great Game. In order to influence the Great Game, you will need a Great Game tracker (see opposite). During your battles, if your army roster includes any **LEGIONES DAEMONICA** units, you will gain Ascendancy points for each of the four gods – Khorne, Tzeentch, Nurgle and Slaanesh. This tracker allows you to keep a tally of how many Ascendancy points each god has at present, growing their domains in the warp, and empowering their daemons. You can use this tracker to keep track of how many Ascendancy points each god is gaining during your games, as well as their overall total.

At the end of each battle, you will recalculate each god's total Ascendancy points and organise them into a hierarchy, from first to fourth position, with the god with the most Ascendancy points taking first place, the god with the second most Ascendancy points taking second place, and so on. Each god will gain new benefits (see opposite), based on their position in the Great Game, that you can use for **LEGIONES DAEMONICA** units on your Order of Battle with their Allegiance keyword. Do not delay in taking the opportunity to use these new benefits though – by the end of the subsequent battle, the balance of power may have shifted again.

After 8 battles, that round of the Great Game will be complete, and your forces will gain additional rewards depending on their god's final position in that round. At the end of each round, after gaining these rewards, each Dark God's Ascendancy points total will be reset based on their final position in the previous round (see The Next Round, opposite).

BEGINNING THE GREAT GAME

To begin the Great Game, each of the Dark Gods starts with the following number of Ascendancy points:

✵	**KHORNE**	4 Ascendancy points
♂	**TZEENTCH**	3 Ascendancy points
✿	**NURGLE**	2 Ascendancy points
♀	**SLAANESH**	1 Ascendancy point

The god with the most Ascendancy points is considered to be in first position, the god with the second most Ascendancy points in second position and so forth down to fourth position.

For the purposes of gaining rewards (see opposite), each god is also considered to have their own Allegiance keyword (e.g. Khorne has the **KHORNE** Allegiance keyword).

GAINING ASCENDANCY POINTS

At the end of each battle, each of the Dark Gods gains a number of Ascendancy points as described below, in the following order: Khorne, Tzeentch, Nurgle, Slaanesh.

- Each god gains D3 Ascendancy points.
- The god that shares an Allegiance keyword with your **WARLORD** gains 1 Ascendancy point. If you won the battle, they gain D3 Ascendancy points instead. (If **BE'LAKOR** was your **WARLORD** for that battle, all four gods gain 1 Ascendancy point each, or D3 each if you won that battle).

If, after a god has gained Ascendancy points, they have the same total as another god, the god you have just rolled for gains 1 additional Ascendancy point. After each god has gained Ascendancy points, make a note of their new position in the Great Game on your tracker.

THE POSITIONS

During each battle while you are tracking the Great Game, each Dark God will gain certain benefits for the units they share an Allegiance keyword with, based on their current position in the Great Game.

First Position
DOMINANT

While a Dark God is in first position in the Great Game:

- Add 1 to the Leadership characteristic of models in **Legiones Daemonica** units from your army that share an Allegiance keyword with that Dark God.
- Once per battle, you can use an Epic Deed Stratagem for 0CP if the unit selected for that Stratagem shares an Allegiance keyword with that Dark God.

Second Position
CLOSE RIVAL

While a Dark God is in second position in the Great Game:

- Add 1 to the Leadership characteristic of models in **Legiones Daemonica Icon** units from your army that share an Allegiance keyword with that Dark God.
- Once per battle, if your **Warlord** shares an Allegiance keyword with that Dark God, you can use the Command Re-roll Core Stratagem for 0CP.

Third Position
FALLING BEHIND

While a Dark God is in third position in the Great Game there are no additional abilities.

Fourth Position
BITTER JEALOUSY

While a Dark God is in fourth position in the Great Game:

- Subtract 1 from the Leadership characteristic of models in **Legiones Daemonica Icon** units from your army that share an Allegiance keyword with that Dark God.
- Each time a model in a **Legiones Daemonica** unit from your army that shares an Allegiance keyword with that Dark God makes an attack against an enemy unit that shares an Allegiance keyword with one of the Dark Gods in first, second or third position, you can re-roll the hit roll.

END OF A ROUND

After 8 battles, the first round of the Great Game will be complete. At the end of that battle, after determining the positions of each Dark God, they gain the following rewards:

First Position Rewards
- Every unit on your Order of Battle that shares an Allegiance keyword with this Dark God gains 3 experience points.
- You can select one **Greater Daemon** model on your Order of Battle that shares an Allegiance keyword with this Dark God. That model gains 1 Exalted Reward, 1 Greater Reward or 1 Lesser Reward from the Favoured Rewards on pages 136-137. Increase that unit's Crusade points total accordingly, as described in the Warhammer 40,000 Core Book.

Second Position Rewards
- Every unit on your Order of Battle that shares an Allegiance keyword with this Dark God gains 2 experience points.
- You can select one **Greater Daemon** model on your Order of Battle that shares an Allegiance keyword with this Dark God. That model gains 1 Greater Reward or 1 Lesser Reward from the Favoured Rewards on pages 136-137. Increase that unit's Crusade points total accordingly, as described in the Warhammer 40,000 Core Book.

Third Position Rewards
- Every unit on your Order of Battle that shares an Allegiance keyword with this Dark God gains 1 experience point.
- You can select one **Greater Daemon** model on your Order of Battle that shares an Allegiance keyword with this Dark God. That model gains 1 Lesser Reward from the Favoured Rewards on pages 136-137. Increase that unit's Crusade points total accordingly, as described in the Warhammer 40,000 Core Book.

Fourth Position Rewards
- There are no rewards for failure!

THE NEXT ROUND

Each Dark God starts the next round with the following number of Ascendancy points, based on their position in the previous round.

A new round then begins, following the same rules as the first.

FIRST	4 Ascendancy points
SECOND	3 Ascendancy points
THIRD	2 Ascendancy points
FOURTH	1 Ascendancy point

FAVOURED REWARDS

If your Crusade army includes any **GREATER DAEMON** units, they can gain Favoured Rewards, based on how well their Dark God performed in each round of the Great Game.

When instructed as part of the Great Game, **GREATER DAEMON** models on your Order of Battle can gain Favoured Rewards. To do so, select one of the entries on the appropriate table shown below or opposite: Lesser Rewards, Greater Rewards or Exalted Rewards. Each model can only gain each Favoured Reward once.

Each time you select a Favoured Reward, increase that model's Crusade points by 1 if it was a Lesser Reward, by 2 if it was a Greater Reward or by 3 if it was an Exalted Reward. Make a note of this on the model's Crusade card.

LESSER REWARDS

AVATAR OF UNREALITY
With every step this malign entity takes, the tortured stuff of reality writhes in agony.

Each time you make a Warp Storm roll (pg 58), if this model is on the battlefield, roll 1 additional D6.

EMPYRIC BEACON
This daemon shines like a beacon in the senses of others of its kind, drawing them inexorably to it.

This model has the **WARP LOCUS** keyword.

FAVOURED FOLLOWERS
This entity's aura of power and corruption draws potent entities into its thrall.

Each time you add a **LEGIONES DAEMONICA CORE** unit to your Order of Battle, you can remove up to 3 Ascendancy points from the Dark God that shares an Allegiance keyword with that unit. If you do so, that **LEGIONES DAEMONICA CORE** unit immediately gains a number of experience points equal to twice the number of Ascendancy points removed.

GREATER REWARDS

INFERNAL MARK

This daemon's patron deity has rewarded it with the merest spark of its divine power, rendering it all the more mighty.

- If this model is a **Tzeentch**, **Nurgle** or **Slaanesh** model, this model knows one additional psychic power from any discipline they have access to.
- If this model is a **Khorne** model, add 1 to that model's Strength characteristic.
- If this model is a **Tzeentch**, **Nurgle** or **Slaanesh** model, once per battle, after successfully manifesting a psychic power, this model can regain up to D3 lost wounds.
- If this model is a **Khorne** model, once per battle, after this model destroys an enemy **Character** model with a melee attack, this model can regain up to D3 lost wounds.

PORTAL KEEPER

Able to fashion metaphysical keys from the raw stuff of the warp, this cunning abomination unlocks the hidden angles and fractures in reality, throwing the doors to the sea of souls open wide.

- If this model is part of your Crusade force and you are the Attacker, then you start the battle with an additional 2 Command points.
- If this model is part of your Crusade force and you are using the Strategic Reserves rule, you can halve the Command point cost required to place units into Strategic Reserves (rounding down).

CROWN OF CONQUESTS

Whether manifesting as a crackling halo of power, an uneven crest of jagged horns, a circlet of burning brass or in some other unholy aspect, this dark gift infuses its keeper with the tormented souls of once-great mortal commanders. With the merest effort of will, the daemon can torture all manner of strategic insights out of its captive advisers.

- Once per battle, if this model is on the battlefield, you can use one Battle Tactic or Strategic Ploy Stratagem twice during the same phase, instead of only once.
- When you select this model to be your **Warlord**, you receive 1 additional Command point.

EXALTED REWARDS

SLAYER OF KINGS

A metaphysical weapon of incredible strength has been bestowed upon this daemon, a jealous thing of tremendous power that infuses its form and aids it in laying low the greatest foes.

- Each time this model makes an attack against an enemy **Warlord** or a unit that has a higher Crusade points total than this model, add 1 to that attack's wound roll.
- Each time this model destroys an enemy **Warlord** or a unit that has a higher Crusade points total than this model, it gains 1 additional experience point at the end of the battle.

LORD OF THE STORM

This blessing renders the daemon a veritable lightning rod for the energies of raging warp storms, allowing it to draw empyric phenomena to itself and focus their fury to a screaming point.

If this model is your **Warlord**, and the Warp Storm ability is in effect (pg 57), while this model is on the battlefield:

- Each time you make a Warp Storm roll, roll 1 additional D6.
- Once per battle round, when you use a Warp Storm effect, reduce the Warp Storm points cost of that effect by 1.

EXALTED SERVANT

Worshipful mortals depict this entity seated at its master's right hand, and whisper in fearful tones of how its matchless deeds have been rewarded by the greatest gifts of their chosen Dark God.

You can use the Exalted Daemon Requisition (pg 132) once for 0RP, but if you do so, you must select this model. If this model is not eligible for that Requisition it cannot be given this Reward. When you do so, that Requisition can be used to give this model an additional Exalted ability. Adjust that model's Power Rating as appropriate and make of note of this on its Crusade card. You cannot use this ability if doing so would cause your total Power Level to exceed your Crusade force's Supply Limit.

PSYCHIC FORTITUDES

When a **LEGIONES DAEMONICA CHARACTER PSYKER** unit gains a Psychic Fortitude, you can use one of the tables below. If you do so, roll one D6 and consult the appropriate table to randomly determine which Psychic Fortitude the unit gains, or choose a Psychic Fortitude from the appropriate table that tells the best narrative for your unit. All the normal rules for Psychic Fortitudes apply (e.g. a unit cannot have the same Psychic Fortitude more than once). As with any Battle Honour, make a note on the unit's Crusade card when it gains a Psychic Fortitude and increase its Crusade points accordingly, as described in the Warhammer 40,000 Core Book.

SLAANESH CHARACTER UNITS ONLY

D6	PSYCHIC FORTITUDE
1-2	**Feast of Rapturous Agonies** *Even as it unleashes the power of the warp upon its victims, this daemon also drinks in the emotional feedback of their blissful suffering to reinvigorate its corporeal form.* Each time this **PSYKER** successfully manifests a psychic power from the Soulstain discipline, it regains 1 lost wound.
3-4	**Phantasmagoric Fugue** *This daemon's curses come disguised behind blessed veils of enrapturing yet unattainable daydream.* Each time an enemy unit is affected by a Witchfire or Malediction psychic power manifested by this **PSYKER**, until the end of the turn, that unit cannot fire Overwatch or Set to Defend.
5-6	**Compulsive Conjuration** *The more this entity channels the power of the warp, the more obsessively it feels the need to do so again and again.* Each time this **PSYKER** attempts to manifest a psychic power from the Soulstain discipline, add 1 to the Psychic test.

NURGLE CHARACTER UNITS ONLY

D6	PSYCHIC FORTITUDE
1-2	**Festering Vitality** *Like an infected wound in the flesh of reality, the warp seeps through this daemon's being, leaving rotten resilience behind.* If this **PSYKER** successfully manifests any psychic powers in your Psychic phase, then until the end of the turn, add 1 to this **PSYKER**'s Toughness characteristic.
3-4	**Epidemicurean** *This entity tastes each new disease it manifests into realspace, refining the brew to perfect contagiousness.* Each time this **PSYKER** successfully manifests a psychic power, if the result of the Psychic test was 7+, after resolving that psychic power, the closest enemy unit within 6" suffers 1 mortal wound.
5-6	**Seeds of Ruin** *The daemon has been sown with spores from Nurgle's empyric garden, heightening its unclean powers.* Each time this **PSYKER** attempts to manifest a psychic power from the Warprot discipline, add 1 to the Psychic test.

TZEENTCH CHARACTER UNITS ONLY

D6	PSYCHIC FORTITUDE
1	**Ninefold Mantra** *This daemon's mind has been expanded with the secret ninefold mantra, that quells all sorcerous flames except those of the Changer of the Ways.* Each time this **PSYKER** attempts to Deny the Witch, a Deny the Witch test of 9 or more is automatically passed.
2	**Tainted Texts** *Gifted with the accumulated lore of many insane and evil tomes, this entity's sorcerous powers have swelled.* Each time this **PSYKER** attempts to manifest a psychic power from the Pandaemoniac discipline, add 1 to the Psychic test.
3	**Storm's Eye** *This strange empyric gift allows the daemon to project its will onto the raging tides of a warp storm, only for it to erupt elsewhere along convoluted channels of ill fate.* Once per battle, after this **PSYKER** manifests the *Smite* psychic power, you can select one enemy unit within range of and visible to this **PSYKER** to suffer the mortal wounds, instead of the closest visible enemy unit.
4	**Implements of Ruin** *The weapons wielded by this daemon are empyric conduits given physical form. As it channels the power of the warp, so they hum with ever greater resonant lethality.* In your Psychic phase, if this **PSYKER** successfully manifests any psychic powers, until your next Psychic phase, add 1 to the Damage characteristic of melee weapons this **PSYKER** is equipped with.
5	**Spiteful Backlash** *A daemonic gift of sentient and spiteful warpflame dances about this entity's corporeal form, lashing out at those who would seek to trammel its sorcery and punishing them.* Each time this **PSYKER** attempts to manifest *Smite* or a Witchfire psychic power, if an enemy **PSYKER** attempts to deny that psychic power but the Deny the Witch test is failed, that enemy **PSYKER** suffers D3 mortal wounds.
6	**Master Manipulator** *This daemon is gifted with the power to interpret the flow of events, foreseeing its own failures and correcting them.* Each time a Psychic test is taken for this **PSYKER**, you can re-roll one of the dice.

BATTLE TRAITS

When a **LEGIONES DAEMONICA** unit gains a Battle Trait, you can use one of the tables below instead of one of the tables in the Warhammer 40,000 Core Book to determine which Battle Trait the unit has gained. To do so, roll one D3 and consult the appropriate table, or choose a Battle Trait from the appropriate table that tells the best narrative for your unit. All the normal rules for Battle Traits apply (e.g. a unit cannot have the same Battle Trait more than once). As with any Battle Honour, make a note on the unit's Crusade card when it gains a Battle Trait and increase its Crusade points accordingly, as described in the Warhammer 40,000 Core Book.

CRUSADE RULES

BLOODLETTERS CORE UNITS ONLY

D3	BATTLE TRAIT
1	**Aspiring Skull-takers** *Driven by an aggressive desire to rise above their station, these daemons seek charnel trophies to prove their worth.* Each time an attack made by models in this unit destroys an enemy **CHARACTER** unit, subtract 2 from that **CHARACTER** unit's Out of Action test at the end of the battle.
2	**Brazen Sinews** *These daemons have been gifted with hissing pistons and brass gears stitched through their infernal musculature.* Add 1 to the Strength characteristic of models in this unit.
3	**Unquenchable Bloodthirst** *Even amongst the daemons of Khorne, these daemons' thirst for spilling mortal blood is remarkable.* Each time this unit is selected for the Frenetic Bloodlust Stratagem (pg 63), that Stratagem costs 1 fewer CPs to use (to a minimum of 0CP).

HORRORS CORE UNITS ONLY

D3	BATTLE TRAIT
1	**Expert Flamecasters** *Gifted with a boon woven from the terror of mortals who perished amidst leaping flame, these daemons perceive just where to hurl their warpfire to cause greatest pain and fear.* Improve the Ballistic Skill characteristic of models in this unit by 1.
2	**Shatterselves** *The very act of banishing these daemons causes their reflected selves within the warp to be spat forth as though bursting through the surface of an infernal mirror.* Out of Action tests taken for this unit are automatically passed.
3	**Fires of Tzeentch** *Conjuring the deadliest sorcerous flame comes naturally to these creatures.* Each time this unit is selected for the Minions of Magic Stratagem (pg 77), that Stratagem costs 1 fewer CPs to use (to a minimum of 0CP).

PLAGUEBEARERS CORE UNITS ONLY

D3	BATTLE TRAIT
1	**Noisome Odour (Aura)** *These daemons bring with them a truly terrible odour. Even a moment in their presence can drive the most stoic mortal creature to recoil in gagging revulsion.* While an enemy unit is within 3" of this unit, subtract 1 from Combat Attrition tests taken for that enemy unit.
2	**Encrusted Scabs** *The hides of these disgusting creatures are covered in a thick layer of congealed pus and ichor, deflecting the blades of their foe.* Models in this unit have a Daemonic Save characteristic of 4+/4+.
3	**Disgusting Resilience** *These daemons shrug off even the mightiest of blows, gurgling a mocking chuckle before striking down their attackers.* Each time this unit is selected for the Revolting Constitution Stratagem (pg 91), that Stratagem costs 1 fewer CPs to use (to a minimum of 0CP).

DAEMONETTES CORE UNITS ONLY

D3	BATTLE TRAIT
1	**Perfect Killers** *These daemons are experts at their deadly task, their every perfect evisceration drawing the eye of Slaanesh.* Each time you make a Warp Storm roll, if any enemy units were destroyed by an attack made by this unit in the previous battle round, roll one additional D6.
2	**Whimsic Wisps** *Like an urge or thought that leaps unbidden to mortal minds, the flickering advance of these daemons cannot be resisted.* Each time a model in this unit makes a melee attack, the target does not receive the benefits of cover against that attack.
3	**Claws of Living Diamond** *The talons of these daemons are as unnaturally beautiful as they are viciously sharp.* Each time this unit is selected for the Razor-sharp Caress Stratagem (pg 107), that Stratagem costs 1 fewer CPs to use (to a minimum of 0CP).

CRUSADE RELICS

When a **Legiones Daemonica Character** model gains a Crusade Relic, you can instead select one of the Relics listed below. All the usual rules for selecting Crusade Relics, as described in the Warhammer 40,000 Core Book, apply.

ANTIQUITY RELICS

A **Legiones Daemonica Character** model of Heroic rank or higher can be given one of the following Antiquity Relics instead of one of the ones presented in the Warhammer 40,000 Core Book. Add 1 to a unit's total Crusade points for each Antiquity Relic it has – this is in addition to the +1 from gaining a Battle Honour, for a total of +2.

Cuirass of Rage

This solid brazen plate covers the daemon's chest and is infused with their fury and scorn at those who attempt to strike them down. Even the mightiest blows are turned aside by its rune-graven surface, leaving no mark.

Khorne model only. Once per turn, the first time a saving throw is failed for the bearer, the Damage characteristic of that attack is changed to 0.

Crystal Tome

Feared even by many of Tzeentch's servants for its reputed sentience, the Crystal Tome is said by some to contain the true name of every being that has ever existed, or even might have but did not. Invoking a creature's true name grants tremendous power over it.

Tzeentch model only. In your Command phase, select one enemy unit within 12" of the bearer. Until your next Command phase, that enemy unit is not affected by the aura abilities of other enemy units.

Shroud of Corruption

This foetid cloth tangles itself about its wearer, clinging like sweat-drenched sheets ensnaring a fever victim in their delirium. Some even claim that it was the receptacle for Grandfather Nurgle's own gushing sternutations, and indeed it does seem to be saturated with the most infectious and clammily mucal of warp maladies.

Nurgle model only. The bearer has the following ability:

Shroud of Corruption (Aura): While an enemy unit is within 6" of this model, at the end of your Movement phase, roll one D6: on a 4+, that unit suffers 1 mortal wound.

Jewel of Excess

Seeming as one perfect ornament amongst many worn by this daemon, the Jewel of Excess is in fact a tormenting prison, housing the souls of every psyker ever slain by the bearer, their power now the daemon's.

Slaanesh Psyker model only.

- Each time the bearer attempts to manifest a psychic power from the Soulstain discipline, add 1 to the Psychic test.
- Add 1 to Deny the Witch tests taken for the bearer.

Bellowing with inchoate fury, Skarbrand hurls itself into battle with a leering Daemon Prince of Slaanesh. Surrounded by baying Khornate hounds and facing an avalanche of savage blows, the arrogant foe's doom is sealed.

LEGENDARY RELICS

A **Legiones Daemonica Character** model of Legendary rank can be given one of the following Legendary Relics instead of one of the ones presented in the Warhammer 40,000 Core Book. In addition, in order to give a model a Legendary Relic, you must also pay 1 Requisition point (if you do not have enough Requisition points, you cannot give that model a Legendary Relic). Add 2 to a unit's total Crusade points for each Legendary Relic it has – this is in addition to the +1 from gaining a Battle Honour, for a total of +3.

G'rmakht the Destroyer

The black blade of this enormous axe contains the essence of G'rmakht, a Bloodthirster whose cyclic imprisonment is an eternal torment. Should the axe's wielder fall, and its death be sufficiently violent, G'rmakht uses their banishment to temporarily unbind its soul-chains, manifesting in the former daemon's place and venting unbridled anger upon any it finds, before the axe's inescapable power ensnares it once more.

Model equipped with axe of Khorne only. This Relic replaces an axe of Khorne and has the following profile:

WEAPON	RANGE	TYPE	S	AP	D
G'rmakht	Each time an attack is made with this weapon, select one of the profiles below to make that attack with.				
- Mighty strike	Melee	Melee	+4	-4	D6
- Sweeping blow	Melee	Melee	User	-3	1

Abilities: Each time an attack is made with this weapon's sweeping blow profile, make 2 hit rolls instead of 1. When the bearer is destroyed, instead of using any rules that are triggered when that model is destroyed, you can instead replace it with a **Bloodthirster** model. This model uses the Bloodthirster datasheet (pg 67) and is treated as a named character, but does not have a Warlord Trait and does not have a Crusade card. At the end of each subsequent Fight phase, roll one D6 for this model: on a 5+, the axe's power ensnares it again, and this model is removed from the battlefield.

Tome of Endless Dimensions

The crystalline pages of this grimoire stream with constantly shifting fragments of words, whose meanings entwine and contradict as they filter through from overlapping but subtly different realities. Should a mortal seek to comprehend these etchings they would be swiftly driven mad by almost-glimpsed snatches of sanity-blasting revelation. To the fluctuating consciousness of a daemon, however, the empowering sorcerous secrets are all too easily gleaned.

Tzeentch model only. Each time the bearer attempts to manifest a Witchfire psychic power or *Smite*, on an unmodified Psychic test of 9 or more, if that power is not denied, after resolving the effects of that psychic power, you can resolve the effects of that psychic power again.

Contagion Blade

Said to have been lost for aeons at the bottom of Nurgle's great cauldron, mortal legend tells how this blade was finally recovered after having absorbed the essence of hundreds of Nurgle's finest contagions. Only the most favoured of the Plague God's daemonic servants have ever been witnessed wielding this malignant blade. The merest scratch from its edge causes countless diseases to bloom within the victim before bursting forth in a fulsome eruption of infectious gore and moistened spores inimical to any unfortunate caught in the blast.

Model equipped with bileblade only. This Relic replaces a bileblade and has the following profile:

WEAPON	RANGE	TYPE	S	AP	D
Contagion Blade	Melee	Melee	+1	-3	3

Abilities: Each time an attack is made with this weapon, an unmodified wound roll of 6 inflicts D3 mortal wounds on the target in addition to any normal damage. If any model is destroyed by these mortal wounds, that model's unit suffers a further D3 mortal wounds.

Tears of Asuryan

When Slaanesh was birthed into the warp by the decadence of the Aeldari, she devoured the souls of many of that ancient race. Tales tell how the Aeldari god Asuryan witnessed the horrible fate of so many of his children and wept bitter tears that crystallised into these rainbow-hued gems. Only rarely is a daemon of Slaanesh encountered bearing such jewels, but should they use one in ritual imitation of She Who Thirsts, the power unleashed is little short of apocalyptic.

Slaanesh model only. Once per battle, in your Command phase, the bearer can shatter a Tear of Asuryan. When they do so:

- You gain 6 Warp Storm points (pg 58).
- Until the start of your next Command phase, the bearer knows all the psychic powers from the Soulstain discipline.

'The Daemons of Chaos are quite literally given form and purpose by the accumulated desires, obsessions and needs of mortal beings. Is it any surprise, then, that these otherworldly entities have as great a capacity for acquisitiveness and ambition as we who so unwittingly empower them? Crucially, they need not even obtain such physical treasures as we mortals squabble over; for them, the mere act of desiring and the symbolic significance of seeking may allow them to manifest the embodiment of the treasures they seek. Woe betide we poor unfortunate mortals when they do.'

- *Sanctus-scholaris First Class Gwethyn Samuela, soul shriven servant of the Ordo Malleus Archivum Infernal*

CRUSADE ARMY

This menacing-looking Khornate daemon army belongs to Toby Liddiard. When not toiling away in the soul-forges — AKA the mould rooms — at Games Workshop's head office, he can be found working on this swift and deadly force.

Toby's mental image of a Khornate daemon army is one of a mass of fast-moving corded muscle and fangs, storming across the battlefield to overwhelm the enemy. He really enjoys every aspect of Khorne's wrathful daemons, from the savage look of their miniatures range, to their uncompromising background and the way they play on the tabletop battlefield. To this end, Toby has crafted a Crusade army based around the Khornate Blood Hunt, a force that seeks to close the gap with its prey – i.e. any other player's army unlucky enough to find itself being hunted – by as direct a route as possible, and then tear them to shreds in hand-to-hand combat.

Unusually for a Crusade army, this force's only HQ choices are a pair of named special characters. However, they have been chosen specifically to fit Toby's narrative, and to lend it real impetus on the tabletop. He sees the Blood Hunt surging across realspace, tearing through the veil to stalk their victims across outlying worlds and fringe colonies before vanishing as swiftly as they came and leaving nothing but carnage in their wake. It is a simple and effective backstory that shows how even a sentence or two of narrative can inspire a unique and striking tabletop collection.

Toby was motivated to collect this army by the current Flesh Hound models. It is unsurprising, then, that he has so many packs of them and plans to add even more as his army's roster grows. Nor is this the only planned expansion for his Crusade army. As the Blood Hunt takes more trophies and its favour with Khorne grows, Toby is planning to pile in more fast-moving daemons, most notably some ultra-heavy shock cavalry in the form of Bloodcrushers. He has plans for some more HQ choices as well, introducing more daemonic leaders of his own creation to take the reins of this ferocious force when Skarbrand or Karanak are called away to other battlefields.

One of the most striking elements of Toby's collection is its extremely effective paint scheme. Calling back to his mental image of Khornate daemons as being covered in rippling muscle, he has perfected a technique that brings that nightmarish vision to life. Coupled with a cleverly applied 'living skull' effect for the models' heads, this makes the army look striking and distinctive. While the army doesn't yet have many conversions amongst its ranks, Toby has done some work to ensure that his Soul Grinders look like true servants of the Blood God. The most obvious example of this is the enormous axe being brandished by one of the infernal war engines. Coupled with the Soul Grinder's curling horns and its brass-and-muscle paint scheme, this simple but effective change ensures that the model looks entirely Khornate in nature and more than ready to rampage across realspace with the Blood Hunt.

WEAPON PROFILES

On these pages you will find the profiles for all the weapons that Chaos Daemons models can be equipped with. Note that some weapons have the Blast ability; this ability is detailed in full in the Warhammer 40,000 Core Book.

RANGED WEAPONS	RANGE	TYPE	S	AP	D	ABILITIES
Bellow of endless fury	12"	Assault 2D6	5	-1	1	Each time an attack is made with this weapon, that attack automatically hits the target.
Bloodflail	12"	Assault 1	x2	-4	3D3	Excess damage this weapon inflicts is not lost. Keep allocating excess damage to another model in the target unit until either all the excess damage has been allocated or the target unit is destroyed.
Burning roar	12"	Assault D6	4	-1	1	Each time an attack is made with this weapon, that attack automatically hits the target.
Coruscating flames	18"	Assault 2	+1	-1	1	-
Death's heads	12"	Assault D3	4	-1	1	Blast
Disgusting sneezes	6"	Assault D6	4	0	1	Each time an attack is made with this weapon, that attack automatically hits the target.
Fire of Tzeentch	Before selecting targets, select one of the profiles below to make attacks with.					
- Blue fire	18"	Assault 3	+3	-4	3	-
- Pink fire	12"	Assault 2D6	User	-2	1	Each time an attack is made with this weapon profile, that attack automatically hits the target.
Flickering flames	12"	Assault D6+3	User	-2	1	Each time an attack is made with this weapon, that attack automatically hits the target.
Harvester cannon	36"	Heavy 6	7	-1	2	-
Heartstring Lyre	Before selecting targets, select one of the profiles below to make attacks with.					
- Cacophonous melody	18"	Assault 6	5	-1	1	-
- Euphonic blast	24"	Assault 1	9	-3	D3+3	-
Hellfire breath	12"	Assault D6	5	-2	1	Each time an attack is made with this weapon, that attack automatically hits the target.
Lash of Khorne	12"	Assault 6	User	-1	2	-
Lashes of torment	6"	Assault 6	4	-1	1	-
Living whip	12"	Assault 6	6	-2	2	-
Phlegm bombardment	36"	Heavy D6	8	-2	3	Blast
Plague flail	7"	Assault D6+3	User	-3	2	-
Putrid vomit	12"	Assault D6	5	-2	1	Each time an attack is made with this weapon, that attack automatically hits the target.
Rod of sorcery	12"	Assault D6	6	-1	2	-
Scourging whip (shooting)	9"	Assault 6	User	-2	1	-
Skull cannon	48"	Heavy D3+3	8	-2	2	Blast. Each time an attack is made with this weapon, the target does not receive the benefits of cover against that attack.
Staff of change	18"	Assault 3	+4	-4	2	-
Streams of brackish filth	12"	Assault 2D6	6	-3	1	Each time an attack is made with this weapon, that attack automatically hits the target.

MELEE WEAPONS	RANGE	TYPE	S	AP	D	ABILITIES
Acidic maw	Melee	Melee	7	-4	3	Malefic 2
Attendants' hellblades	Melee	Melee	User	-3	2	Malefic 4
Axe of Dominion	Melee	Melee	+3	-3	3	-
Axe of Khorne	Each time an attack is made with this weapon, select one of the profiles below to make that attack with.					
- Mighty strike	Melee	Melee	+4	-4	D6	-
- Sweeping blow	Melee	Melee	User	-3	1	Each time an attack is made with this weapon profile, make 2 hit rolls instead of 1.
Baleful sword	Melee	Melee	+1	-3	3	Malefic 3
Foul balesword	Melee	Melee	User	-3	2	Each time an attack is made with this weapon, an unmodified hit roll of 6 automatically wounds the target.
Barbed tail	Melee	Melee	User	-3	3	Malefic 1
Bileblade	Melee	Melee	User	-3	2	Each time an attack is made with this weapon, you can re-roll the wound roll.
Bilesword	Each time an attack is made with this weapon, select one of the profiles below to make that attack with.					
- Mighty strike	Melee	Melee	+1	-3	D6	Each time an attack is made with this weapon profile, an unmodified hit roll of 6 automatically wounds the target.
- Sweeping blow	Melee	Melee	User	-3	1	Each time an attack is made with this weapon profile, make 2 hit rolls instead of 1.
Biting maw	Melee	Melee	User	-1	2	-
Blade of blood	Melee	Melee	User	-3	3	-
The Blade of Shadows	Each time an attack is made with this weapon, select one of the profiles below to make that attack with.					
- Sweeping strike	Melee	Melee	User	-3	1	Each time an attack is made with this weapon profile, make 2 hit rolls instead of 1.
- Piercing strike	Melee	Melee	+4	-4	D3+3	Each time an attack is made with this weapon profile, invulnerable saving throws cannot be made against that attack.
Bladed axle	Melee	Melee	+2	-2	2	Malefic 4
Bladed horn	Melee	Melee	User	-2	1	Malefic 4. Each time the bearer fights, if it made a charge move this turn, then until that fight is resolved, change the Strength characteristic of this weapon to +2.
Coiled tentacles	Melee	Melee	+1	-2	3	Malefic 3
Daemonic axe	Melee	Melee	+2	-2	3	-
Disc blades	Melee	Melee	4	0	1	Malefic 1
Diseased claws and teeth	Melee	Melee	User	0	1	Each time an attack is made with this weapon, an unmodified hit roll of 6 automatically wounds the target.
Dissecting claws	Melee	Melee	User	-2	2	-
Distended maw	Melee	Melee	+1	-1	3	Malefic 1
Doomsday bell	Melee	Melee	+1	-1	2	-
Exalted Seeker tongues	Melee	Melee	4	0	1	Malefic 8
Fanged maw	Melee	Melee	User	-1	2	Malefic 1
Foul mouthparts	Melee	Melee	5	-2	2	Malefic 2
Gnarlrod	Each time an attack is made with this weapon, select one of the profiles below to make that attack with.					
- Mighty strike	Melee	Melee	+1	-3	3	Each time an attack is made with this weapon profile, an unmodified hit roll of 6 automatically wounds the target.
- Sweeping blow	Melee	Melee	User	-2	1	Each time an attack is made with this weapon profile, make 2 hit rolls instead of 1.
Gore-drenched fangs	Melee	Melee	User	-2	1	-
Great axe of Khorne	Each time an attack is made with this weapon, select one of the profiles below to make that attack with.					
- Mighty strike	Melee	Melee	x2	-4	D3+3	-
- Sweeping blow	Melee	Melee	User	-3	2	Each time an attack is made with this weapon profile, make 2 hit rolls instead of 1.
Hellblade	Melee	Melee	User	-3	2	-
Hellforged sword	Melee	Melee	+1	-3	3	-
Iron claw	Melee	Melee	x2	-3	D6	-
Lamprey bite	Melee	Melee	+2	-3	2	-
Lashing tongue	Melee	Melee	4	0	1	Malefic 2
Lopping shears	Melee	Melee	+1	-3	2	Each time an attack is made with this weapon, an unmodified hit roll of 6 automatically wounds the target.
Malefic talons	Melee	Melee	User	-1	2	Each time the bearer fights, it makes 1 additional attack with this weapon.
Marotter	Melee	Melee	User	0	1	Each time an attack is made with this weapon, an unmodified hit roll of 6 automatically wounds the target.
Nurgling claws	Melee	Melee	2	0	1	Malefic 7
Piercing claws	Melee	Melee	User	-2	1	-

MELEE WEAPONS	RANGE	TYPE	S	AP	D	ABILITIES
Plaguesword	Melee	Melee	User	-2	1	Each time an attack is made with this weapon, an unmodified hit roll of 6 automatically wounds the target.
Prehensile proboscis	Melee	Melee	4	-2	1	Malefic 4
Putrid appendages	Melee	Melee	User	-2	2	Each time an attack is made with this weapon, an unmodified hit roll of 6 inflicts 2 mortal wounds on the target and the attack sequence ends.
Ravaging claws	Melee	Melee	User	-2	2	-
Ritual dagger	Melee	Melee	User	-1	1	-
Scourging whip (melee)	Melee	Melee	User	-2	1	Malefic 6
Screamer bites	Melee	Melee	6	-3	2	Malefic 6
Seeker tongues	Melee	Melee	4	0	1	Malefic 4
Serrated claws	Melee	Melee	User	-3	2	-
Sharp quills	Melee	Melee	User	0	1	-
Slaughter and Carnage	Each time an attack is made with this weapon, select one of the profiles below to make that attack with.					
- Mighty strike	Melee	Melee	x2	-4	D3+3	Each time an attack is made with this weapon profile, invulnerable saving throws cannot be made against that attack.
- Sweeping blow	Melee	Melee	User	-2	2	Each time an attack is made with this weapon profile, make 2 hit rolls instead of 1.
The Slayer Sword	Melee	Melee	User	-3	3	Each time an attack is made with this weapon, invulnerable saving throws cannot be made against that attack.
Snapping claws	Melee	Melee	User	-4	3	Malefic 4
Soulpiercer	Melee	Melee	x2	-4	3	Each time an attack is made with this weapon against a CHARACTER model, this weapon has a Damage characteristic of D3+3.
Soul-rending fangs	Melee	Melee	User	-2	2	-
Staff of Tomorrow	Melee	Melee	+2	-3	2D3	-
Staff of Tzeentch	Melee	Melee	User	-2	3	-
The Trickster's Staff	Melee	Melee	User	0	1	Each time the bearer is selected to fight, you can select one melee weapon an enemy INFANTRY model within Engagement Range of it is equipped with. Until that fight is resolved, this weapon has the same profile as the selected weapon.
Warpclaw	Melee	Melee	User	-2	2	Malefic 4
Warpsword	Melee	Melee	User	-3	D3+3	Malefic 2
Witstealer sword	Melee	Melee	+2	-3	3	Each time an enemy model loses any wounds from an attack made with this weapon, until the end of the battle, each time that model makes a melee attack, subtract 1 from that attack's wound roll.

POINTS VALUES

You can use this section to determine the points (pts) value of each unit in your army. Each entry lists the unit's size (i.e. how many models the unit can contain) and how many points the unit costs. If an entry has a unit cost of 'x pts/model', then the unit costs x points for every model in that unit. You must then add points for each weapon, or item of wargear, that is included in that unit if it is listed in that unit's entry (weapons and wargear not listed in a unit's entry cost no additional points to include in that unit).

POINTS

KHORNE

💀 HQ

Bloodmaster (pg 68)
Unit size..1 model
Unit cost.. 90 pts

Bloodthirster (pg 67)
Unit size..1 model
Unit cost.. 310 pts

> **Exalted Abilities (pg 62)**
> Indomitable Onslaught......................+40 pts
> Master of the Blood Tide....................+20 pts
> Rage Unchained..............................+35 pts

Karanak (pg 70)
Unit size..1 model
Unit cost.. 100 pts

Rendmaster on Blood Throne (pg 69)
Unit size..1 model
Unit cost.. 140 pts

Skarbrand (pg 66)
Unit size..1 model
Unit cost.. 330 pts

Skullmaster (pg 69)
Unit size..1 model
Unit cost.. 130 pts

Skulltaker (pg 68)
Unit size..1 model
Unit cost.. 110 pts

▶ TROOPS

Bloodletters (pg 70)
Unit size..10 models
Unit cost.. 130 pts

✠ ELITES

Bloodcrushers (pg 71)
Unit size...3-6 models
Unit cost...45 pts/model

⚡ FAST ATTACK

Flesh Hounds (pg 72)
Unit size..5-10 models
Unit cost...19 pts/model

👑 HEAVY SUPPORT

Skull Cannon (pg 72)
Unit size..1 model
Unit cost.. 100 pts

🏰 FORTIFICATIONS

Skull Altar (pg 73)
Unit size..1 model
Unit cost.. 50 pts

TZEENTCH

💀 HQ

The Blue Scribes (pg 83)
Unit size..1 model
Unit cost.. 90 pts

Changecaster (pg 84)
Unit size..1 model
Unit cost.. 80 pts
• Staff of change ....+5 pts

The Changeling (pg 82)
Unit size..1 model
Unit cost.. 100 pts

Fateskimmer (pg 82)
Unit size..1 model
Unit cost.. 140 pts
• Retinue of Horrors ....+5 pts
• Staff of change ....+5 pts

Fluxmaster (pg 83)
Unit size..1 model
Unit cost.. 110 pts
• Staff of change ....+5 pts

Kairos Fateweaver (pg 81)
Unit size..1 model
Unit cost.. 320 pts

Lord of Change (pg 81)
Unit size..1 model
Unit cost.. 300 pts
• Baleful sword ....+10 pts
• Rod of sorcery ....+10 pts

> **Exalted Abilities (pg 76)**
> Architect of Deception ....+35 pts
> Master Mutator..................................+30 pts
> Nexus of Fate....................................+20 pts

▶ TROOPS

Blue Horrors (pg 84)
Unit size..10 models
Unit cost.. 70 pts

Pink Horrors (pg 85)
Unit size..10 models
Unit cost.. 150 pts

✠ ELITES

Exalted Flamer (pg 86)
Unit size..1 model
Unit cost.. 75 pts

Flamers (pg 86)
Unit size...3-6 models
Unit cost...25 pts/model

⚡ FAST ATTACK

Screamers (pg 87)
Unit size...3-6 models
Unit cost...30 pts/model

👑 HEAVY SUPPORT

Burning Chariot (pg 87)
Unit size..1 model
Unit cost.. 120 pts
• Horror infestation ....+5 pts

NURGLE

HQ

Epidemius (pg 98)
Unit size .... 1 model
Unit cost .... 90 pts

Great Unclean One (pg 96)
Unit size .... 1 model
Unit cost .... 300 pts

Exalted Abilities (pg 90)
Bountiful Gifts .... +25 pts
Hideous Visage .... +20 pts
Revoltingly Resilient .... +30 pts

Horticulous Slimux (pg 99)
Unit size .... 1 model
Unit cost .... 140 pts

Poxbringer (pg 97)
Unit size .... 1 model
Unit cost .... 90 pts

Rotigus (pg 95)
Unit size .... 1 model
Unit cost .... 320 pts

Sloppity Bilepiper (pg 98)
Unit size .... 1 model
Unit cost .... 85 pts

Spoilpox Scrivener (pg 97)
Unit size .... 1 model
Unit cost .... 100 pts

▶ TROOPS

Nurglings (pg 100)
Unit size .... 3-9 models
Unit cost .... 20 pts/model

Plaguebearers (pg 100)
Unit size .... 10 models
Unit cost .... 150 pts

✠ ELITES

Beasts of Nurgle (pg 101)
Unit size .... 1-3 models
Unit cost .... 80 pts/model

⚡ FAST ATTACK

Plague Drones (pg 102)
Unit size .... 3-6 models
Unit cost .... 45 pts/model

🏰 FORTIFICATIONS

Feculent Gnarlmaw (pg 103)
Unit size .... 1 model
Unit cost .... 75 pts

SLAANESH

☠ HQ

Contorted Epitome (pg 114)
Unit size .... 1 model
Unit cost .... 160 pts

Infernal Enrapturess (pg 113)
Unit size .... 1 model
Unit cost .... 80 pts

Keeper of Secrets (pg 112)
Unit size .... 1 model
Unit cost .... 280 pts

Exalted Abilities (pg 106)
Diaphanous Panoply .... +35 pts
Epicurean of Agonies .... +25 pts
Insatiable Onslaught .... +20 pts

The Masque of Slaanesh (pg 113)
Unit size .... 1 model
Unit cost .... 90 pts

Shalaxi Helbane (pg 111)
Unit size .... 1 model
Unit cost .... 300 pts

Syll'Esske (pg 114)
Unit size .... 1 model
Unit cost .... 200 pts

Tormentbringer on Exalted Seeker Chariot (pg 115)
Unit size .... 1 model
Unit cost .... 120 pts

Tormentbringer on Hellflayer (pg 117)
Unit size .... 1 model
Unit cost .... 110 pts

Tormentbringer on Seeker Chariot (pg 116)
Unit size .... 1 model
Unit cost .... 100 pts

Tranceweaver (pg 116)
Unit size .... 1 model
Unit cost .... 70 pts

▶ TROOPS

Daemonettes (pg 118)
Unit size .... 10 models
Unit cost .... 120 pts

✠ ELITES

Fiends (pg 118)
Unit size .... 3-6 models
Unit cost .... 35 pts/model

⚡ FAST ATTACK

Hellflayer (pg 120)
Unit size .... 1 model
Unit cost .... 75 pts

Seeker Chariot (pg 121)
Unit size .... 1 model
Unit cost .... 65 pts

Seekers (pg 119)
Unit size .... 5-10 models
Unit cost .... 20 pts/model

♛ HEAVY SUPPORT

Exalted Seeker Chariot (pg 121)
Unit size .... 1 model
Unit cost .... 85 pts

UNDIVIDED

☠ HQ

Be'lakor (pg 125)
Unit size .... 1 model
Unit cost .... 420 pts

Daemon Prince of Chaos (pg 126)
Unit size .... 1 model
Unit cost .... 140 pts
• Daemonic axe .... +10 pts
• Hellforged sword .... +10 pts
• Wings .... +35 pts

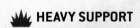 HEAVY SUPPORT

Soul Grinder (pg 127)
Unit size .... 1 model
Unit cost .... 190 pts

GLOSSARY

Below you will find a glossary that contains a number of terms used in this Codex.

Allegiance Keyword (pg 56): A LEGIONES DAEMONICA unit will have one or more of the following Allegiance keywords: KHORNE, TZEENTCH, NURGLE or SLAANESH. If a unit has the <ALLEGIANCE> keyword, you must replace this keyword with one of those listed above.

Ascendancy points (pg 134): A resource gained by each Dark God if your Crusade army is influencing the Great Game.

Favoured Rewards (pg 136): Additional abilities that can be gained by GREATER DAEMON units from your Crusade army based on performance in the Great Game. These come in three types: Lesser Rewards, Greater Rewards and Exalted Rewards.

LEGIONES DAEMONICA Detachment (pg 53): A Detachment in a Battle-forged army where every model has the LEGIONES DAEMONICA keyword (excluding models with the UNALIGNED or AGENTS OF CHAOS keyword).

Loci of the Gods (pg 133): A new kind of Battle Honour that GREATER DAEMON or HERALD units can gain.

Malefic Weapon (pg 56): A melee weapon that the bearer can use to make attacks in addition to the melee attacks they make with other weapons.

Maximum number of models: A unit contains the maximum number of models if it includes every model it possibly can, as described on its datasheet (excluding models representing wargear).

Psychic power type: A psychic power's type is written in bold at the start of its rules. There are three types of psychic power described in this Codex: Blessing, Malediction and Witchfire.

Stratagem label: A Stratagem's labels are written beneath its title and can include: Legiones Daemonica; Battle Tactic; Epic Deed, Strategic Ploy; Requisition; Wargear. A Stratagem can have more than one label (e.g. a Stratagem with 'Legiones Daemonica – Wargear Stratagem' has both the Legiones Daemonica and Wargear labels).

Warp Storm points (pg 58): A resource gained during the battle if every unit from your army has the LEGIONES DAEMONICA keyword (excluding models with the UNALIGNED or AGENTS OF CHAOS keyword).

PSYCHIC DISCIPLINES

Pandaemoniac discipline (pg 78): A psychic discipline TZEENTCH PSYKER units can know powers from.

Warprot discipline (pg 92): A psychic discipline NURGLE PSYKER units can know powers from.

Soulstain discipline (pg 108): A psychic discipline SLAANESH PSYKER units can know powers from.

Noctic discipline (pg 124): A psychic discipline LEGIONES DAEMONICA PSYKER or DISCIPLES OF BE'LAKOR PSYKER units can know powers from.

RELICS

Relic of Khorne (pg 65): A Relic available to LEGIONES DAEMONICA KHORNE CHARACTER models from your army, if it is led by a LEGIONES DAEMONICA WARLORD.

Relic of Tzeentch (pg 80): A Relic available to LEGIONES DAEMONICA TZEENTCH CHARACTER models from your army, if it is led by a LEGIONES DAEMONICA WARLORD.

Relic of Nurgle (pg 94): A Relic available to LEGIONES DAEMONICA NURGLE CHARACTER models from your army, if it is led by a LEGIONES DAEMONICA WARLORD.

Relic of Slaanesh (pg 110): A Relic available to LEGIONES DAEMONICA SLAANESH CHARACTER models from your army, if it is led by a LEGIONES DAEMONICA WARLORD.

STRATAGEMS

Disciples of Be'lakor Stratagem (pg 129): A Stratagem available if your army is a Disciples of Be'lakor Army of Renown. All Disciples of Be'lakor Stratagems are considered to have the Legiones Daemonica Stratagem label (see left).

Legions of Khorne Stratagem (pg 63): A Stratagem available if your army includes any LEGIONES DAEMONICA Detachments in which every unit (excluding models with the UNALIGNED or AGENTS OF CHAOS keyword) has the KHORNE keyword. All Legions of Khorne Stratagems are considered to have the Legiones Daemonica Stratagem label (see left).

Legions of Tzeentch Stratagem (pg 77): A Stratagem available if your army includes any LEGIONES DAEMONICA Detachments in which every unit (excluding models with the UNALIGNED or AGENTS OF CHAOS keyword) has the TZEENTCH keyword. All Legions of Tzeentch Stratagems are considered to have the Legiones Daemonica Stratagem label (see left).

Legions of Nurgle Stratagem (pg 91): A Stratagem available if your army includes any LEGIONES DAEMONICA Detachments in which every unit (excluding models with the UNALIGNED or AGENTS OF CHAOS keyword) has the NURGLE keyword. All Legions of Nurgle Stratagems are considered to have the Legiones Daemonica Stratagem label (see left).

Legions of Slaanesh Stratagem (pg 107): A Stratagem available if your army includes any LEGIONES DAEMONICA Detachments in which every unit (excluding models with the UNALIGNED or AGENTS OF CHAOS keyword) has the SLAANESH keyword. All Legions of Slaanesh Stratagems are considered to have the Legiones Daemonica Stratagem label (see opposite).

UPGRADES

Exalted Bloodthirsters (pg 62): An upgrade that bestows new abilities on a BLOODTHIRSTER unit for an additional cost.

Exalted Lords of Change (pg 76): An upgrade that bestows new abilities on a LORD OF CHANGE unit for an additional cost.

Exalted Great Unclean Ones (pg 90): An upgrade that bestows new abilities on a GREAT UNCLEAN ONE unit for an additional cost.

Exalted Keepers of Secrets (pg 106): An upgrade that bestows new abilities on a KEEPER OF SECRETS unit for an additional cost.

WARLORD TRAITS

Khorne Warlord Traits (pg 64): A Warlord Trait available to KHORNE WARLORD models.

Tzeentch Warlord Traits (pg 79): A Warlord Trait available to TZEENTCH WARLORD models.

Nurgle Warlord Traits (pg 93): A Warlord Trait available to NURGLE WARLORD models.

Slaanesh Warlord Traits (pg 109): A Warlord Trait available to SLAANESH WARLORD models.

REFERENCE

Below you will find a bullet pointed summary of several Chaos Daemons rules. In most games, you may find referencing this summary is all you need to resolve a rule, but if not, follow the page reference to read the entirety of the rule.

<ALLEGIANCE> KEYWORD (PG 56)
When you include a unit with the **<ALLEGIANCE>** keyword, nominate which Dark God it owes allegiance to.

- Replace every instance of the **<ALLEGIANCE>** keyword on that unit's datasheet with the name of your chosen Dark God.

DAEMONIC PACT (PG 53)
- If your army includes one **LEGIONES DAEMONICA** Detachment, and the combined Power Ratings of all units in that Detachment is 25% or less of your army's Power Level, then until the end of the battle, every unit in that Detachment gains the **AGENT OF CHAOS** keyword.

DAEMONIC LEGIONS (PG 53)
- If your army only contains **LEGIONES DAEMONICA** Detachments, and includes any **GREATER DAEMON** units, one of these must be your **WARLORD**, unless your army also includes **BE'LAKOR**.
- For each **GREATER DAEMON** unit included in a Detachment, you can include 1 **HERALD** unit with the same Allegiance keyword in that Detachment without that **HERALD** unit taking up a Battlefield Role slot.

EXALTED UPGRADES
- If your army includes any **LEGIONES DAEMONICA** Detachments (excluding Auxiliary Support, Super-heavy Auxiliary or Fortification Network Detachments), then when you muster your army, you can upgrade any **GREATER DAEMON** models from your army to be exalted.
- That **GREATER DAEMON** model gains an Exalted ability, depending which Dark God they owe allegiance to.

MALEFIC WEAPONS (PG 56)
- A malefic weapon is any weapon which includes the 'Malefic' ability in it's profile, followed by a number.

DAEMONIC
A unit with this ability has the following abilities:

DAEMONIC INVULNERABILITY (PG 56)
- Instead of a normal Save characteristic, as described in the Warhammer 40,000 Core Book, each **LEGIONES DAEMONICA** datasheet has a Daemonic Save characteristic (abbreviated to DSv on that datasheet's profile line). This characteristic has two values. The first characteristic is used when a melee attack is allocated to that model. The second characteristic is used when a ranged attack is allocated to that model. In either case, this saving throw cannot be modified.

DAEMONIC TERROR (PG 57)
- While an enemy unit is within 6" of this unit, subtract 1 from its Leadership characteristic and subtract 1 from any combat attrition tests made for it.

MANIFESTATION (PG 56)
- During deployment, you can set that unit up in the warp instead of setting it up on the battlefield.
- Unit can then arrive during Reinforcements step of one of your Movement phases.
- When unit arrives, set it up on battlefield more than 9" from any enemy models or wholly within 6" of a **WARP LOCUS** model from your army.
- If that **WARP LOCUS** model has an Allegiance keyword, the unit being set up within 6" of it must have the same Allegiance keyword.

WARP STORM (PG 58-59)
- If every unit from your army has the **LEGIONES DAEMONICA** keyword (excluding models with the **AGENT OF CHAOS** or **UNALIGNED** keywords), then at the start of each battle round, you can make a Warp Storm roll. To do so, roll eight D6.
- For each 4+, gain 1 Warp Storm point (WSP).
- Warp Storm points can also be gained via other rules. No matter the source, you can only gain Warp Storm points from such a rule if every unit from your army has the **LEGIONES DAEMONICA** keyword (excluding models with the **AGENT OF CHAOS** or **UNALIGNED** keywords). Warp Storm points can be spent during the battle to gain additional effects. Each effect will specify how many Warp Storm points it costs.

THE GREAT GAME

ASCENDANCY POINTS

Khorne

Nurgle

Slaanesh

Tzeentch

POSITIONS

1ST

2ND

3RD

4TH